AFRICA
O-Ye!

To the memory and the music of

Alhadji Bai Konte (c.1921-88)
and
Luambo Makiadi (1938-89)

AFRICA
O-Ye!

A celebration of African music
by
Graeme Ewens

with an introduction by
Manu Dibango

GUINNESS PUBLISHING

Edited and designed by Sango Publications, London

Designer: Megan Green

Electronic pagemaking: Roger Burnett

Research and additional material supplied by:
Mamello Pheko
Charles Easmon
Phil Stanton
Florence Tity Gnimagnon
Rick Glanvill
Gary Stewart

Picture credits and acknowledgements: p224

First published in 1991 by Guinness Publishing Limited
Publication copyright © Guinness Publishing Limited 1991

Published in Great Britain by Guinness Publishing Limited,
33 London Road, Enfield, Middlesex

Typeset in London
by Henderson Print and Design

Printed and bound in Italy by New Interlitho SpA, Milan

'GUINNESS' is a registered trade mark of Guinness Publishing Ltd

A catalogue record for this book is available from the British Library.

ISBN 0-88112-977-3

Contents

Abeti Masikini

Music in Motion

" African music is in the image of Africa. There is variety but it is divided, left to stand for itself. There is no music industry structure to support it because Africa is not structured. But music exists, and everywhere in Africa you will find it. That alone is not special to Africa. What is special is that Africa has a long historical relationship with sound, and a communion between sound and the visual stronger than in any other culture. The sound carries the rhythm and movement creates the images. The way an African moves compared with the environment is different from the Western conception.

Music in Africa is defined by two main factors: there is the African environment and African society. The environment gives us an image and also a vision. It affects the way a person sees himself and the way he moves through life, a life which is measured by a number of musical events, with music for birth, initiation, marriage, death and after the mourning.

For three-quarters of the African population the environment is the countryside not the town, but when we consider modern African music we form our judgement on what we know about people who live in the city. It is only the small minority of urban Africans, one quarter of the population, who have the possibility to become involved in artistic, or musical development. Like most musicians who are known outside their country, I was born in a town, not a village. Yes, even 57 years ago there were towns in Africa, and Douala was a small town.

But an African's spiritual home is his village. In the village, music is indivisible from life. There is no art. 'Art' is a Western concept. In traditional Africa the word has no meaning. When we speak of art we speak from a Western point of view. As I, and many other musicians such as Youssou N'Dour, Mory Kante, Miriam Makeba and Hugh Masekela have tried to make clear: African artistic values are not the same as Western artistic values.

In Africa 'art' is something which functions differently from Western ideas of artistic function. In the past when they made sculpture in Africa it was not to sell. It was something sacred, which is in principle something secret, a sacred secret. The sacred is the spirit of the people. It cannot be sold. If you had a sculpture in the house for divinity or fertility, you could not just decide to sell it. Some things are not suited to the Western notion of commerce. In the West great artists like Leonardo used to be commissioned, their work was paid for. But in Africa creative work was not bought and sold.

'Artist' is already a limited concept; creator is a better word. Before, you had no artists in Africa, but you had people who created, and they were everywhere. At the moment people are forced to sell everything, including their heritage, because the economic system has changed. Even in show business it is not easy. We say 'the show is good, but the business is bad'. We shall have to see what happens with the Africans. They are becoming culturally mixed up people because they are now 'consumers' not the producers in life. This is the real problem that confronts all creative Africans, which we must reflect on.

Africa has already absorbed several shock encounters with the outside world: first there was slavery, then colonisation, then independence and now democracy. It has all happened so fast. What took two thousand years to happen in Europe has taken maybe 30 years in Africa. And we have never been completely equipped for what we need to do. But I think it is an interesting time for Africa, because with all the communications in the world, everyone knows what is going on, and everything is changing. Once the world was too big, now it is so small. Communications give the chance for everyone to reflect on anything that is happening, whether in the bush or in the cities like Kinshasa, Sydney or Paris. Perhaps this holds some hope for Africa.

Life has changed completely. People who moved to the towns have joined a multitude of strangers of different origins. The town provides a unity for these different people; a common language, and a community that supports a large population. Outside the towns people live in small groups and speak their own private dialect. It is very different. Now those people living in the towns are experiencing an evolution which is both positive and negative, but necessary. It is the nature of humanity, evolution. There must be a period of adapting for each stage of evolution, but things are moving fast.

Already the influence of the town has reached the village. You have two-way traffic between town and village, village and town. You have a sound that arrives in the town and returns to the village, changed. The echo which comes back is not the same as the original. When a note arrives in town from the village, the town returns it with electronic delay, with reverb, limiter and all the studio technology, but it is the same note that came from the village. When the village takes a sound from the town, there is a chemistry they add which transforms the sound again.

In the villages today people are informed; they have their transistors. They keep their traditional music for cultural activities and their work. They listen to the village singers but at the same time they listen to Franco, they hear what Manu is doing, or what is happening with Fela somewhere. Although they don't know us, they have heard of us, and heard our music.

Now everyone knows the modern music. And even the folklore music is moving. Traditional musicians are human, they live in the modern world, and their music is not fixed, it changes. Traditional music has definitely been affected by modern music, because the same people listen to both. The tradition will always be there, of course, but like a person, it evolves, develops. Just as the fishermen still use canoes, they now have canoes fitted with outboard motors.

Whether the people who play modern music are the same people who play traditional music varies throughout Africa, depending on the people's custom, their colonial history and their religion. In West Africa you have *griots*, who are mainly Muslim. And in those countries they have a strong cultural tradition, and a different educational system. You do not find griots in Central Africa. Also there are fewer Muslims, the cultures are different. So there is a difference in the conditioning between myself and say, Mory Kante. Originally all Africans were animist. But he has been conditioned by his culture which is Muslim. I have been conditioned by Christianity. He is from a family of griots, I'm from a family of civil servants.

When I first played with non-Africans, it was not for a musical advantage but as one of life's adventures. For a musician it is normal to play with others, because music has no frontiers. It is man who makes the frontiers. Now if I go to play in the USA, I go not as an African but as a musician. But the people see me first as an African. Yes, I am an African but is it the African they want to hear or is it the musician? Sometimes it's the African they want, sometimes the musician. Artist or African, it depends on the people. Some always see African musicians as 'African musicians' not musicians from Africa. But it's changing now, which is good, because for a long time I've been fighting against this stupid situation. Of course a musician has the sound of his environment. But you listen first to see if you like his playing, before asking where he comes from. If you judge everything by its colour, nothing has changed.

People who are curious search for sounds; they seek out harmony and melody because they are curious. Your curiosity can be limited by your environment, or you can expand it to take in things from outside; a bigger curiosity for a bigger world. The extent of your curiosity should not be determined by the village, or the town, or a city in another continent. The musician moves in these circles, but he moves to break out of his limits. Now when the circles touch you have negative and positive effects. Whether you break through depends on whether the cycle is right when you arrive. If you arrive at a good moment it's fine, if you arrive at a bad moment it's not so good. That is nature. It is another rhythm to synchronise with, whether you are a musician or not. **"**

Manu Dibango

Africa O-Ye!

The sounds of Africa have been seeping through into the mainstream Western pop consciousness for some time and now, at last, the African contribution is being recognised in the West. Since the late 1980s, musicians from Algeria, Mali, Guinea, Senegal, Cameroon, Nigeria, Zaire, Zimbabwe and South Africa have all had varying degrees of success with international record company contracts. Most other African countries have been represented on radio and in discos and nightclubs far away from their borders, while video clips, televised music travelogues and live shows have broadened audiences' appreciation. The Western world has started to wake up to the vibrant contemporary sound of Africa, where modern instruments and hi-tech production standards blow away any misconceptions about primitive 'jungle drums'.

The idea of Africa without music is unthinkable. However modern the interpretation, African pop is rooted in a musical continuum that accompanies every formal and informal moment of life; as if it has been there all along, with musicians of succeeding generations tapping the ever-flowing stream, interpreting it in an individual way.

In its traditional forms music accompanies almost every activity, from birth to burial, while in contemporary popular guise it is proving to be a lively form of cultural expression. As non-African listeners soon realise, the African pop spectrum is wide, with styles that vary from region to region. It is not just dance music, but it can be taken for granted that the rhythms will be strong and fluid enough to stimulate the spine; that guitars, synthesizers, saxophones or whatever combination of instruments will weave a sensuous fabric from rhythm and melody and that voices will exude emotion of soulful intensity.

Dancer with Fatala, from Guinea

In trying to describe music in non-technical terms commentators necessarily turn to metaphor and analogy such as the familiar image of an 'inter-woven' fabric of rhythms and melodies which 'mesh' together into a complete whole. This is fine as far as it goes but the carpet analogy is two-dimensional and frays at the edges. A better image for African music would be a three-dimensional shape with room for the spaces between the notes, so essential to any music and fundamental to an appreciation of African idioms. It is more like a net or a web, an image which also illustrates the sense of helpless entrapment that can overcome those 'wrapped up' in the music.

Much contemporary African music has been called 'transitional', bridging the gap between the traditional and the modern; the village compound and the nightclub dancefloor; the bush and urban environments, which have an equal pull on the affections and allegiances of today's young Africans. This 'Celebration of African Music' looks at the development of those styles which have crossed over cultural boundaries to find an audience in other parts of Africa or farther afield. As Manu Dibango describes it, African music spreads out from its cultural base in circular ripples, within which musicians are confined. After breaking out of the first circle, the traditional village culture, musicians must then appeal to national and regional audiences before qualifying for international recognition. Even then they remain tied to the French, English or Portuguese cultures of their colonisers.

No African popular music exists in a vacuum; it is always related in one way or another to the cultural background of the performers. As the music is generally vocal-led, the language colours every aspect; it sets the pace and gives a sense of place, enabling most African music to be identified geographically. The environment has helped to define culture, with geography, topography, climate and even vegetation affecting the language, the kind of instruments played and the style of dancing. The construction of instruments is obviously limited by the choice of plant and animal materials available, and even direct physical expression can be restricted by the thickness of the undergrowth. A BBC radio report from Cameroon included an interview with a man who could tell where someone came from by the way they danced; those who lived in forest communities were more restricted in their leg movements than people from the open savannah. And it is tempting to think the nasal wail of musicians from the arid Sahara region reflects something of the desert climate.

The popular music of the continent is in most cases the product of two parents, one internal and African, the other external or alien. The strongest connections lifting music from its traditional context have been with displaced musical relatives from the New World, such as jazz, calypso, rumba and reggae. African pop styles have become centralised, clustered around the main cultural or commercial centres, so there is 'Manding swing' or 'electro griot' music from West Africa, the 'Swahili sound' from East Africa, 'jive' from the south, Muslim music from the north, *makossa* and 'liberation' music in between, and pan-African syntheses like 'highlife' and Congo-Zairean rumba or *soukous* which have radiated furthest from their points of origin. Of the many popular music styles in Africa, these are really the only ones which have spread to new audiences outside their cultural base.

Popular music is by definition commercial, depending for its existence on the basic ingredients of a music business, particularly the means of production and distribution, and a clientele willing and able to pay for the music. These factors only come together in about half a dozen African capitals which have (or have had) a viable music business, and despite the low chance of success they attract countless young hopefuls seeking a career in music. One observer writing about Kinshasa in 1990 pointed out that the Zairean capital was set to become the largest French-speaking city in the world by the end of the twentieth century, and was not being facetious when he suggested the musical ambience might be one of the main attractions for would-be urbanites coming in from the regions.

The difference between contemporary popular music and traditional idioms is often vast but there is a continuity of purpose identified by Ray Lema, 'fusion' keyboard player and ex-director of the Zairean national ballet: "Music is a social game where every member of a tribe has a place of his own, and that's the purpose of the game, to find one's place in society."

Each of the pop idioms or 'style clusters' featured in the following chapters represents a peak of achievement in fusing traditional Africa with the prevailing technology. Each has earned the right to exist while many others have been lost, diverted, misplaced or forgotten. African music is constantly reviving itself, however, referring back to its roots while embracing new developments in instrument and recording technology, and there remains a multiplicity of styles waiting to be revived, reinvented or recuperated. The most enduring pan-African styles have thrived not only because they started in the right place at the right time, but also because they were examples of outgoing music, deliberately tailored to help the widest inter-ethnic or non-tribal audience find a place in the modern world.

Nyoka Longo, Zaiko Langa Langa

The Heartbeat of Africa

To say that music is a part of life in Africa is an understatement. In many African cultures music has a greater significance than human life. It is often believed to have pre-dated the existence of man and remains the main conduit for communication with the gods. It certainly pre-dates history. Even the young pop musician who has never played traditional music and likes to dance to American soul carries a weight of cultural baggage, memories from the collective subconscious and the conscious expression of his people, and understanding music's potential as a language will be part of the load. In that baggage the African musician has a complete survival kit, a fund of forms and contents, but it is also a burden to be carried through life. From the African perspective music is heavy with meaning.

Music was probably a language some time before words had literal meanings. The Christian religion believes that 'In the beginning was the word'. Could that word not have been a song? Music is so much a part of mortal life that no major African language has a word for 'music' in general — only for the various forms it takes. There are countless words for indigenous musical styles, dances and songs, most of which either describe the music's function, the instrument it is played on, or the occasion on which it is used. But for most purposes the catch-all European word 'music' (*musique, muziki*) is now used throughout the continent.

Africa is a land of languages. There are at least 2,000 ethnic sub-groups speaking as many dialects of the main language families. Their customs, traditions and beliefs vary widely, despite similarities in the way of life and social organisation across the continent. The main language groups, are the Bantu-speaking peoples of Central and Southern Africa, the Nilo-Saharan from the

Language of the gods: the human body is the most ancient and versatile of instruments

northeastern region, and the Niger-Congo language speakers of West Africa. Within these, whole nations of inter-related peoples have developed and several empires have been established by the major 'tribes' whose names should be on every school child's roll call of African dynasties, including the Kingdom of the Ashantis, the Manding Empire, the Congo Kingdom and the Zulu Nation. Each sub-group, 'tribe' or clan of the main groups has its own music, most of which has a specific function in the community. This applies not only to 'folklore' or 'cultural' music but also to transitional, modernised variants and outright commercial dance music.

Devotional music is a crucial element of worship, regardless of denomination

The voice is the original musical instrument and it is no coincidence that singing is still the most important feature in almost all popular music, but the human body was also adaptable as a hand-clapping, leg-slapping, and 'human beat box' instrument thousands of years before being taken up by twentieth-century hip-hoppers. With the beginnings of language came the lyric, crucial to most traditional music where the message is usually served by the medium. Within small ethnic sub-groups traditions are preserved through the continuity of the music, but songs that are handed down are prone to changes in content and interpretation. In popular music designed to reach outside a small community, songs must still be relevant to the primary audience. Many pop singers and composers have inherited the cloak of immunity which covers traditional musicians such as West African *griots*, allowing them an ambiguous freedom to criticise, satirise and moralise on sensitive issues. Under African military regimes musicians have often been more outspoken than politicians,

Music for pleasure: Zairean group TAZ Bolingo blaze a trail for women in African popular music

although total immunity is never guaranteed. Topicality, poetic or oratorial elegance and wit are essential talents for the social commentator, but the measure of success for a 'popular' musician is being accepted and enjoyed by people who don't understand. And no matter what the language, African listeners have an ear for a good voice.

An important vocal construction is call-and-response singing, a pattern common to many types of African music and Black music in the West. This form of musical dialogue usually consists of a short phrase from the lead voice or instrument answered by the chorus or other instruments and so it progresses, exchanging words or musical phrases in a kind of shorthand abstract conversation, although literal meaning is never far away. Even purely instrumental African music sometimes has a narrative story line behind it. In Uganda certain xylophone tunes have unspoken lyrics which must be learned in order to play the pieces properly. And in contemporary African pop, bass and guitar lines usually follow the melodic pattern of the songs.

Ashanti drummers playing the 'fontomfrom'

Melody has often been identified by musicologists as less important in African music than rhythm and harmony, but the interplay and 'impersonation' between melody and rhythm is one of African music's powerful fascinations. Melodic instruments and vocal lines are as dependent on rhythmic pulse as the so-called rhythmic or percussion instruments which invariably manage to create a kind of parallel melody of their own. In contemporary pop the song content does not always dictate the form of the music. The important musical language of Lingala is tonal but accents are often bent in favour of a tuneful line, which might be stretched with added syllables to fit the melody.

Some languages are so tonal that a sequence of notes played on certain instruments can have literal meaning. An obvious example is the talking drum, but even guitar and saxophone phrases have been 'interpreted' by music fanatics as subtle threats, insults or warnings to rival musicians. When the Africans' love of word play is taken into account these meanings can be stretched indefinitely. Making witty, topical puns with secret, 'in-crowd' significance can be fun enough with words; when sounds are used the scope is even greater.

Sound Objectives

There is a continuity of life in Africa which is difficult for an outsider to comprehend and historical facts barely give an idea of the cultural span of the continent. The oldest remains of man's ancestors, calculated to be some one and threequarters of a million years old, were found in East/Central Africa. Around 3400 BC the world's first great civilisation was established in Egypt. By the first century of the modern calendar it is believed the Bantu people began to migrate from what is now southern Zaire to settle

Fanfare players returning from a funeral in Kinshasa

'Roots' rhythms are often a product of the daily grind

throughout Africa south of the Equator. About 1100AD, the stone city of Zimbabwe was constructed, while in West Africa the gold-rich empire of Ancient Ghana was about to be absorbed into the Songhai Empire of Mali which reached its zenith in the early 1300s. The African coast was not explored by Europeans until the Portuguese in the late fifteenth century. This was about the time Columbus 'discovered' America, although there is some evidence to suggest that Africans arrived in the New World centuries before him. In the sixteenth century the colonial era began, but the interior of the 'Dark Continent' was not investigated by Europeans until Mungo Park's travels in 1795. During those millennia African society changed very little.

Many forms of African music bridge the gap between traditional customs, possibly thousands of years old, and modern city life. The most culturally specific music, which does not cross over from one people to their neighbours, has often grown out of particular activities — from pounding maize, paddling a dugout canoe, gathering crops or building houses to punishment, healing, seasonal celebrations, naming ceremonies, initiation, circumcision, storytelling, children's play, education, hunting, worship, war, weddings, wakes, installation of chiefs or kings, overcoming natural disasters and so on.

In one of the most widespread uses for music, it accompanies the spirits of the recently deceased and celebrates their arrival in the land of the ancestors. During funerals there might be sad music provided by professional mourners but this is usually contrasted with exuberant celebration. As an African must strive never to offend the spirits of the ancestors, so displays of sadness are often balanced with happiness, pride with shame and strength with weakness. This helps explain how songs of personal grief can often display a kind of euphoria.

Some of the functions of traditional music have been continued in popular idioms. As the Nigerian juju superstar Sunny Ade explained, his brand of juju music retains its usefulness even though it has been refined. "We use the music to preach, we use it to teach, we use it to educate. It is not entertainment all alone, because when you play juju music you are playing traditional music which has been around for decades, being refined. You refresh the memory of the people, even those who are not born by that time, and teach them what has been in existence from before our forefathers. And at the same time you make sure that it belongs to our culture and heritage."

Music is also a medium for personal expression, either following a creative impulse or for more practical purposes. A sub-group of the Akan people of Ghana have an annual religious festival when they are encouraged to release their pent-up aggression and ill-feeling through song. During the week-long event, common people and those in authority can be freely criticised by anyone who has a score to settle. In Zaire, the Pende people virtually sing their way through life, even conducting council meetings and criminal trials in song.

Physical activities like work often provide their own momentum for the music, setting the tempo and dictating the rhythm precisely, and where tools are used they sometimes double as instruments adding their own voice to the aural atmosphere. Africa is alive with sound, from the swish of the besoms at dawn, when millions of women across the continent sweep the loose sand from outside their doors, to the digitally precise squeaking of flying fox fruit bats hanging in the mango trees at dusk. In The Gambia women still pound their rice or millet every day in large

A gathering of chiefs at an installation in Senegambia griots are called to play at all formal and social occasions

The Drummers of Burundi: court musicians invited to join the global rock and roll circus

mortars, heaving their heavy pestles in a rhythmic upswing and letting them fall back onto the grain with a satisfying thump that reverberates through the dirt floor of the compound. To make the work more pleasurable they clap their hands while the big sticks hover in the air, sometimes three women working together in perfect synchronisation.

A form of functional music to have survived and thrived in popular idioms is the praise song. Originally reserved for chiefs, kings and rulers, contemporary musicians now sing the praises of businessmen, sports stars, commercial sponsors and of course, presidents and their political parties. Often wealth alone is sufficient reason to praise a subject, particularly where the custom is for patrons to 'dash' money to the singers. In West Africa this is widespread, from the Alhadjis stuffing dalassis or CFA francs into the sound holes of koras, to the lace and silk-robed Yoruba businessmen who 'spray' bandleaders with wads of negotiable currency or the Zairean mamas who fondly thrust a single note into the hands of a grinning *atalaku* shouter. Anyone can participate and as the praise can come before or after payment noone need feel neglected.

As Sunny Ade pointed out, "When you are entertaining guests there must be music, and you can easily praise a particular subject, on the opening of a new house, installing a king". Fortunately for Ade and the other Yoruba superstars there is a large royal community in Yorubaland. "As they say in the proverb 'Any king that reigns and his time is good, let his name be written for life. Any king that reigns and his time is bad is going to be

15

Postures of politics: one of the Zairean ruling party's many 'animation' teams sing and dance the president's praises

Member of The Gambian National troupe: dance is indivisible from the expression of music

written for life." Praise singers are open to lobbying and commercial pressure, and the level of 'goodness' is often established on the basis of 'no pay, no praise'. Indeed, if a West African *griot* is dashed money by a stranger, particularly a foreigner, about whom he knows no personal details or family history his only recourse might be to praise the patron for his generosity.

Among some peoples there are specialist musicians who learn their skills through childhood at the hands of a master who might also be related. Already familiar to Western listeners are the griots of West Africa and court musicians attached to royal families such as the Drummers of Burundi. Their exclusive, hereditary roles make the musicians virtual professionals. But to the majority of traditional musicians, their particular music is so specific, and so integral to their society, that commercialism would be inconceivable. Against this background it is not difficult to see that older people in particular often have an ambivalent attitude to popular music. The fact that it is now marketed like other consumer goods has helped improve the popular musicians' standing, and while the old snobberies and taboos remain, the music itself is usually found to be acceptable.

Dorothy Masuka, the Zimbabwean singer who grew up in South Africa, felt communal disapproval at her chosen career because artistes were not expected to behave like "normal human beings". She described it as a battle to make people accept that music could be a profession. "Eventually, I'm not rich, I'm not poor. That's when they started seeing it as a real job. They would ask, 'Where does she get her money?' and my mother would say 'She's singing, she gets paid', and they started to think about it positively."

There are many kinds of music which are open to all comers, but there are always rules, and most traditional music can only be played by certain initiates. Women, for instance, although steeped in rhythmic work patterns and as physically capable as most men, are rarely permitted to play anything but percussion instruments. They often sing, but their regular part in music is to dance.

Dancing is so crucial to music (even in its more sombre vein), that to 'play' music can mean to dance, or clap along as well as to play an instrument. It is the participation which counts, with artistic interpretation, grace, humour, physical skills and the ability to improvise valued and admired. Dance is often claimed to be the original art form, even pre-dating song, and in Africa it is indivisible from music, which might be a solo voice or percussion instrument or it might be mute, only heard instinctively by the dancers. As Manu Dibango has observed, people move with an image of their environment, and the perceptive craftsmen who created the famous bronze figures of Benin, Nigeria could apparently tell the occupation of a person by the way he or she danced. "Dance in Africa is not a separate art, but a part of the whole complex of living," the American dancer Pearl Primus once said. It certainly complements all other art and craft disciplines, which in Africa are rarely separated from each other, or from life in general. Dance is a form of multimedia living theatre, involving the design and cutting of cloth shown off on the body and on certain

Dancers from Kivu bring traditional flare to an urban festival

Senegambian fiddlers with molo, single-stringed instruments

17

A Zambian plays a slit log drum: a 'talking drum' type found throughout Central Africa

occasions the clay, raffia and painted creations of mask makers and costumiers.

The language of dance can express a range of meanings, and some such as the *adowa* from Ghana are used for both sad and festive occasions. Among the Akan, dance language has a lexicon of symbolic movements which can be made with all parts of the body. E.A. Duodu of the University of Ghana has published a list of some 40 such gestures for many occasions. They run from congratulations, through expressions of love, loyalty, reverence, guilt and innocence to an arm gesture which tells the drummers they have been promised a drink and another which means 'I regard you as a toilet roll'. Ritual dancing, as a form of personal expression or physical release, tends to be more improvised. Dance's spiritual function keeps people in touch with their ancestors through contact with the earth and brings the living together in one mystical experience, in which control of the body is given up to music.

Throughout Africa it would be impossible to find someone who has never participated in music for pleasure and African childhood sometimes appears to be a continuous dance which even the elders can tap into. For whatever reason, people in Africa like to dance and as modern life renders more traditional expressions redundant, popular music fills the void.

The Texture of Sound

Africa is far more than just a land of drums. It has a huge variety of instruments made from natural materials whose diversity is only limited by the people's imagination. Versions can be found of almost all the instrument types known to man, including drums of every size and shape. As there is special music for particular activities so the types of instruments have their own significance; several are thought to be representative of gods, either as actual embodiments of the deities or as gifts to mortal man from specific spirits. The *mbira* thumb piano from Zimbabwe, the *marimba* xylophone from Southern Africa and the West African *kora* harp are all examples of such gifts which can speak the language of the gods and therefore have great spiritual significance.

Musicologists prefer to relate instruments with others of their

A Tanzanian 'marimba': where the name refers to both thumb-pianos and xylophones

Xylophones, common to many sub-Saharan peoples, combine melody and percussive attack

kind in 'family' groups. The family of stringed instruments, classed as chordophones, is divided into those which are plucked, struck or played with a bow. Plucked instruments like the guitar are common throughout Africa and have left their mark on modern music perhaps more than even the drums. The earliest harp was a one-string bow, a type of which is still played in Angola and Central Africa. The sound is obtained by striking the tensed string with a stick. Presumably the musical properties were discovered by early hunters as they heard the bow string twang past their ears, although some musicians have suggested it might have been the other way round, when an instrumentalist found the tension on his bow string could send his stick flying. Sometimes calabash gourds have been added as sound resonators and some, like the fabled 'earth guitar', use a hole in the ground covered with a resonating membrane.

The one-string bow evolved in many directions, leading to the development of fiddles, guitars, harps and zithers. Strings were originally gut, plant fibre or strips of animal hide. Sound boxes, necks and bridges were made out of anything available, including animal horns, calabashes, carved wooden boxes, turtle shells and even human skulls. The *kora* harp/lute is one of the most impressive stringed instruments found in Africa, both in appearance and in the enchanting quality of the melodies that a skilled

The guitar has proved to be a 'natural' instrument for Africa. Musicians start on home-made versions (below) in the absence of the real thing. Playing in Europe, the Kenyan Zak Sikobe enjoys superior technology

player can coax from its calabash sound box. It is a large instrument, with a hard, rosewood neck up to 4ft long, and a calabash (gourd) sound box up to about 2ft in diameter, similar in structure to its five-string cousin the *ngoni.* Another which has crossed over into 'transitional' music is the *nyatiti* lyre from Kenya and Uganda.

Some of the most distinctive African instruments are idiophones, in which the sound is generated from the body of the intrument. These are mostly percussion instruments used for playing the vital accents which give music its dynamic, including percussion and clapping sticks, slit-log drums, bells, rattles and gongs. There are also two very important families of melodic instruments which fall into this group; the xylophone, in which pre-tuned keys are hit with a mallet, and the thumb piano in which the keys are plucked with fingers and thumb. Frequently called a *sanza,* the thumb piano is more properly known under a variety of African names including *kalimba, likembe, marimba* or *mbira.* From The Gambia to Mozambique various versions can be found, and in Zimbabwe the mbira has been especially vital in bridging traditional and popular culture.

Thumb piano is a useful descriptive name for this hand-held instrument, in which metal tongues are arranged in a keyboard design on a resonator base or soundboard. The size, shape and construction varies from large, painted West African kalimbas based on cutaway petrol cans to figuratively carved, pocket-sized likembes from Zaire and the impressively business-like *mbira dzavadzimu* from Zimbabwe. Some are built on sardine cans or packing cases, while those on solid bases are frequently played inside calabashes or turtle shells to amplify the sound. As with some other instruments the rather gentle melodic tones are accentuated by the distinctive buzzing of rattles such as shells or bottle tops fixed to the resonator. The number of keys varies from as few as seven to more than twenty, although a three-keyed instrument is played in Ethiopia and in the north of Zimbabwe some instruments have more than 50 keys.

The sound of the thumb piano is similar to the wooden-keyed xylophone, *marimba* or *balafon,* which in many cultures is often played in accompaniment. In Tanzania both instruments share the name marimba, which in some southern African traditions is the name of the mother of the universe. It is an instrument of great antiquity and the origins of the instrument are clearly part of creation mythology. There are many types of xylophone in Africa, including those with free-floating keys, sometimes laid over the

Rock iconography on the wall of a bar in Freetown, Sierra Leone

Acoustic touch: Senegalese singer Baaba Maal strums a Western made 'box' guitar

player's knees, and stone instruments. The most ubiquitous design, with hardwood keys bound on to a framework with calabash resonators fixed beneath, can be found across sub-Saharan Africa, most notably in Mozambique where it is known as *tsimbila.* In the same instrument family are *lokole* slit-log drums, found throughout Central Africa in all shapes and sizes.

Drums are usually considered to be the primary African instrument. They are certainly more significant, more widespread and more various than anywhere else. In forest areas where there are plenty of wide, mature trees, large wooden drums are common and often played in batteries, as in Burundi. In the open savannah grasslands, smaller logs, wooden frames or other materials are used, including earthenware pots, gourds, turtle shells and garbage cans, anything with an open mouth to stretch the skin over and a resonating space behind. In some ethnic groups drumming is restricted to certain classes of society, and is often an hereditary role. In other nations anybody can drum on certain instruments but most cultures have drums which are, or were, reserved for sacred functions. Most drums have a fixed pitch; others can be tuned by altering the tension of the skin during play. The hourglass shaped, doubled-headed talking drums from West Africa are made to speak by changing tension on the thongs which link the two skins. With the instrument held under one arm, the player squeezes the speech from the drum. Other types of talking drum in West and Central Africa are large free-standing pairs in different sizes with complementary tones or voices, which are played with sticks.

The last group of traditional instruments, which have had much less effect on contemporary music, are the aerophones or wind instruments. The range of materials includes wood, metal,

Impressive adowa drum band from Ashanti region, Ghana

horn, bamboo, clay, gourds and sea shells, made into a variety of trumpets, flutes, whistles and pan-pipes. Islamic cultures use reed instruments, although these have not penetrated south of the Sahara. Panpipes, with two to twenty individual pipes bound together, are thought to have spread across Africa from ancient Greece. Horns, trumpets and flutes come in a wide selection of shapes, sizes and tones. Some of the largest are found in eastern Zaire, where ivory trumpets up to eight feet long have been noted. As in the West and the Arab world, the use of horns is mostly reserved for ceremonial occasions.

The horn sound, found rarely in traditional music, was re-invented by a generation of dance bands. Fela Kuti's sax section play call-and response with soloists

Traders and Technology

Traditional instruments are rarely used in electrified popular music, with the notable exception of the West African kora and the mbira of Zimbabwe, featured in the music of 'pop stars' such as Mory Kante and Thomas Mapfumo. Such music which has been refreshed from within the culture, including *mbalax* or juju, is essentially 'tribal' in character and appeal. It is living traditional music which has caught up with modern technology. Traditional drums, particularly the hour-glass talking drums of the Yoruba and the Wolof, and various percussion instruments find their way into popular music groups, but in general most of the widely different African pop idioms are delivered on the standard Western pop equipment of drum kit, electric guitars and bass, possibly with the addition of synthesizer and trumpet and saxophone sections.

The European guitar has been known and played in Africa for centuries, since being introduced by Portuguese traders. It proved so adaptable to regional and local styles that since its general availablity after World War Two, the guitar has become the instrument of Africa. Acoustic, 'box' or 'dry' guitars, have been copied and improvised in all manner of materials and shapes, often taking features of the banjo, an American instrument of African origin.

Another less likely European contribution, the accordion, was distributed by traders all over Africa during the early years of this century. The instrument was one of the ingredients of the earliest Nigerian juju music, and accordions have been heard in places as far apart as Algeria, Sierra Leone, Nigeria, Gabon, Zaire, Kenya and Madagascar. Probably the last fling for the antiquated instrument came in the late Sixties' South African style of Accordion Jive, but the flavour survives in much of the keyboard and synthesizer playing of today's popular dance bands.

Africa entered the modern world under the yoke of colonialism. Spiritual beliefs had been supplanted by Christian and Muslim religions, and cultural development was further inhibited by European notions. In many cases the use of traditional instruments was discouraged, although rarely prohibited outright. In West Africa, the 'White man's Graveyard' indigenous culture was allowed to thrive while White settlers were discouraged. In the 'Scramble for Africa' when the continent was divided up by the Europeans in the mid-nineteenth century, the French and British had taken the biggest slices. Their different approaches ensured that francophone nations looked to Paris as the cultural capital, where there is now a homogeneous African community linked to all the French-speaking countries. The English- speaking countries of West Africa make less of a community and there traditional cultures have usually been preserved more intact. But in East Africa, where White settlers dominated, indigenous culture has been treated with less respect.

The most successful pop music within Africa crosses over 'tribal' boundaries to appeal to an inter-ethnic audience, and those idioms inevitably have plenty of international content. The strongest examples, such as West African highlife, Congo-Zairean rumba, South African *mbaqanga* and lately pan-African reggae, all began with artistes copying dance music imported from the Americas. Once a pan-African audience for these styles had been established, innovative musicians began to refresh and re-Africanise the music with elements of their own language and 'folklore'. Three generations on, the most popular African music bears little obvious relation to the original grandparents, but the family lineage can be traced back. Creating those fusions and keeping them alive is a matter of continually making the connections between the cultural memory bank and the changing external world.

The fatuous arguments about music's authenticity have thankfully died down in recent years as listeners have come to realise that almost all African popular music is a synergetic product with an effect which exceeds the sum of the indigenous and foreign components. It is pointless to condemn any kind of 'fusion' music for a lack of authenticity. The authentic music is the music people listen to and live with, not that which is preserved in a state of near-death to be pulled out each year to mark some 'traditional' festival or other in a tourist village.

Neverthless two of the most solid and mature popular music forms in Africa, Congo-Zairean rumba and Manding swing, are products of deliberately closed systems in which musicians were encouraged to create a post-independence national music from internal resources rather than outside fashions. Presidents Mobutu Sese Seko of Zaire and Sekou Toure of Guinea, two of Africa's most controversial heads-of-state, both inaugurated programmes of 'authenticity' to meld a unified nation of disparate people by focusing on indigenous rather than foreign culture. Under social conditions which were often oppressive, chosen musicians were given the artistic freedom to educate and guide their audiences along party lines, often through a process of self criticism. In Africa, music is functional and it is only authentic if it does its job; communicating with the man in the *trotro* bus, the market mammy or the youth on the disco floor. In creating a new audience, groups such as Osibisa and Toure Kunda have delivered authentic Afro-rock. Alpha Blondy and Lucky Dube play African reggae, authentically.

The South African trumpeter Hugh Masekela, who has played across the globe, made the point for many musicians at the end of the Eighties. "Look at samba, look at salsa, look at Zairean music or highlife which fascinated me very much. It's all Western influenced. If you look at modern Western music, it's all African influenced. The fulcrum is African-American. The age-old diaspora of the African people confuses some of us, and we say salsa is the real Latin-American music, but the thing is we are all living in a universal world today and the criteria should be what is good and what is bad, because good music and bad music are two different things. But if people insist that music doesn't have enough bone in the nose, or the lips are not big enough, or the nose is not flat enough, at that point instead of being culture it becomes tribalistic or racial. I get tired of it. I've been a musician since I was five and I think very few people except musicians 'know what's happening about music'. But musicians are not great at talking about music. I think they're good at playing it."

Accordions, introduced by Portuguese traders, were commonly used for social dance music in many countries, including Madagascar (below) but the electric guitar is now the sound of Africa. A member of Woya (right) strolls through a market in Ouagadougou

Rapping for Africa: Kris Parker of Boogie Down productions, providing Afrocentric 'edutainment'

Contexts and Connections

Black Music is always in flux. That is its nature. Always progressing, developing, fusing, reverting and ceaselessly borrowing from itself. And whatever the latest rave in one particular place, there is sure to be another whole movement struggling to life in a different part of the Black diaspora. Whether it is rap, acid house music, dancehall reggae, blues, rumba or the myriad forms of jazz, it has its roots in Africa. That is not to say it tries to imitate African music. Kids in the Bronx, Brixton or Trenchtown might not even recognise contemporary African dance music, because they are not attuned to it. Just as many Africans will have no time for the sounds of a different people or neighbouring country. While the traditional music of other cultures remains alien, popular music consumers have readily accepted calypsos played by Ghanaians, rumbas by a Congolese band or reggae from a South African. Yet all will proudly espouse their Africanness, and the need to keep in touch with their roots. As the radical rapper Kris Parker, aka KRS One of Boogie Down Productions, proclaimed from the Bronx, New York: "One thing we must understand in the 1990s is it's all about Africa – African consciousness, African physicalness, African mentalness, African heartness."

The main musical styles from the New World which were quickly taken up back in Africa were jazz and soul from the USA; calypso from the Caribbean, rumba from Spanish-speaking Cuba, and *merengue* from Dominica. Later American fusions like funk and hip-hop have kept the channels open, while reggae has built probably the largest African following for an 'imported' music. More recently the hi-tech *zouk* music from the French Antilles islands of Martinique and Guadeloupe (Martiloupe music) had an invigorating effect on the West African music scene.

Voice of the Diaspora

The transportation of slaves from Africa to the Americas which started in the sixteenth century has led to a widely diffused Black culture. Most of the young men and women exported to America came from the coastal regions of West Africa, although many were prisoners taken in inter-tribal wars and brought from the interior to the ports by local traders. From the Gold Coast (Ghana) region, Ashanti and Fanti people were shipped out to North America and the Caribbean by predominantly British slavers. The South American population was more of Bantu origin, with Spanish and Portuguese slavers operating further south, although Yorubas were also shipped in large numbers to Cuba and Brazil.

In spite of some colonists' policy of breaking up tribal groups to prevent organised dissension, some African music was preserved. In the so-called Latin countries of the Caribbean and South America, where slaves were more often kept as tribal units, they were also allowed to maintain their social identity and culture. The Spanish and Portuguese encouraged slaves to participate in Catholic church activities, but did not restrict their spiritual or social music. Little original African music has survived intact, but some distinctive instruments have been handed down, particularly the *marimba* (xylophone) in Cuba and South America, and two instruments which are played in both Angola and across the ocean in Brazil – the *berimbau* single-string bow harp known in Angola under many names including *mbulumbumba*, and the *cuica* or *pwita*, a tension 'drum' that howls when the skin is twisted by a stick attached to the inside.

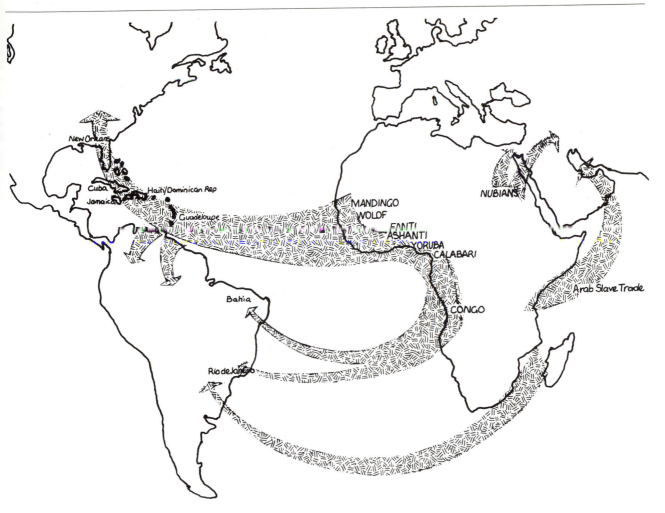

CHAPTER TWO

New Orleans

Cuba

Jamaica

Haiti/Dominican Rep

Guadeloupe

MANDINGO

WOLOF

FANTI

ASHANTI

YORUBA

CALABARI

NUBIANS

Arab Slave Trade

CONGO

Bahia

Rio de Janeiro

Origins and destinations of Africans transported during the years of the Slave Trade, showing major ethnic groups

In the English-speaking colonies most instruments were either banned or abandoned during the journey and Africans had to re-create a folk tradition using improvised instruments. The most important was the banjo, claimed to be an all-American instrument but based on the West African *gonje* or *gouje* gourd guitar. Some slaves reportedly arrived in the New World carrying European-made violins which presumably had been given or traded by early explorers — possibly in exchange for the person's freedom — and the fiddle became a familiar sound in the slave quarters during the rare snatches of leisure time.

One kind of music which did survive the brutality of slavery was, appropriately, the worksong, often accompanied by the sound of thumping hoes, slashing machetes or the hammering of construction gangs. Examples of mining and digging songs still exist in Brazil and Jamaica. Other connections with the motherland have been kept alive in song lyrics. A late nineteenth-century example which survived in Trinidad in the pre-calypso style called *kaiso* is *Congo bara*, an ironic lament sung in French, for a cruel slave driver who died in prison after fighting with the police.

African communities in some countries formed ethnic social clubs or 'nations' which preserved many aspects of their culture, some even recognising 'royal' families. There are also religious groups, of which the most established are the Yoruba cults dedicated to the god Shango, which have survived in Cuba, Brazil and Trinidad and have also been revived in the United States. In Bahia in northern Brazil the Yoruba presence, preserved as much in custom as in the people's blood, is so strong the region is known as the 'Rome of Africa'. The 'Afro-blocs' or 'Afoxes' are political and percussion societies with literally thousands of members who turn out to play the *bata* during carnival. In Cuba there are also Ekpo cults kept alive by descendants of Efiks and Ibibios from southern Nigeria. Since the abolition of slavery many of these societies opened up their membership and in Spanish and Portuguese colonies, where there was less segregation, White people were accepted as members. In Haiti the *voudoun* religion remained true to its African origins. It was banned on the country's independence in 1804, but like the Jamaican *obeah* cult, outlawed after the slave revolt of 1760, voodoo still thrives in secret.

In the USA, African music was virtually eliminated by the slave owners. Tribal groups were split up and drums were originally prohibited because of their ability to speak, and therefore be used for subversion, although music was permitted at work to boost productivity. The first African-Americans were not encouraged to share the Whites' religion, and neither were they allowed to preserve their own customs. Along with the drums, dancing, defined as crossing the legs while in motion, was forbidden on most plantations, except once a year at Mardi Gras or carnival.

Despite the cultural confinement suffered by African-Americans, they refused to let their music stagnate. In areas where social exchange was possible, the 'feeling' or inflexion of Black music began to insinuate itself into the Whites' dance music. On the other hand that music was taken up by Blacks who subtly transformed the waltzes to their own tastes. Travelling minstrel shows, with repertoires containing ballads, early blues and operettas, were at their peak at the end of the nineteenth century. The first Dixieland bands also appeared; with trumpets, clarinets, trombones, tubas, banjos and drums. The trumpet became popu-

Dreaming of America: bar paintings in Sierra Leone express the envy of Western culture common to African youth

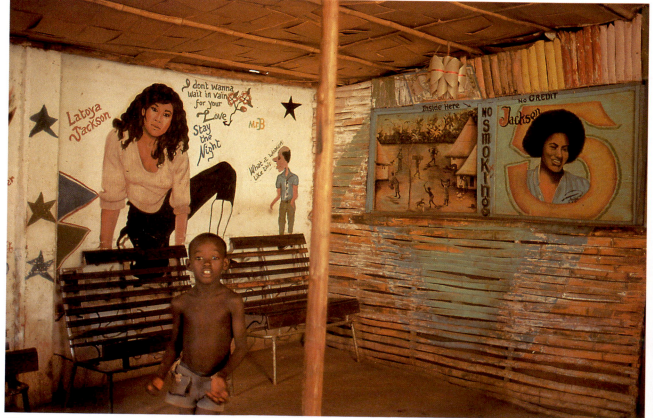

'Jogo da Capoeira': a Brazilian dance with highly acrobatic movements accompanied by the berimbau single-string bow harp which originated in Angola

lar as the first solo voice to stand out from the ensemble.

During the eighteenth and nineteenth centuries, Africans or aspects of their culture mingled in high-brow society, participating in some of the grandest classical music. In 1795 George Bridgetower, a third generation African-American, played violin with no less a figure than Beethoven; 50 years later Gottschalk, the first internationally respected American composer, incorporated Black folk music into pieces titled *Bamboula* and *Chanson Negre*. In 1907 Harrry L. Freeman became the first African-American composer to conduct a symphony orchestra.

Ironically, by the time African culture was beginning to find a modicum of 'respectability' abroad, the slave trade was also at its peak with some twenty million Africans having been brutally uprooted to the Americas. When Livingstone started exploring the African interior in 1849, the West African city of Freetown (Sierra Leone) and the state of Liberia had been established as homes for freed slaves. There were already many thousands more in America who had earned their release, and by 1863 Abraham Lincoln had, theoretically, emancipated the remainder.

America, Home of the Free

The most important developments in Afro-American music have come from the USA, particularly since the dawn of the age of electricity. African and anglophone music had never meshed as satisfyingly and as naturally as Afro-Latin music, and African-Americans, already denied access to drums, had to create completely new forms. Jazz, which transformed European structured music with African techniques of interweaving rhythm and melodies, call-and-response patterns and 'vocalising' with instruments, became the first all-American art form.

Roots of the blues: guitarist Ali Farka Toure, a fan of John Lee Hooker, knows both sides of the story, from Malian folklore to downtown Chicago

There was also the folk music of the poor, less-sophisticated, usually rural people, expressed in the blues, the 'Devil's music' in which solo singers, usually accompanying themselves on guitar, reflected on the hardships of life. The often topical content and the independent minstrel life had similarities with the social role of west African griots, and so did the music, according to Malian 'blues' guitarist Ali Farka Toure. With little money available, instruments for social music sessions were often improvised in a very African fashion including items such as washboard percussion, bath tub bass and a jug blown across the neck to sound like a tuba. Kazoos were also common for this type of dance-blues or 'juke' music. There was another more genuine form of Devil's music in New Orleans, from the 'devil-worship' rites of the Arada people from Dahomey (now Benin), close neighbours of the Yoruba. The Arada rites are a major part of voodoo and also have a connection with the funeral marching bands of New Orleans.

Parallel with the Devil's music was the religious alternative taking place in the church communities which were always strong and expressive. Many Africans were far from heathens, having already been exposed to missionary zeal before their capture and transportation. The new hymns and gospel songs created in America had strong African influences and the allegorical nature of spirituals allowed them to become a form of underground communication, and a focus of cultural identity. However processed the content, the communal expression and hidden significance of religious music proved a binding cement in the social and family structure of Black American life.

And then there was jazz, a proto-highlife music if ever there was. Jazz is an American art form; it has also been described as the summation of the Black man's experience. It is arguably the most important development in the history of music, establishing a context for improvisation in which musical instincts of all persuasions can find a space. Through the spectrum of the jazz rainbow anything from uninhibited primal screams to the most artful, scored compositions can be worked in alongside each other. In the middle ground the sound of Africa is always evident.

Originally jazz was dance music, restricted to the Black milieu of cheap dancehalls, bars and bordellos. The early New Orleans jazz was a fusion of the ragtime piano style with blues, spirituals and the brass music of marching bands common at the start of the twentieth century. Under Spanish and then French rule until the nineteenth century, the city had an almost Latin atmosphere, with a rhythm of life more Caribbean than American. Out of ragtime evolved the local boogie-woogie style of piano playing, in which short phrases are repeated to create cross rhythms greater than the sum of their parts, a technique shown to have strong links with African xylophone playing. Even before World War One, ragtime and proto-jazz had found appreciative audiences in English-speaking Africa, particularly South Africa and the Gold Coast (Ghana).

The New Orleans style was not the only form. King Oliver, the top trumpeter took his band to Chicago where he was joined by Louis Armstrong, the first virtuoso jazz musician, soon to become famous among Africans as a symbol of Black achievement. In 1929 Armstrong inaugurated mixed race music when he took the stage with White musicians. In Chicago, the first large jazz bands, divided into sections of instruments, generated a craze for dancing, and during the Prohibition (1919-1933) and the Depression years of the 1930s a taste of the 'high life' became a popular antidote. Swing was mass appeal music covered by countless imitators of the great bandleaders, Count Basie and Duke Ellington. The music of the swing era gradually became more Africanised, using short, repeated phrases or riffs, and incorporating Afro-Latin dance elements such as the *rumba, conga,* and *samba.*

In the 1950s the bebop revolution took place. This was not the usual evolution of Black music where styles are borrowed from one side and blend into another. It was a musical revolution in which the historic flow of past influences was cut off. From now on jazz was no longer music for dancing. As White culture successfully assimilated swing music, many Black musicians combined their resentment with a progessive attitude, bringing an artistic, spiritual and physical intensity which was unprecedented. In reaction to the 'big bland' sound, bebop was the music of individuals and small improvising combos. In the 1940s the main breakthroughs were made by the saxophonist Charlie Parker and trumpeters Dizzy Gillespie and Miles Davis, whose frantic instrumental solos virtually doubled the speed of the music, making it too complex for many listeners. The spiritual realm of the 'universality of Black music' was further explored by people like John Coltrane, Albert Ayler, Ornette Coleman and Don Cherry.

Several jazzers have visited Africa over the years since Armstrong's 'homecoming' to Ghana, although few penetrated the heart of the continent south of the Sahara. The pianist Randy Weston worked and played in Morocco during the Sixties and Dizzy Gillespie also landed in North Africa to record his *Nights in*

Seminal blues man Muddy Waters: one of a generation of Americans whose music filtered back to West Africa

Tunisia. Few musicians followed the 'Roots' route back to the homeland, although Roy Ayers' collaboration with Fela Kuti brought horn-men Lester Bowie and Arthur Blythe in touch with Afrobeat. One horn player who had already voyaged over several continents before arriving in West Africa in the early 1980s was the trumpeter Don Cherry, a precursor of 'world music' who tapped a fund of traditions, cross-pollinating them with those of his African-American heritage. In Mali he acquired a four-string *dousso n'goni,* a hunter's guitar, which expanded the range of sounds and textures available to him.

The African-American dance root was kept alive in the regenerated form of Rhythm and Blues (R&B) which had established itself with record buying African-Americans. The electric guitar, pioneered by jazz man Charlie Christian in the 1930s, was quickly taken up by blues musicians and the brash, urban environment of the industrial cities hardened the music, giving it an added vitality. Regional tastes differed, and recognisable styles came about in the major towns with large Black populations.

After World War Two the R&B chart, initiated by *Billboard* magazine in America, brought together gospel, ballads, boogie-woogie, jug and juke bands, jump blues and swing blues. While swing bands now played almost exclusively to Whites, and jazz innovators plied their trade in small, exclusive 'art' circles, R&B had become the music of the people. Many of the R&B idioms, particularly acappella vocal music, boogie-woogie and the hard, urban blues of guitarists such as Chuck Berry and Bo Diddley fused with country music and ballads to become rock and roll. After jazz, rock and roll proved to be the most influential fusion, but as it spread across the globe in the new age of electronic communication, it soon became White music. Meanwhile Blacks reclaimed their cultural identity with soul.

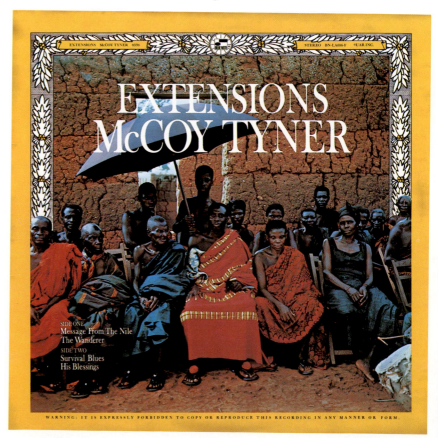

Sleeve for record by pianist McCoy Tyner, a graduate of John Coltrane's band and exponent of the 'universality of Black music'

Don Cherry, precurser of 'World Music', brought his *ngoni* instrument to the jazz and rock milieu

Dancing in the Streets

Soul, which grew up in the eastern and mid-western cities of the USA during the early Sixties, went right back to the basic ingredient, the voice. Reclaiming many R&B ingredients, soul's most immediate ancestor was gospel music. Most of the best soul singers such as Aretha Franklin and Wilson Pickett had developed their talents in church gospel choirs during their childhood. A powerful voice was required to express the drama, intensity and painful emotion of a good soul song. It could be cracked or croaking, as long as it overflowed with emotion. A solid beat and big, brassy horn arrangements were essential, although the tempo varied from super-fast dance ravers to slow, dreamy ballads. Live soul reviews backed up the intensity with flamboyant dance routines and extravagant costumes, while 'sweetening' effects, such as overdubbed violins and multiple vocal harmonies created a plush 'sophisticated' atmosphere.

In Africa, the raw emotion of soul touched a nerve, while the contemporary production values made the music sparkle invitingly. One of the biggest soul successes was the Percy Sledge release, *When a Man Loves a Woman,* which enabled Sledge to tour East and Central Africa several times during the Seventies. Other big names like Otis Redding, James Brown and Wilson Pickett were heard across the continent. Pickett headlined the influential 'Soul to Soul' festival in Ghana in 1974, supported by Roberta Flack, the Staples Singers, Carlos Santana and Ike and Tina Turner amongst others. The loudest response from Africa was Manu Dibango's *Soul Makossa* classic, although soul continues to inspire countless musicians across the continent.

James Brown's funk style, relying on repetitive riffing with steady bass and drum lines, was a kind of neo-African music, showing a direct line of descent. Brown obviously saw the value of the African connection which he re-established by playing in Nigeria, Zaire and Kenya. With its dependence on rhythm, dance and ritual, the permutations of funk were explored by several jazz artistes, before it too was assimilated into the mainstream to become a familiar pop dialect which has coloured much contemporary Western music. In Africa Brown's music had a direct effect on Fela Kuti and, for a while, on the great Zairean dance orchestras.

In the early Eighties the mechanical disco of artistes like Donna Summer and Barry White brought a whiff of hi-tech sophistication to young, urban Africans. But the biggest international icon across Africa during the 1980s was Michael Jackson. An idol of the youth in anglophone countries and envied everywhere, the young Jackson was a particular phenomenon in Nigeria, where at the height of 'Michael Mania' his picture on a magazine centre spread would be ripped out and sold for the same price as the magazine.

At the start of the 1990s rap was still being marketed in the West as if it were a new music, but the style had been around since the late Seventies when New York disc-jockey Grandmaster Flash began voicing over hard funk instrumental tracks, 'scratching' with the stylus and skipping the disc by hand to repeat choice phrases. This was the start of a new street culture associated with graffiti artists, flamboyant sports clothing and unashamed egotism. It was mainly verbal, with no instruments and a minimal creative vision, but it was a great opportunity for expression. Hip-hop had rediscovered the original instrument, but given it the texture of a silicone chip. Hip-hop rhythms and rappers had developed an aura of controversy by the time the 'Afrocentricity' movement appeared around the tenth anniversary of the first rap attack. Top rappers like KRS One, Queen Latifah, and others tried to snap the more mindless devotees to attention by calling on their listeners and rivals to think about where they were going and where they were coming from.

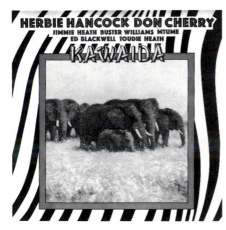

The music took on the function of self-healing as well as education. In 1990, Queen Latifah, a twenty-year-old New York rapper, mixing hip-hop with reggae and house music, claimed: "Hip hop is the most positive and enlightening music out there. It's rappers that talk the most about crushing apartheid, about staying away from drugs and about racial equality and homelessness. Why? because each of us has experienced these problems." A female contemporary of Latifah's, Monie Love from South London joined New Yorkers including the Jungle Brothers and Black Watch, a Black consciousness movement fronted by Queen Mother Rage, X-Clan and Isis, who summed up the new awareness: "Perhaps we have got into who we are, our African descendency, so we carry ourselves differently."

Return of the Rumba

The music which cut the widest swathe through Africa during the infancy of its music business was known generically as 'rumba'. The popular music of South America and Cuba was always an easier blend of African social music with Spanish and Portuguese idioms already influenced by North African Moors since they occupied Spain in the eighth century. A few hundred years later Spain established its trading base on the Canary Islands, whose original inhabitants were also of North African origin. From there they could sail directly to Cuba. Ships of all the colonising countries often made their last landfall at the nearby Goree Island off Senegal, where the slave prison's 'last doorway' led straight into the holds of the merchant ships.

The music which prospered in the more relaxed Latin colonies, including Dominican and Haitian *merengue, beguine* from the French Antilles, *tango, candombey* and *samba* from South America, blossomed with the introduction of recording in the Thirties and Forties and was known in West Africa almost immediately. In Cuba the idiom which had closest relations with Africa was the *son,* a variant of rumba which had a lasting influence on African popular dance music. The *muntuno, cha cha cha, bolero,* and *salsa* were also popular, especially in francophone or Hispanic countries where Anglo-African jazz had less influence. From Senegal to Mozambique 'rumba' is still loved and enjoyed but nowhere more so than in its original homeland of Zaire, Congo and Angola, where the Cuban bandleader Rafael Ley in particular inspired the first generation of 'Congolese rumba' artistes.

The son, a sound which dominated Cuba for fifteen years from the mid-Twenties, was literally a song and dance format, with the vocal action confined to the first part and an instrumental second section given to 'animation' and dancing, which the Congolese developed into the characteristic *sebene.* Before World War Two, Latin music had infiltrated the dance repertoires of bands in many

The legendary Louis Armstrong, first generation jazzman, on his 'return' to Africa in 1956 is greeted in Ghana by comedian Ajax Bukana and highlife trumpeter E.T. Mensah (left)

The 'Wicked Pickett', seen by a Sierra Leonean bar artist, touched a nerve throughout the 'Land of a Thousand Dances' during the Sixties

African countries, but the vital commercial boost came in the early Fifties when the EMI label released its famous series of 'GV' discs throughout Africa. Most of these classic Latin singles were pre-war recordings and the B-side of the first disc was *El Manicero* (The Peanut Vendor), still part of every African band's warm-up overture and one of the most recorded songs of all time.

Throughout the francophone zone the biggest band by far during the Eighties was Kassav, frontrunners of a vital hi-tech music called zouk. They became a supergroup in France and their homeland in the French Antilles islands of Martinique and Guadeloupe. The zouk fusion had started in the previous decade in Guadeloupe when Georges and Pierre Decimus came together with guitarist Jacob Desvarieux to play a funked up version of the local folk music, featuring a bamboo percussion instrument called the *ti-bois,* blended with available modern idioms. Previously the most popular music in the Antilles had been beguines and *mazurkas,* sweet but frenetic music like a rumba album played at 78rpm. Then Haitian music had its day before being surpassed by *cadance* and in the Seventies, *discocadence.*

The African connection is a strong one. Desvarieux had lived in Senegal as a child: the ti-bois is an instrument also found in Cameroon, and, as keyboard player Jean Claude Naimro says, the zouk bass line also comes from Cameroon. Naimro had worked with several Cameroonians including Manu Dibango and Toto Guillaume and recalls Cameroonian hits in the Antilles like *Ami* and Sam Fan Thomas' *African Typic Collection* on which he played. He also acknowledged the source of the Congolese ingredient as Ryco Jazz, who spent four years in Martinique in the late Sixties. Kassav hit the big time in 1989 with a series of shows at the Zenith in Paris. Their music caught on with several Zaireans, notably Pepe Kalle and Kanda Bongo Man. The big sound of zouk was slick and chic but, as Naimro said, zouk is a craze, and into the Nineties its steam seemed to be running out.

Islands in the Sun

The folk music of the Caribbean contains many elements of European tradition, including tunes, rhythms and words which are now archaic in their homeland. Trinidad had an especially chequered colonial history with Spanish, British and French colonists and even an Asian influence from the large minority of 'east Indians' living there. Early calypsos were sung in French and only in the late nineteenth century did English become the norm. Calypso was originally a Port of Spain underworld custom which had evolved from 'kaiso', a verbal jousting game which livened up the old work songs. Kaiso songs were being recorded on the island from the mid-1920s onward. With scandalous lyrics, expressing an outrage that is sometimes mock, sometimes deadly serious, calypso is a form for polemic and gossip similar to many forms of African music today.

The role of the calypsonians and their relish for lyrical invention, in chastising villains and celebrities, making lewd innuendoes or savage social comment, can be likened to the role of the griot in West African society. Calypso was well known in Africa by the 1930s but after World War Two it enjoyed worldwide popularity with Attila, The Lord Pretender, Roaring Lion, Lord Invader, Mighty Sparrow and Lord Kitchener, and the American pop interpretations of carnival songs like *Rum and Coca Cola* from the Andrews Sisters and *Island in the Sun* by Harry Belafonte. Africa

Zouk group Kassav stormed West Africa in the Eighties with a hi-tech presentation of Antillean fusion

provided a keen audience for this new idiom, with its acoustic guitars and melodious quality. E.T. Mensah, S.E. Rogie, Gentleman E.K. Vikey and other West Africans took readily to calypso which blended with their own rhythms to become highlife. Calypsonians returned the interest with songs like Lord Invader's *I'm Going Back to Africa.*

Today's harder dance version, *soca*, retains the jaunty quality,enlivened by brash horns, synthesizers echoing the steel pans, which themselves recall African xylophones, and occasional African guitar sounds. Songs by performers like David Rudder, Gypsy and Ed Watson are the regular 'copyright' fare of many dance bands in anglophone Africa. Arrow, a regular visitor to Sierra Leone, Bally and Black Stalin are some of the many Caribbean artistes who have recorded songs with African themes.

The first Third World hero, whose name, image and music are household currency throughout the Black diaspora, was Bob Marley who led the penetration of reggae music into Africa, Europe, America and beyond. The growing interest in pan-Africanism and Black consciousness which gathered momentum in the States during the 1960s provoked an exchange of Caribbean and American culture. West Indians had absorbed American

The first Third World hero: Bob Marley's music and memory inspired a generation of African reggae artistes

The Harder They Come: Jimmy Cliff made himself at home in several African countries during the late 1980s

R&B from the radio and Jamaicans adapted it to their own tastes, leading to the ska or bluebeat rhythm which later evolved into reggae. Developed from the 'mento' social music of the early African inhabitants, the music, with its characteristic offbeat drumming and dominant bass lines caught on quickly in Britain and filtered back through to the States during the 1970s. The early pioneers of ska included the likes of Prince Buster, and Toots Hibbert and the Maytals, whose music kept an up-beat expectant feeling.

The beat turned fully inside out for rock steady and 'dub', with the silence of empty space taking a solo role. There was also a jazzier stream nurtured by guitarist Ernest Ranglin and sax players Roland Alphonso and Tommy McCook. Jimmy Cliff, a pioneer of commercial reggae, visited several African countries in the Eighties including a long personal journey down the west coast, recording with Cameroonian and Zairean musicians. Marley played Zimbabwe and Benin, Burning Spear visited Nigeria (unhappily), while the London-based Misty in Roots toured frequently in Zimbabwe and West Africa.

Although reggae rhythms were quickly taken up by musicians from every continent, the significance of the music to Jamaicans is closely related to the Rastafarian religion. This 'Back to Africa' persuasion owes its existence to the teachings of Marcus Garvey who established the Black Star shipping line in the 1920s to enable Jamaicans to return to Africa. The specific homeland was to be Ethiopia. During the 1970s and 1980s, Rastafarianism became the most supportive cultural atmosphere for Black youth in many countries. But religious accessories of dreadlocks, ganja, Ethiopian national flag and images of Haile Selassie are for many, if not most 'dreads' secondary to the music. As happens quickly to most 'rebel' music, reggae was assimilated into Western pop, after having matured within its own sub-culture.

The return of all these various musical forms to Africa was dependent on hardware — first the instruments brought in for religious or ceremonial bands or as trade goods. When radio became viable in Africa the music received its first life-giving slap to the backside. It howled lustily. African popular music was born.

AFRICAN ROOTS..

ACT 1

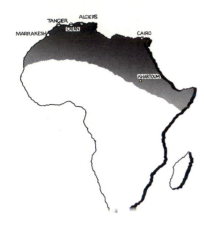

Islamic Inflexions

Throughout North Africa and way beyond the Sahara desert, the wailing call of the muezzin atop the mosque tower has been heard at sunrise and another four times a day since the Arab penetration of Africa began about 1300 years ago. That voice, language and tonality have influenced music far from Mecca, in sub-Saharan Mali, Senegal and Nigeria and as far down the east coast as Tanzania and Madagascar. Many African music enthusiasts draw the line at the Sahara and say that Arabic music is not real African music. Culturally there are vast differences, but countries such as Egypt, Algeria and Morocco are members of the Organisation for African Unity (OAU) and regularly represent the continent at its second major past time, football. It is often a matter of convenience to Maghreb Arabs whether they consider themselves Africans or not. At home they preserve their differences but outside Africa they might be ready to present a more united front.

The influence of Arabic and Islamic culture on some parts of Africa has been profound, but often the further away from Mecca, the less orthodox the religious beliefs. One important distinction is that the suppression of physical expression evident in Arab countries has never been so enthusiastically accepted by Africans south of the Sahara. Outwardly Islam is often devoutly maintained and koranic classes, at which dozens of small children sit reciting the holy book in the early evening darkness, are a familiar sight throughout much of Africa. These schools often provide the only formal education available and when the local language is unwritten, the decision to become literate in Arabic is often seen as a more 'African' gesture than learning to write the language of the old Western colonial powers. In many sub-Saharan societies, Islam has been adapted to fit in with older animist beliefs and customs.

Contemporary North African music, in common with other regional styles, is as much a product of the colonial presence as a development of traditional social music. Apart from the Arab conquest which combined commercial activities like slave and gold trading with a religious crusade, the main external inputs have come this century from the French empire. All the North African countries are French oriented; even in anglophone Egypt the middle classes preferred the French language and Mediterranean culture. There was also a brief Italian colonial presence in Libya and Ethiopia.

The colonial influences included a taste for large orchestras and Western instruments such as the violin, which became notable in cinema theme music from Egypt and, to a lesser extent, from Algeria and Tunisia. The neo-colonial stimulus was perceived as a two-edged sword. The instruments, studio and broadcasting technology were keenly accepted, but at the same time strong cultural pressures led to a resistance by many musicians to the conventions which accompanied the technology. This was partly due to orthodox Islamic thinking and partly a desire to look inward and express something more relevant than an imitation of Western pop.

One of the the biggest music stars of any time, the Egyptian female singer Oum Kalsoum, earned her fame through the newly-introduced medium of radio but was aware of the need to maintain 'authenticity'. She set the tone for the modern music early on. "We must respect ourselves and our art," she once said. "The Indians

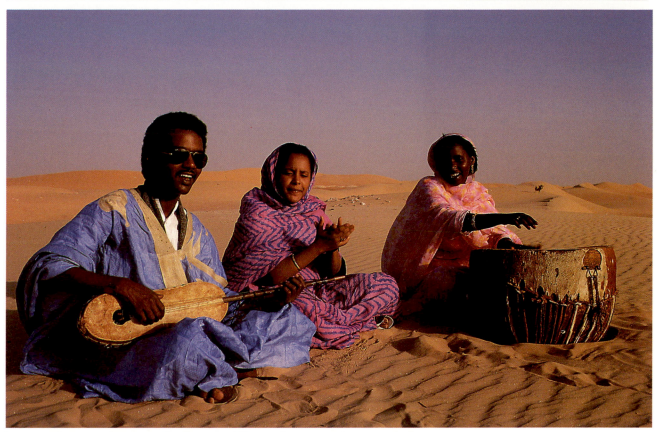

have set a good example for us. They show great respect for themselves and their music is known throughout the world. This is the right way." Arabic music has maintained its identity quite rigidly in the decades since, and most musicians followed Kalsoum's 'right way'. Many artistes, however, were obliged to take a different route, particularly following the influx of tourists to the region since the late 1960s. In the resort towns and holiday villages of Tunisia and Morocco which catered for European sunseekers, and on Egyptian packaged-pyramid tours, one effect was the crass exploitation of local culture as cheap cabaret entertainment, while other musicians knocked up quick versions of instruments to sell to passing tourists.

But some highly innovative modern sounds have come out of the North African, or western Arabic, region since the 1980s, notably Algerian *rai* music, which has established a keen following in Europe, and similar crossover experiments which fuse the roots music of the Maghreb with contemporary house, funk and reggae rhythms and production methods. Of the international dance fusions which have started to make an impression, rai is the most obviously successful but artistes from almost every other Maghreb country have taken the fusion route, combining their own regional music with modern production methods and Western electronic instruments, including the synthesizer. Pioneers include the Algerians Cheb Khaled and Chaba Fadela, the Moroccan group Lem Chaheb, and individuals such as Alisha Kandisha, Hassan Erraji, and the Egyptian Sooliman Gamil, while the young Tunisian songstress Amina has made her mark on the French commercial pop charts and was joint winner of the 1991 Eurovision Song Contest.

Countries in the desert interior have evolved their own music but their isolation and inferior technology have hindered develop-

Mauritanians Khalifa Ould Eide and Dimi Mint Abba, whose Moorish music, with echoes of sub-Saharan culture, is becoming popular throughout North Africa

ment. Musicians from Sudan and Ethiopia have appealed to Western listeners since the late Eighties, while Mauritania only came to international attention in 1991 when Dimi Mint Abba and her troupe toured Europe. Abba accompanies herself on the *ardin* a 14-string calabash instrument similar to the *kora* of Senegal and Mali. A large flat drum, tambourine, Berber vocals and flamenco elements set the music in the Maghreb zone, although the freedom and variety of expression suggest the less inhibited character of Black Africa.

From Mecca to the Maghreb

The Arab conquest of the Middle East and North Africa (Maghreb) had begun around 700AD. Spreading out from what is now Saudi Arabia the empire soon stretched from the Pyrenees on the Spanish/French border to the River Indus. and eventually all

Instruments of Islam

The instruments of the Arab world and North Africa are believed to have been the original models for almost all Western instruments from the guitar to the trumpet. There is a huge variety, some of which are very local, but three main instruments which appear throughout the Islamic world are the oud lute, the kanoon zither and the nay flute.

The oud is used throughout the Middle East and a great part of Africa from the Horn down as far as Zanzibar. Originally it had four strings, two with Persian names and two Arabic names; a fifth string was added later to allow two octaves to be played. The modern oud has ten or twelve strings arranged in pairs like a twelve-string guitar, and is played with a plectrum, although in North Africa four pairs of strings are also common. In contrast with the ancient oud, the modern instrument has no frets. The gunbri, (right) a type of lute with two strings plucked with fingers is also found widely in Morocco, Egypt and Sudan. One of the most impressive stringed instruments of all is the kanoon or Qanum, a large, table-sized zither with 72 strings grouped in threes and played with a plectrum. A similar but smaller zither, the santur uses

half as many strings.

Of the bowed instruments the rabab also known as the rebec in Europe, is a one or two-stringed fiddle found across North Africa to Ethiopia and down the east

coast to Tanzania. Another crucial instrument is the Sudanese tambura, a bowl lyre similar to the smaller instrument found in Kenya and Uganda. It has been carried as far as the Gulf and India usually in the hands of Suda-

nese slaves. True harps had become virtually extinct in the Arab world by the eighteenth century and now survive only in parts of eastern Zaire and Uganda.

The most common wind instruments are flutes, gasba, used for all kinds of folk idioms including the trance music of the Maghreb and Turkey. Double-reed shawms or oboes are also used in ensembles where their penetrating wailing sounds achieved with non-stop circular breathing techniques are found suitable for all sorts of social and formal occasions.

Trumpets originated in the Middle East and spread through Europe and Africa. They were taken up enthusiastically by Hausa kings in northern Nigeria and Cameroon, where the kakaki long brass horns sometimes measure up to six feet long. As in Europe trumpets were originally retained by the nobility for fanfares and military purposes.

Not many kinds of drum are used in Islamic music but the ones to have made the most impact are percussion frame drums (tambourines), the darbouka bowl drum, cymbals and kettle drums, which have also found their way into Western music.

the countries north of the Sahara, except Ethiopia, were united under the sign of the crescent. The empire continued to spread down the east coast of Africa where slave trading centres were established during the tenth century, and out into the Indian Ocean where all the islands, including Madagascar, were converted. The Arab penetration continued south into Central Africa until the nineteenth century, and there is evidence to show that they reached inland at least as far as the stone fortress city of Zimbabwe.

The music played today shows a cultural continuity which goes back to the days before Mohammed, who lived from 570-632 AD. Classical Arab music was itself a fusion of pre-Islamic Arab and Asian music with Persian and Turkish elements acquired during the spread of Islam. The so-called Islamic 'art music', a mainly vocal classical tradition based on the koran, is a sophisticated highly formal idiom which still thrives, but a greater influence on social music comes from the huge variety of traditional folk styles, which have often survived through continual use at family or group celebrations like marriage, naming ceremonies or harvest festivals.

The ubiquitous oud: seen here in the hands of Abdel Gadir Salim

Throughout the Muslim countries common instruments can be found many thousands of miles apart. The most ubiquitous is a lyre known universally as the *oud* by people from Morocco to Zanzibar, believed to have been the original guitar, lending its name to the 'lute', and said by the Somalis to be the instrument 'in which all other instruments can be heard'. Lyres, flutes and frame drums are played throughout the region, even by nomads. In the towns, instruments such as harps, long-necked lutes and shawms are also common. The more remote peoples have usually kept the strongest hold on ancient customs. The Berbers and the Gnaoua of the western Maghreb, show a more African identity while the nomadic Bedouin from the Sahara desert maintain what are believed to be pre-Islamic Arabic characteristics.

The Berbers (or Moors), who used to account for about one third of the North African population, have a language so different from Arabic that it is said to be impossible for a foreigner to learn one and then the other. Many Berbers converted to Christianity before the arrival of Islam; St Augustine who introduced Christianity to Britain was a Berber. They have traditionally maintained closer contact with sub-Saharan African peoples than the Arabs have, and they have inter-married with Africans in a way that offended the European-minded Arabs. In Morocco especially the French colonisers worked these differences into their policy of divide and rule.

In Islamic music the voice is the most important sound and the Arabic language has given it a nasal, almost whining, inflexion which carries throughout the lands where Arabs have left their religion, even affecting the sound of local languages. In classical Arab culture 'art music' refers to the vocal expression of Arab-Islamic literature. Performers are appreciated for the way they improvise, embellish and interpret texts within the rules and conventions of the form, using the full capacity of their voices to scream, holler and roar as well as croon and whimper. Islamic music uses a modal system in which certain notes in a scale are stressed. There are countless modes or formulas and the singer has only to refer to the theme before launching into a new composition.

With the formulation of the laws of Islam, music performance was limited to readings of the koran, the call to prayer and certain family celebrations. Although music was apparently played at the prophet Mohammed's own wedding and at that of his daughter, the law makers who followed him virtually outlawed it. Singing passages from the koran was just acceptable but it has always been referred to as 'reading', however musical the delivery. Music is still discouraged in theory by many Muslim sects, although only the most fundamentalist believers try to restrict it in practice. Certain 'philosophical' sects such as the Sufis, respect music and have incorporated it into their ceremonies, while the dervishes of Morocco and Turkey rely on wailing pipes and non-stop rhythms to whip them into a trance state during their flamboyant whirling displays.

During the Golden Age of Islam, professional musicians were earning huge salaries and became as famous as the rulers who employed them. The first major star, who toured extensively in the eighth century, Ibn Misjah reputedly maintained a pure Arab form, and did not succumb to light-hearted and frivolous foreign influences. There was always great debate about modernising the music, and taking it away from its original moral high ground. One who did help its development was the eminent performer Ziryab , the 'Blackbird', who was exiled to the Maghreb and moved on into Spain where he became the founder of Andalusian or Hispano-Arabic music. The music of the western Arabs was already different from the Middle East varieties which dominated cultural life throughout the Islamic empire. Female singers have often been the most popular artistes in Egypt, Algeria and in further flung centres of African Mohammedanism. In the pre-Islamic period women were often prominent instrumentalists, but because of religious constraints they are now rare.

Egypt's Music City

Cairo, which has had a commercial music business since the start of the twentieth century, is the commercial and cultural centre of North African music. For several generations artistes from all over the region have gravitated to Cairo in order to establish themselves in the Arab world. Although Egypt has more in common with the Middle East than with Africa, much of the culture has been assimilated through the Arabic language into various African societies.

The strongest classical art music comes from Egypt, and popular performers like Oum Kalsoum, Farid el Atrache and Mohammed Abdul Wahab have been among the greatest stars of modern music, popular wherever Arabic is spoken. The European influence was also strongest in Egypt, where violins were first incorporated into a new popular fusion by large *firquah* orchestras of a type still popular today. Egyptian feature films, made prolifically from the 1920s onwards, created a demand for these large orchestras, which became a strong musical force, producing from their ranks stars such as Farid El Atrache, his sister Ashmahan and Abd Al-Halim Hafiz. There was also a modern culture of theatrical melodrama which remained popular up until the mid-1970s. Television was launched in the Sixties but it was not widely available until the 1980s, by which time it had become quite progressive with several popular music shows. As well as the secular urban entertainment music, the Islamic tradition was maintained through sung recitations of the koran, often by women singers in the villages. Such was the way Kalsoum started her illustrious career.

With at least ten sophisticated 24-track studios in Cairo, Egypt produces the best and most commercial of Arabic music. It

اذكريـني

سلوا قوس التلة

أم كلثـوم

Oum Kalsoum, the 'Great Lady' of Arabic music, enjoyed and adored by one of the largest audiences for any musician

also has historical credentials as one of the first music industries to be set up in Africa. British companies had begun selling wax cylinder recordings in Cairo and Alexandria in the last decade of the nineteenth century. In 1904 the first locally-made products were on the market and by the start of World War One, the Odeon label's catalogue included some 450 titles. Other big European companies including Pathe and Gramophone soon joined the market, and two locally-owned companies also became involved; Baidophon, which moved from Beirut in the 1930s when singer Mohammed Abdul Wahab became a partner, and Mechian, a Cairo-based company that provided the main support for many of the region's musicians.

An independent radio station was launched in the Twenties but when Egyptian National Radio was set up in 1934 artistes were able to make longer recordings in which they could improvise and extemporise more freely than when restricted to one side of a disc. Radio became the most popular format for epic artistes like Oum Kalsoum, whose broadcasts were enthusiastically recorded by thousands of entrepreneurs, especially during the early Seventies when the first cassette recording 'studios' found a ready market and started the craze for piracy which has hardly diminished. Very few discs are now released in Egypt and production has been limited to cassette releases for some years.

The only rival to Oum Kalsoum had been Ashmahan, a princess of Lebanese origin and sister of the film star Farid el Atrache. Her singing of classical Arabic verses was coloured by a dramatic European influence which made her attractive to almost all the composers who supplied songs to Kalsoum, and during the Thirties Ashmahan became a major star in all the media. She died in a car crash in 1944 in what were thought to be suspicious circumstances connected with war-time intelligence operations.

A celebrated composer who wrote for both women was Mohammed Abdul Wahab, creator of some of Kalsoum's most lasting works at the request of President Nasser. Wahab, who was born in 1907, made his debut in a theatrical troupe where in a high, pre-pubescent voice he sang the lead vocals for the 40-year-old star from behind a curtain, until the day he was accidently exposed to the audience and the act was ruined. From then on he made his talents public and his voice evolved into one of the most admired in Egypt. A successful populariser of modern music, Wahab credited Sayed Derwish as the real pioneer who took elements of folk music and the film and theatrical styles of the Thirties and blended them together. Able to adapt from recording to theatre and musical comedy, Wahab, who died in 1991, had become the most respected composer in the country and an undisputed star.

During the austerity years of President Gamal Abdel Nasser, who became leader of modern Egypt and the Arab world in the Fifties, the tendency was to reject outside influences and look inwards to Arabic culture. A musician who made good use of that heritage was Sooliman Gamil who played an extraordinary mix of orchestral and folk styles. "I began to experiment with Egyptian folk music instruments in my compositions for cinema and stage in 1963," he said. "My objective in using these instruments was to extract the capacity of the innate dramatic expression of thousands of years ago, in the simple structure of these instruments dating back to Pharaonic times."

The first youth-oriented dance music with an urban beat only came about in Egypt as late as the 1970s, following Nasser's departure. There were two main threads, al jeel and *shaabi*. Al jeel, meaning 'the generation', was a jazzy fusion of Nubian, Bedouin and Egyptian rhythms interpreted on a mixture of traditional and

The Great Lady

Oum Kalsoum, who died in 1975 at over 70 years of age, was undoubtedly the greatest star of Arabic music this century. Coming from a humble village background, Kalsoum was loved as much for her singing as for her contact and empathy with the people. She was taught music by one of the local masters of her village, but was unable to attend koranic school because her father was too poor to pay the fees.

While still a girl she was invited to Cairo to sing at the wedding of a businessman. The musicians who accompanied her were so impressed they persuaded her father to help her on a musical career, which she started in 1921. For five years she performed with only her father and brother accompanying her in public, although she recorded for Odeon with anonymous studio musicians.

By 1926 she was a celebrity in fashionable Cairo and her earning power grew dramatically -- she could reportedly command £300 for one recording. Self-educated and compe-

*tent, Kalsoum's career took off when she started her own radio show. Every Thursday evening for many years she brought the Arab-speaking world to a halt, for what was known as 'Oum Kalsoum night'. She later be-*came an executive at the radio station and also had a successful career as a film star during the Thirties and Forties.

Kalsoum's songs, which were mostly epic lyric poems, would typically last between 30 and 60 minutes, beginning with an instrumental introduction for ten minutes or so and then rapturous applause for several minutes when she appeared on stage, followed by a reverent silence as she began to sing in her smooth, flexible wide-ranging voice. She was invariably accompanied by large orchestras with numerous violins, cellos and a piano, as well as many Egyptian instruments, which were seldom very audible in the mix.

Her career spanned 50 years and Kalsoum had become an institution by the time of her death. Several million people turned out on the streets of Cairo for her funeral.

modern instruments and was identified as the music of the students and educated youth. The pioneer was Hameed Sharay who later became a producer of artistes such as Hanan and Ehab. Sharay, who is half Libyan, came into the Egyptian music scene in the 1970s, following Colonel Ghaddafi's purge of foreign culture in which Western musical instruments were reportedly destroyed. There is an important Nubian ingredient in al-jeel which is non-Arabic, and Nubians, who come from the south of the country, were represented by such singers as Mohammed Mounir, Amr Dieb and Khedr.

Nubian music has its own champion in Ali Hassan Kuban, a native of the Nile region, who revolutionised Nubian traditional music by using Western techniques and instruments including saxophones and even bagpipes, set against complicated rhythms and rural chants. Known as the 'Captain of Nubian music' Kuban sold millions of records and cassettes in his home province and in the capital, often reworked versions of classic Sudanese and Egyptian favourites. Originally trained as a clarinettist, Kuban started his career playing in the orchestra for the opera *Aida* as well as performing traditional music, before he formed his own band and carved a glittering career which included playing at the birthday celebrations of the Egyptian president.

Music on the market in Cairo, the recording capital of Islamic music, where records are almost non-existent

The other popular style which surfaced in the 1970s was the more urban rough-edged sound known as *shaabi* (people's music), which revived a name used a generation before in Algeria and Kenya. An early protagonist of the Egyptian version was Ahmad Adaweer, who improvised coarse, nonsensical freestyle lyrics in the traditonal form *mawal*, which provoked interest and amusement in the night club milieu and the poor quarters of Cairo during the early Seventies. An urban expression of the previous generation's pastoral music, shaabi was faster and rougher than the more genteel contemporary, al-jeel. It was heralded as the start of a working class sound, and predictably, was disapproved of by the bourgeoisie who have preferred to ignore its existence for the last twenty years. What makes shaabi stars like Hassan el Asmar, Shabaan Abdul Raheem, Shaabeeni an Talaat and Sami Ali especially popular is the topicality of the lyrics combined with often irreverent, obscene performance. Sami Ali, who performs with the belly dancer Saha Hamdy brought shaabi into the 1990s with a provocative song *Egyptian Rap* which was banned by the authorities because of its sexual explicitness.

Ya Rai!

Algerian cultural life was also shaken in the mid-1980s by the controversy over a vibrant rebellious pop music which talked openly of sexual desire, alcohol and other 'vulgar' Western preoccupations. Known as *rai* (opinion), the music surfaced in and around the port city of Oran which had a reputation as the most cosmopolitan city in this relatively liberal Islamic country. In the words of an Algerian disc-jockey, "We are not fundamentalists. If we want to go to the mosque, we go to the mosque. If we want to go to the pub, we go to the pub." Relations between the sexes, however, are strictly moderated by Islamic practices. Effectively banned from public media until the mid-Eighties, rai immediately became popular not only with the youth of Algeria and the North African quarters of Western cities, but also with the hipper dance crowds in Parisian clubs where it was introduced alongside reggae, hip-hop and hot tropic dance music. The commercial and production centre of rai is Paris, where sophisticated recording techniques have lifted this previously ethnocentric music into the international spotlight.

The music which embraced electric guitars, organs and drum kits and eventually synthesizer and rhythm machines, came of age in the cabarets and nightclubs of Marseille, Lyon and Paris, where expatriate Algerians dressed in fancy European party clothes dance through the night, moving their hips and waving their hands to the sultry rhythms and paying well over the odds for bottles of whisky. The name 'Cheb' adopted by the young male singers means 'boy' or ' good looking' and is intended to show an irreverent attitude in contrast with the respectful title 'Cheikh' accorded to singers of the earlier generations. The women are known as 'Chaba'.

The roots of rai lie in Bedouin oral tradition, in which the nomads' chanting was punctuated by shouts of 'Ya rai', and the secular Algerian version of shaabi flute and percussion music of the Thirties and Forties. Rai was initially the preserve of women cabaret artistes who eventually began to sing of physical desire and other such unseemly enthusiasms with apparent immunity. The women, while often outrageously direct in their lyrics, were accompanied by the same instruments used for the shaabi music which remained popular with the older generation, particularly in Algiers. The young generation revolutionised the sound, and in the process they also smoothed out the lyrics, making the images of sensuality more subtly opaque, less outrageous than the older womens'. Rai was quickly accepted as a pan-Maghreb sound. The Algerian basis was complemented by Arabic, African and Spanish ingredients and especially, via French cabaret and radio, elements of polka, and rock. While the Arabic lyrics have gradually been adapted to suit a more homogeneous youth culture, so too has the music's development been spurred by international influences. In the Thirties, the Cheikhs had begun this process when they added Western instruments like violin and accordions to the shaabi accompaniment of oud, gasba (shepherds' flute) and Bedouin percussion. But from the start the female stars such as Cheikha Remitti El Ghilzania made the running.

Remitti was by all accounts a powerful and impressive figure. In a well-worn, husky voice she sang of the pleasures of bed to her audience of male drinkers in the series of bars which she would tour each night, accompanied by her retinue of musicians. She

Chaba Fadela: set the tone for rai music in the Eighties

Performing in the West, Chaba
Fadela revels in bright lights and
hi-tech stage sets

acquired her name from the French cries of 'remettez' (more!) which followed her performances. When she was recorded by Pathe in 1936 her fame spread across the Arab world, but her sphere of influence was always in Algeria.

Following Oum Kalsoum's inspiration, new styles of urban music sprang up across the Maghreb, and in Oran Belaoui Al Haouri brought together Andalusian, Egyptian and local folk music in a form he called *wahrani,* a prototype for pop-rai. But it was not until the 1970s that traditional instruments gave way to electric guitars. The first Western instrument to make its mark was the trumpet of Bellemou Messaoud. A big star by the time of Algerian independence in 1962, Messaoud and the singer/accordionist Bouteldja Balkacem are credited with recording some of the earliest hits of the new generation pop-rai.

Bellemou Messaoud was born in a town south of Oran in 1947. He taught himself to play acoustic guitar before enrolling at a Spanish music school in the town, where he studied trumpet and saxophone, and also became leader of the local brass band. During the Sixties he began to follow the rai musicians, especially the women singers, whose raw style was confined to the bars and bordellos. The cheikhas were reputedly exotic creatures, sometimes flaunting tattooed bodies, and several of them were known to be prostitutes.

Despite continuing struggles between nationalists and the French throughout the 1950s, Algeria was considered the most developed country in Africa. Its citizens had all the rights of their 'compatriots' across the Mediterranean, and French radio had kept Algerians up to date with European cabaret music. Bellemou formed a band playing covers of international favourites to club audiences. After Algerian independence he abandoned that style to concentrate on bringing rai music into the modern world.

Bellemou Messaoud (behind) with Cheb
Ourrad Houarri

Linking up with a traditional bass drummer and a *darbouka* player, he began the fusion of Latin and European elements to create 'pop-rai', which was first played at weddings and private functions before it was launched on the public as pre-match entertainment for the town football club.

L'Ensemble Bellemou's fame soon spread through the Oran region. In 1968 they were 'discovered' by a record producer who cut three singles with the band accompanying Bouteldja Balkacem. As his career developed Messaoud became known as the father of Rai and after several up and coming singers had passed through his band it was subtitled the 'School of Rai'. He mysteriously stopped recording for eight years from 1975, although he continued performing. When he returned to the studio to pick up on his recording career he found the modern music had moved too far from its origins. While he still plays rumba, flamenco and waltz music when it suits him, Messaoud prefers to keep them separate and not to mix up the musics too much. "Today you get rock-rai, disco-rai, anything rai. Some I like, some I don't. I just continue to play what pleases me."

Producer Rachid Baba Ahmed brought rai into the hi-tech era in the mid-Eighties releasing records out of Paris which quickly caught on in Holland, Germany and Scandinavia, spreading into the anglophone world with the British release *Hada Raykoum* by Cheb Khaled. Other top stars included Cheb Mami, Cheb Hamid, Cheb Sahrahoui and his wife Chaba Fadela, Chaba Zahouania, Chaba Faylia and one of the rare groups, Rana Rai. One of the younger success stories was that of Cheb Kader, a Paris-based Moroccan who became a champion of the 'Maghrebbin' immigrants living in France with his rock-rai crossover, using rock bass lines and drum sounds. Other artistes working out of Paris on similar fusions are Cheb Tati and the group Carte de Sejours. But as rock/rai crossover artiste Jimmy Wahid said in 1991 "The problem with the music business in Paris is racism. But we sing in French and mix it up, so it is not obviously too Arab."

The first rai artiste to break the anglophone barrier was Cheb Khaled in 1986

At home in Algeria orthodox religious opinion was against this openly controversial music but, despite official disapproval, influential Algerian businessmen actively helped to promote rai as an exportable commodity, and the authorities reluctantly lifted the television and radio ban in 1985. Big festivals in Oran, Algiers and in France gave prominence to rai artistes like Khaled and Mami. But there was also official pressure on musicians to moderate the sensuality and irreverence of their compositions. This ambivalence resulted in the figurehead, the 24-year-old Cheb Khaled, being effectively banned at a crucial point of his career.

Hit-shot rai producer Rachid Baba in the studio with Cheb Hamid

While appearing to revel in his rebelliousness, Khaled's troubles were caused by his frank lyrics, delivered against sensuous, revolving rhythms which combine the eroticism of a belly dance with the trance inducement of dervish music. Such statements as 'Whisky is Arab, Beer is European' and 'Hey mama, your daughter, she wants me' do not go down well with traditional Muslims. Although less controversial, Cheb Mami was an early admirer of Khaled. He claimed that while some singers are more outrageous than others, there is an underlying morality to the music which should not be overlooked in the rush to strip away taboos. Rejecting the street wise stance of Khaled, the Paris-based Mami affected a suave, debonair image. In 1991 he moved to Los Angeles where he recorded with producer Hilton Rosenthal, fresh from working with the 'White Zulu' Johnny Clegg.

The role of women as frontrunners of rai has continued into the Nineties with several female singers among the most popular artistes. Chaba Fadela came to prominence at the end of the Seventies with her huge hit *Ana Ma H'lali Ennoum* (I Don't Like Sleeping Anymore) which set the tone for the music's future in the age of the synthesizer. Having been introduced into the club and cabaret circuit in the coastal towns, Fadela soon became a national celebrity. In 1983 she married Cheb Sahraoui and took two years off the stage to start a family. In 1985 she returned in a duet with her husband. The song *N'sel Fik* was recorded in the western Algerian town of Tlemcen where producers Rachid Baba and Fethi had started to develop the slick contemporary sound, with a technique of recording the improvised vocals before adding the musical backing. The partners later opened the country's first 24-track studio.

Chaba Zahouania, the 'mystery woman' of rai, is of Moroccan origin. Even though her family are strict Muslim fundamentalists who banned her from public appearances and photographs, she has risen to the top of her trade, selling hundreds of thousands of her own solo recordings and having duetted with many of the top Chebs including Khaled, Mami, and Hamid. In 1990 she released *Nights Without Sleeping*, also produced by Baba and Fethi and with a model standing in for her on the cover photograph.

Rai is one of the few African idioms to have benefited from the so-called 'world music' movement, bringing an undemanding but genuinely 'exotic' product to international audiences who enjoy it for its mood. The lyrical content, however, has continued to upset various authorities at home and in 1991 Islamic fundamentalist pressure caused rai festivals to be outlawed once again. In an appeal for tolerance the Algerian journalist Bouziane Khodla pleaded the case for rai's defence. " Although it is true that rai is about alcohol and sex, adultery and carnal pleasure, life and death good and bad, it really is only expressing genuine and deeply held frustrations. It doesn't preach about sin, it only throws light on it. It attempts to heal the pain of a generation which is in search of the truth about itself."

Moroccan Roll

Moroccan music had a moment of brief glory in the Western pop world during the 1960s heyday of the Rolling Stones, when guitarist Brian Jones visited the country and 'discovered' the master musicians of Joujouka. A traditional 'cafe' ensemble playing wailing double-reed shawms and drums, they induced the trance like state which Jones was known to be seeking. Processed through spacey phasers and released on the Stones' own label it was briefly taken up as a kind of hippy mantra. The musicians were unable to capitalise on the fleeting exposure, although they eventually visited Britain in the early 1980s, and the connection was re-established again in 1989 when the Rolling Stones returned to Morocco for a television documentary.

There was a thriving bohemian-intellectual community of foreigners living in Tangiers and American jazz musicians occasionally showed up among them, including the pianist Randy Weston, and the trumpeter Don Cherry. The 'free jazz' alto saxophonist Ornette Coleman made interesting connections with his own system of 'harmolodics' when he visited Morocco in the Seventies and actually played with the Joujouka musicians and released an album. Other travellers were returning to Europe with tales of the Gnaoua people, 'real Africans' whose music was more rhythmic and danceable. The music adventurer Mim Scala set off in a mobile studio for their mountainous homeland. The mobile finished up at the bottom of a canyon but Scala delivered the tapes and the music was released in 1977.

Morocco, situated at the only strategic crossing point between Africa and Europe, is well placed to absorb direct inputs from the whole of North Africa and from across the Straits of Gibraltar. The Moors had ruled Spain for some 300 years, and the cultural connections were once again opened up in the late 1980s when the first Maghreb-flamenco fusions made themselves heard. Moroccan folk music, based on ancient repertoires and often played by large orchestras, had resisted the influx of Western instruments like violins, accordions and guitars, although it had assimilated influences from other Arab countries as far as Egypt. To a lesser extent its rhythms had been refreshed by those carried over the Sahara by traders and slaves, particularly the Gnaoua, a people of Bambara origin from south of the Sahara, whose rhythms and percussion instruments have infused the regional folk music. Often Moroccan folk songs are identical with those of neighbouring Algeria, although there are subtle differences in style and delivery, with the Moroccans considered to play faster and more rhythmically.

The first to bring a new approach to the music after the end of World War Two was Mohammed Fuiteh who used eastern modes and sang in simple everyday language. Others soon followed and with the launch of the national broadcasting service in the 1950s, a new market opened for contemporary performers. One of the first stars of the new system was Abdel Wahab Dukali who toured Algeria in 1962 and went on to settle in Cairo, from where he pumped out hits across the Arab world. Abdelhadi Belkhyat, a contemporary of Dukali, took the same route, although he had returned to Morocco by the end of the Sixties. Before retiring from music in 1989 he toured as far as Afghanistan.

Moroccans who made their careers outside the country included several rai singers in Algeria and France, and others who centred their careers in Cairo. One group called Sfataim apparently have followers in Israel. But Morocco was not totally bereft

Gnaoua musicians in Marrakech, Morocco, where Arabic, African and Spanish cultures meet

of pop music. In Tangier, Sheik Abdu Rashid, who once danced with the Duke Ellington band, provided a focus for 'jazz' and pop music. In the 1970s the country's pop heroes were the innovative Ness el Ghiwan, Jil Jilala, and Lem Chaheb, who earned their popularity by re-interpreting rural folk music, only cautiously adding the alien sounds of Western instruments. Their lyrics, however, were beginning to address the problems of modern living.

More recently those Moroccan musicians making fusion music have turned less to Africa but rather north towards the European capitals and their technology. As well as France, there is a large North African community in Berlin. Prime movers in the Rock-Maroc hybrid, Lem Chaheb are one of Morocco's rare pop groups, a five-piece outfit who use guitar and *buzuki*, traditional percussion, electric bass and rhythm machine. In Berlin, they collaborated with the German group Dissidenten. "It's quite natural to get to like Arabic music", said flute player Friedo Josch on their 1985 record release *Sahara Elektrik.* "You just go round the corner to the shish kebab shop and that's the music you'll hear on the tape recorder."

Hassan Erraji's band, Arabesque, play a blend of Moroccan, flamenco and European jazz, evolved after many years touring Europe. Erraji, who was classically trained, plays *kanoon* (zither) and *al ghita* (clarinet) as well as violin. His music is based on traditional folk or classical songs given a distinctly personal treatment which he has developed since he first moved to Belgium in the late 1960s. Erraji played throughout Europe with Arab musicians for years before crossing cultural barriers to create his Arab-jazz fusion. A very individual musician, he does not represent a particular style although a Lebanese musician, Ali Rabdou Khali, has independently arrived at a similar sounding fusion. The Spanish flamenco connection is also explored by Juan Pena Lebrijano and Orchestra Andalusi de Tangier Encountros who continue a cross-cultural tradition developed over many centuries of contact with Spain.

Sidi Seddiki is a young musician and poet from Rabat, who arrived in London in 1980. Born into a relgious family, Sidi was steeped in koranic culture, but also became adept at a range of local percussion and stringed instruments. Once he had moved into the Ladbroke Grove area of London, Sidi could not avoid hearing a full range of 'street' music, predominantly reggae, but

Ethiopian musicians show imagination in customising a Western drum kit

also rock, funk, rap and jazz. With his guitar and an ever-changing line up of musicians Sidi started his career playing at weddings and parties for the local Moroccan community. He describes his repertoire as conservative, with compositions covering grand themes like love, piety and spirituality, although his delivery is light-hearted and dynamic. He takes elements from many folk traditions including shaabi and Spanish music. Sidi's first album was recorded in London with a mix of Moroccan and European musicians, including jazz bassist Charlie Hart, playing a selection of stringed instruments, keyboards, horns and percussion.

Sudan and the Horn

In the bad old days of Empire the Sudan was a huge swathe of territory which stretched almost across Africa south of the Sahara. In West Africa, French Sudan was the name for what is now Mali; the British ruled territory of Egyptian Sudan also spanned the cultural divide between Arab and Black Africa. The long-running civil war has intensified animosities between north and south, whose different peoples and cultures have reasserted either Arab or African identities. The north, including the capital Khartoum, is the economic focus and the southern, African territories have remained largely undeveloped, and until today quite resistant to Islamic *sharia* law. Khartoum is so close to Arabia and to Egypt that it was the natural direction for the earliest expansion of Islam. In northern Sudan cultural life follows standard Islamic patterns, while people in the far south maintain an ancient way of life that is quintessentially African. Contemporary Sudan is one place where African and Arab cultures make incongruous and incompatible co-citizens.

The Sudanese music business is centred on radio and television broadcasting. There is a market for cassettes but no records. As there is no system of copyright control, live performances and broadcasts are always bootlegged. Successful artistes therefore have to make the most of those appearances and people like Kabil and Hanana Boulou Boulou receive huge payments. Most of the popular music is played by large orchestras delivering a blend of Egyptian styles with European influences and instruments. The accordion is especially popular, as it is in many other parts of Africa. The biggest stimulus to Sudanese music has come from the Institute for Music and Drama, founded in 1969 in Khartoum by Mahi Ismael, 'curator of Islamic music traditions'. Among the popular stars Abdul Aziz il Mubarak, who has toured in neighbouring countries and abroad, uses Western electric bass and drums for city performances and gives a more traditional presentation for rural audiences. He and his co-singer Abdel Gadir Salim are both graduates of the Institute, as is Muhammed Gubara.

On some old maps almost the whole of Africa was labelled Ethiopia. The country which now uses the name was called Abyssinia and has one of the oldest documented histories in Africa. Settled originally by Arabians, Ethiopia converted to Christianity in 200AD. Absolute power rested in the hands of imperial dynasties until 1930 when Haile Selassie became Emperor. He was deposed in 1974, since when the Muslim Eritreans, whose land was annexed by Selassie in 1962, were fighting for self-governance. Nonetheless a lively popular music scene still survived in Addis Ababa up until the fall of the Mengistu regime in 1991. The top band was the Roha Band, formed after the 1974 revolution, who collaborated with most stars such as singers Mahmoud Ahmed and Neway Debebe on record sessions and

Moroccan jazz fusionist Hassan Erraji

Aster Aweke links Ethiopian tradition with American soul delivery

played regularly in the big hotels.

A new voice appeared in 1989 via the USA, where Aster Aweke had been entertaining the Ethiopian community in Washington for some twelve years. A singer with a strong, fruity voice, Aster has created her own modernised form of Ethiopian music reflecting her life in the States and the inevitable inspiration of soul artistes such as Aretha Franklin and Anita Baker, to whom she has often been compared. Her early cassette releases and singles have found their way back to the home country and into the neighbouring Arabic cultures of Sudan and Yemen, where she also has many followers. Aster has had the violin and oboe sound transferred into a soul-type horn system of riffing. The fuller, more rounded tones of the Amharic language in which she sings contrast with the nasal sounds of Arabic speaking singers.

Somalia is the only African country with one people, one language and one religion. The Somalis, a traditionally nomadic people, were among the earliest converts to Islam in the eighth and ninth centuries, and they have a venerable tradition of oral poetry, in which complex verses cover all the great themes from love songs to battle hymns. More rhythmic than pure Arabic music, Somali music is also dependent on the oud. The most popular form of social music is *quai,* associated with the chewing of *quat* a mild stimulant narcotic leaf, which is played on flute, violin and bongo drums or Asian-style tablas added to oud. Colonial inputs from the British and Italians include accordions and harmoniums, which have been played there for over 100 years. Sudanese music is also popular and some elements of pre-Islamic culture remain.

During the 1950s Columbia made records for the local market, recording artistes like Abdul Quadir Junicomar and H.M. Timayere. The father of the modern music was Muhammed Mooge who was killed by his own government while fighting with Ethiopian based rebels in 1983. The most popular oud player of recent times is Ismael Hudaide, and the top female singer is Margol. Contemporary popular musicians now use saxophones and trumpets, Western drum kits, electric guitars and cheap synthesizer keyboards with in-built rhythms, to generate a sound known appropriately as 'metallic' by the traditionalists. Overall, the music can be placed geographically in the East African style cluster, particularly as the south of the country is the northernmost base for the *taarab* music so popular down the Swahili coast.

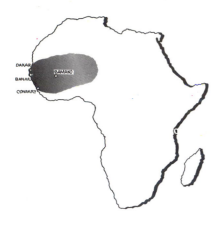

Sounds of The Sahel

The music of the Sahel region, where the 'real' Africa begins, broke into the Western pop mainstream in the late Eighties when Mory Kante's kora/fusion version of *Yeke Yeke* topped domestic hit parades in several European countries and lingered in the dance charts further afield. Around the same time Salif Keita, the renegade from a royal family who took the dirt road into music, rose from regional fame to international acclaim with *Soro,* one of the landmark albums of 'world music'. The age of the 'electro-griot' had arrived. Both carried big reputations into the 1990s but these two artistes merely represent the tips of one iceberg. The Manding minstrels were not the first from their region to break out of the francophone world into the lucrative English speaking market. The soaring cries of Youssou N'Dour rising out of his elliptical *mbalax* music were already known around the globe. With the Amnesty World Tour he had performed on five continents alongside Sting and Bruce Springsteen and with the English pop star Peter Gabriel he had made a 100-city tour of the USA. In Britain, France and Scandinavia he was already known and loved, not to mention right down the length of the west African coastline.

Most of the music heard coming out of the Sahel region, down as far as the Guinea coast, is transitional music, that is living traditional music which has been boosted by Western techniques and instrumentation, rather than fused with imported idioms. Although, as elsewhere in Africa, it was through playing foreign music on imported instruments that musicians found the inspiration to up-date their own folk music. In the Fifties, the only popular dance music available was foreign, and Latin music hit closer to home than French, or even American, idioms. Cuban records were distributed throughout Africa by HMV on the GV series, whose releases were usually known by number only, without reference to artistes or song titles. GV discs provided the early inspiration for the post-war generation of West African musicians from Senegal down to Congo. There was also a more direct connection supplied by Cuban cruise ships which sailed along the west African coast, complete with rumba orchestras who stopped off ashore to play at dances and inspire the local musicians.

Indigenous popular music only came to life at the time of the French colonies' independence in 1960. Since the Thirties all the francophone countries of the region had been administered as regions of French West Africa run by African prime ministers, several of whom served in the French government. Leopold Senghor, the poet, politician and proponent of 'Negritude', became the first president of Senegal, which had been probably the most democratically run colony in Africa. Although Dakar was a 'developed' cosmopolitan city, with its own university since 1950, there was little attempt to popularise indigenous music. In the 'quartiers' of the capital, traditional music, in particular the role of *griots* and the drumming groups who accompanied social and sporting events, continued to thrive. The first of the newly electrified music was heard across the region via the powerful national radio station of Guinea-Conakry, a fiercely independent state which recognised the propaganda value of music and which broadcast a substantial quota of modernised folklore and popular dance tunes.

The rumba dance orchestras, which appealed to francophone audiences more than to English-speaking Africans, eventually

The *bala* xylophone: provides rolling cross-rhythms central to Manding swing

Senegalese 'electro griot' Ismael Lo: one of the Sahel region's fusion enthusiasts at home amongst the baobab trees

provided the inspiration to interpret traditional music in a contemporary way. If saxophones, electric guitars and organs could be used to play rumba, or 'jazz' music then they could also help to augment the folk music of the region, which is universally known and respected.

The most impressive traditional instruments are the Manding people's 21-string *kora* and the hardwood *balafon* or xylophone, which 'speak' the same language. There are obvious differences of inflexion, reflecting the variations in dialect throughout the region but the overall swing of Manding/Bambara music is a direct interpretation of one or other of these instruments whose patterns can be recognised in the great orchestras like Bembeya Jazz, the Rail Band and Super Biton. Such instruments are usually the preserve of griot families, whose role is stronger in the Sahel region than anywhere else in Africa. Griots, from the hereditary caste of *jali,* musicians, praise singers and oral historians, have continued to ply their trade uninterrupted by colonial or other controls and have thus preserved an invaluable line of descent from the ancestors. Griots remain true to the roots of their music because they are tied to it for life, and after. They are often easily recognisable by their family names, the most common of which are Kouyate, Diabate (Jobarteh), Suso and Damba. Konte or Kante, although carried by some well-known musicians, denote families of blacksmiths.

Manding culture is the most widespread in the region, reaching from the Bambara in northern Mali to the Malinke on the coast of Guinea and Dioula in Cote d'Ivoire. The Manding people have lived as close neighbours with other ethnic groups for many years but in the capital of Senegal, the richest, most developed country in the region, the Wolof people are culturally dominant. While kora and balafon are familiar to Wolofs, their griots, known as

Gambian griot and kora player Malamini Jobarteh with an early singing partner, Sirifo Camara

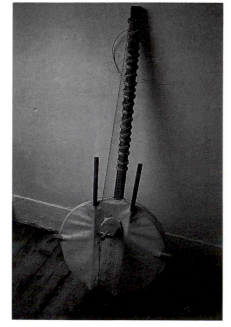

gewel play smaller, simpler instruments such as *molo* and *xalam* lutes but the most prominent contribution to Wolof folklore comes from the *sabar* drums which, along with the Jola people's *buga-rabu*, set the tone of the characteristic mbalax. Minority peoples of the region whose music has recently become known farther afield include the Pulaar-speaking Fula and Tukulor from northern Senegal, the Jola (Diola) and the Dogon of Mali.

The 21-string kora is ancient, but its music is very much a living tradition and in the West African homelands of the Manding people it is an important symbol of cultural continuity, bridging the gap between ancient custom and the modern world. The earliest written reference to the kora was made by Mungo Park in 1798, but as he was the first Westerner to venture into the heart of the Manding empire that does not help to measure its antiquity. The premier kora player was Jalimadi Wuleng, praise singer to the court of Kalefa Saane in the early nineteenth century.

In Mandinka legend the instrument arrived some 400 years ago, originally in the possession of a spirit, who was tempted to give it to its first mortal owner in exchange for some sweet fruit. Since then it has been used exclusively by griots. Their traditional role as court musicians is now outmoded but griots are still patronised by the rich and powerful and their relevance, particularly to the illiterate rural populace, is as strong as ever. Griots are called to all the major social events in the community, being indispensible at child-naming ceremonies, weddings and inaugurations of chiefs and officials. Griots are supposed to be the first to hold a baby and the last to touch a corpse before burial.

In the tiny West African state of The Gambia the kora is particularly important as a symbol of national culture and pride, and kora musicians are regularly called overseas to promote the country's small but important tourist industry. Kora playing soloists, duos and trios have toured in Europe, America and the Soviet Union, while the national troupe, which keeps up a regular schedule of domestic engagements, has also visited Europe. Such exposure not only attracts visitors to the region, but also provides a much needed opportunity for musicians to record and market their music. The growing interest in African music has ensured a steady demand for the restful sounds of the kora and musicians such as the late Alhadji Bai Konte, his sons Dembo Konte and Malamini Jobarteh and grandson Pa Jobarteh, Kausu Kouyate and Amadu Bansang Jobarteh have received international acclaim for albums of traditional music. The Gambian style is dramatic and flamboyant, following the inflexions of the nasal, Islamic-sounding vocals which reach to haranguing peaks, reflecting the griots' ability to harass as well as praise their listeners. Music from the eastern areas has a more reflective 'swinging' style.

The Guinean kora player Jali Musa Jawara has proved lastingly popular in Europe since his 1983 record of mellow music, featuring the instrument accompanied by guitars and balafon. The Malian musician Toumani Diabate came to notice with an album of instrumental numbers in which the complexity of sound, with its cascades of tonal scales, was such that the sleeve notes pointed out there was only one instrument being heard, and no double tracking.

Jali Musa Jawara: popular recording artiste with a more traditional approach than his brother Mory Kante

The delicate, rippling sound of the kora is also to be found in much of the electrified popular music of the region, whether in its own right, transposed to guitar or used as a synthesized effect in high-tech studio recordings. In fact some of the most 'progressive' African pop music comes from the Sahel region, with 'crossover' artistes like Salif Keita and the French-based Senegalese group Toure Kunda making extensive use of the kora 'sampling' ability of synthesizer keyboards. Players like Mory Kante from Guinea, Ama Maiga from Mali and Foday Musa Suso from The Gambia have been incorporating the authentic kora sound into a soul fusion for several years often complete with electronic drums, guitars and brass arrangements.

The repertoires of both traditional and modern exponents of the instrument draw on the vast pool of historical compositions, mostly delineating the rise and fall of various dynasties, during the ancient Songhai and Manding empires. The success of a griot within his own community is based as much on the style of delivery as the content, and while the core of historical knowledge is respected, each puts his own signature to the story line and the music. Some of the griots playing today will also be writing their names into future compositions as curators of ancient traditions, which in many parts of Africa are being allowed to wither away.

Giants of Manding Swing

The Orchestre Bembeya Jazz 'International' of Guinea is one of the continent's musical legends. The first African national orchestra to have succeeded as a popular band, they generated an international reputation while working in a country which was closed from contact with the West throughout the Sixties and Seventies. When Guinea opted for independence in 1958 it became the first self-governing francophone country in Africa. But by establishing total autonomy the president, Sekou Toure, ensured the ex-colony would remain outside the French sphere of influence, and the economic union of countries which used the convertible CFA franc. One of the most radical of African presidents, Sekou Toure established a closed system under a policy of 'Authenticite', in which the revival of Guinean culture was considered paramount, and he encouraged the formation of local orchestras to 'animate' the culture of the regions. He also established Enimas, a national distribution service for musical and sporting goods which made instruments available in the regions.

When Bembeya Jazz was founded in 1961 they joined such established groups as Kelitigui and his Tambourines, Balla and his Balladins, Horoya National Band and the cultural troupe Keita Fodeba, formed in 1953, which featured Mory Kante's elder brother on guitar. Bands appealing to younger tastes in the Seventies and Eighties include Kaloum Stars, Ambience Melody and Messagers.

Guinean music is gracious and stately, befitting its origins in the court music of the ancient Manding Empire. The elastic rhythms and silky melodies are distinctive of the Malinke language, a cousin of Bambara and Mandinka. In Bembeya's interpretation, the folklore music of the region was augmented with instruments and arrangements taken from the rumba orchestras, to create a classical music which is also highly danceable. Dynamic orchestration, fulsome brass and lazy, insinuating rhythms are their hallmark, but the virtuoso guitar playing of Sekou 'Diamond Fingers' Diabate, made a lasting impression, swooping and soaring through a series of solos which make surprising reference to a lexicon of rock and jazz cliches. The guitar histrionics may be dazzling but they do not obscure the sterling work of the orchestra who provide the solid foundations of this dignified musical construction.

Bembeya Jazz was founded in the forested Beyla region of northern Guinea, some 1000km from the capital Conakry, and was named after a river of the region. With equipment provided by a regional administrator the group began as a collection of amateurs with limited experience of modern instruments but a wealth of vocal talent. In 1963, the year they cut their first recording, Bembeya were joined by singer/composer and showman, Aboubacar Demba Camara, who soon became leader and featured soloist. The following year the group won a gold medal at the national music festival and in 1965 they were chosen to represent Africa at the Tri-Continental festival in Cuba. At the time most West African bands played rumba, but when the Latin star Tino Barosa heard Bembeya's interpretation he reportedly cried with joy.

The band also played in a variety of other styles including Congolese but soon they were required, for political reasons, to incorporate more indigenous music into their repertoire. In 1966 they won another gold medal in Conakry, following which the band was nationalised, making the musicians civil servants, and the headquarters was moved to the capital. During the Seventies the band was at its height, playing free shows throughout West Africa sponsored by the Guinean government. They also toured in other African countries as far afield as Tanzania, and visited Moscow several times.

But in April 1973 Bembeya was shattered when Camara, their leader, inspiration and solo singer, was tragically killed in a car crash, coming from a show in Dakar, Senegal. Camara was recognised as contributing 70 per cent of the spectacle and his death totally demoralised the band, who spent three years looking throughout the region for replacements. The group re-formed in 1977 for the FESTAC festival of Black arts in Lagos, Nigeria, where they won yet another prize for orchestration, and the lead guitarist Sekou Diabate was voted top guitarist, acquiring the sobriquet 'Diamond Fingers'. They toured Africa once more to new-found popularity, but the band was shaken yet again by the death of another key member, bass player Mory Kouyate II, and Bembeya retreated from the music scene for a second time. In 1979, with a new line-up containing five of the original members and ten others, the group was totally reconstructed and trumpeter Mohammed Ashken Kaba installed as band leader.

With such a disrupted history, Bembeya maintained their international reputation more by hearsay than first-hand experi-

In The Gambia kora music is an accompaniment to daily life

ence. In 30 years as a major musical force, the group have released only a dozen albums for the international market. It was not until 1985 that Bembeya made their first serious foray into Western Europe, touring and recording two albums in Paris, and returning home as Bembeya 'International'.

One of the region's seminal dance bands, Bembeya Jazz brought their Manding swing to Europe in the mid-1980s

Also founded in 1961 in the capital Conakry was another national institution, Les Amazones du Guinea, certainly the first, and for a long time the only, female orchestra in Africa. In the beginning they numbered some 30 women playing instruments like violin, cello and banjo, but in 1965 they modernised, swapping the orchestral instruments for dance band equipment such as saxophones and electric guitars. The full complement when on tour was cut back to fifteen musicians, with three guitarists, three saxophonists, percussionists, singers and dancers. Their repertoire is based not only on the folklore of Guinea, but of Africa in general, and everywhere they have visited from Zaire to Kenya or Senegal, they aim to soak up a taste of that country's music. Soukous, Afrobeat, ndagga, salsa and reggae are well within their capacity. Their real success started when they appeared at FESTAC in 1977. "All of Africa was there to hear us, and from there we received invitations to many countries," said the leader 'La Reine' (Queen) Niepo Habbas, who plays a stylish lead guitar.

Wall painting in the Bembeya Club, in the Guinean capital, Conakry

Several of the women compose or re-interpret songs to be sung in Malinke, Fula, Susu and regional dialects. The flavour of the music is essentially the same as Bembeya's, and indeed the second guitarist and solo recording star Sona Diabate is the sister of Bembeya's Diamond Fingers. "None of the women had ever played with any other group", said Habbas. "I myself took up playing at the age of about twelve or thirteen, studying with some other girls under the doyen of Guinean music, Keletigui Traore, a great musician who originally formed Les Amazones."

Even more surprising than to find a band of African women is to discover that they are all serving members of the police. "When

Vocal power from Les Amazones du Guinea: Fatou Cissey, Mah Sylla and Condette Kouyate

we are not playing, we perform the normal duties at the port, the airport, in the banks, in each brigade of the gendarmerie. We are not just traffic wardens", explained Habbas, "we also play an active part in catching criminals and thieves. In the evenings we rehearse our music." At home in Guinea they play regularly for official functions or to welcome visiting delegations for the president. They also tour the provinces carrying their spectacular show to the people.

As a national, state-sponsored band Les Amazones have an educational or propaganda function and perform songs that cover social issues such as the need to work together, the dangers of alcohol and the emancipation of women. Most of the women are married, yet they claim there is no conflict between their roles. "The husbands have confidence in us, and the public also trusts us," said Habbas. "It is a question of organisation and the husbands are used to it."

Minstrels of Mali

Mali has had several fine orchestras in the African custom of big dance bands, seven of which are state-sponsored orchestras serving each region of this vast country which reaches down from the Sahara to the Guinean border. Like Guinea, Mali was also cut off from Western influences following independence and this large, inland country developed its modern cultural identity behind closed doors. In the late 1980s some superb soloists emerged on the international scene, notably Salif Keita, Ali Farka Toure and a cluster of female stars, and some of the country's orchestras gained a new lease on life.

Within Mali, Cuban music had been popular since the Fifties, having penetrated from Senegal, although there was another more direct connection established in 1965 when L'Orchestre Maravillas de Mali was formed in Havana, Cuba by Malian students who took up the local rumbas, sons, montunos and boleros for their own amusement. When they returned home at the end of their studies the musicians scattered, but not without a few more Latin ingredients being blended into the Manding music. Malians were also inspired by the brassy dance band highlife which could be heard on radio from the southerly anglophone neighbours, and which the whole region was dancing to in the Fifties and Sixties

The first band to combine these various elements into a new synthesised pop music was Super Biton from the Segou region. Formed in 1954 by bandleader and trumpeter Amadou Ba around members recruited from the Segou Jazz band and the regional orchestra, Super Biton evolved their mature sound in the early Sixties and achieved consistent national success through two decades, winning first prize for orchestras at every biennial cultural festival between 1968 and 1976. During the early 1980s they made several trips to Europe and recorded their second album in France. There are few bands finer at interpreting the balafon-inspired Bambara music, with Ba's trumpet-led, jazz-inspired horn parts, synthesizer solos and laconic guitar licks bringing a characteristic sparkle.

One of the region's most celebrated orchestras, the Rail Band of the Station Buffet in Bamako, was formed in 1970 by a director of the state-run railway, with sponsorship of the Ministry of Information, in order to safeguard and promote the country's culture. In those days state sponsorship was practically the only way for a band to exist. Equipment was difficult to obtain and despite the relative security of the job, there were frequent personnel changes. Among the singers in the original front line was Salif Keita who went on to spread Manding culture throughout the world. He was soon joined by a fourteen-year-old Guinean, Mory Kante, who was also to touch the summit of European success. Mory Kante came from a family of blacksmiths, which included a senior brother, Kante Facely, who was a guitar maestro. As a child Mory played balafon before leaving home to study at a 'school of oral tradition' in Bamako where he learned the basics of his kora technique. He joined the Rail Band as a small boy, playing

The first female band in Africa: Les Amazones were recruited from the women's gendarmerie

Mory Kante moved from village compound to 'acid house', scoring Africa's biggest European hit

guitar at the time when the band were beginning their fusion of traditional and electric music. When Salif Keita was absent for a while in 1973, Kante took over as vocalist and launched his career as a singer and composer whose first hit, *L'Exile de Soundiata,* about the founder of the Manding Empire, spread his fame across the region. In 1975, the band journeyed to Nigeria, and on their return released four albums. But within two years the grave economic situation in Mali had driven Bamako's two major bands to Cote d'Ivoire in search of work.

Soon after arriving in Abidjan, Kante left the band to form his outfit which came to include as many as 70 musicians and dancers, performing musical comedy theatre based around tales of the ancestors. Among the cast was another brother, Jali Musa Jawara, who began his own recording career a few years later. In the Ivorian capital Kante cut his first solo hit record in 1981, followed by a grand tour of the West African region which opened the way for his first visit to Europe. The Rail Band, meanwhile had returned to the Bamako station venue, where they kept up the mix of pumping bass, swirling keyboards, phased electric guitars and full-throated horn playing.

Kante had by now widened his horizons and following his return to France, where he played with the Milieu Branche, he began his personal research into the future development of a 'modern, authentic music', leading to the eventual release in 1984 of the album *Mory Kante a Paris* on which Cameroonian and Ivorian musicians were prominent. This early example of kora-funk included Kante's first version of *Yeke Yeke,* the traditional song which was to make his fame a few years later. "I want to prove to everyone that all the major dance developments come from us, from salsa to breakdance," he said then. "African music is the origin of all dance music today."

'Electro-griots' on charge

In Paris Kante developed into a 'serious' musician, whose credibility was boosted in 1984 by his contribution to the pan-African famine relief project, Tam Tam Pour L'Ethiopie, in which he collaborated with Manu Dibango, Salif Keita and other franco-phone African artistes. Then in 1988 came the acclaimed album *Akwaba Beach* with the new arrangement of *Yeke Yeke.* Ironically the version released as a single, which made a bigger impression on the European pop charts than any previous African release, had lost a lot of the African content in the pared-down 'acid house' style production.On the mix selected for British release the kora had all but disappeared.

Running on parallel tracks with the Rail Band for several years were Les Ambassadeurs, who lived up to their name by taking Malian music on to the international stage. Formed in the early Seventies, the band came to prominence in 1973 when Salif Keita joined. In collaboration with guitarist Kante Manfila, Keita pushed the new Malian music to its limits, resulting in a stunning new fusion which was still in contact with its roots. When the band left Mali in 1977 for Abidjan, a young Guinean guitarist, Ousmane Kouyate, had been recruited to the team.

Starting out on accordion and balafon, Kouyate had been encouraged by his griot father to take up guitar. In 1972 he began agricultural studies at Kankan university in Guinea but soon dropped out and found his way to Bamako where he joined Les Ambassadeurs. When co-leader and guitarist Kante Manfila and Keita went different ways Kouyate stayed with Salif, who estab-

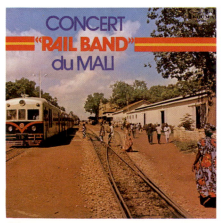

Salif Keita, Prince among Paupers

Of all the hopeful artistes bringing the Manding sound out of the Sahel region, the first international success came to Salif Keita, the albino singer from Mali with the searing voice and mellifluous melodies. His 1987 record release Soro was one of the most critically acclaimed albums made by an African. He appealed to all the right 'taste makers' and it seemed that after being taken up by Island Records his star would ascend.

Keita was born into an aristocratic family in the village of Djoliba, close to the capital, Bamako. As an albino he felt lonely and rejected by society, and took up the life of a wandering griot, which was not in keeping with his family background.

His extraordinary voice, however, helped him rise above adversity to become the most popular singer in the region.

In 1970 he joined the Rail Band but broke away after three years to link up in Les Ambassadeurs de Bamako with guitarist Kante Manfila. Their fusion of Manding musical tradition with the popular dance sounds of Cuban and Congolese rumba and elements of blues and soul, ensured the band's wide acceptance at home.

In 1977, following several popular recordings, their reputation had travelled to Guinea, where the president, Sekou Toure, awarded a national honour to Keita. He returned the compliment by singing Toure's praise in his most successful song, Mandjou, which was followed with another regional hit, Primpin, after which the band left Mali for the music capital of Cote d'Ivoire.

Seeking a wider international forum, Keita eventually quit Les Ambassadeurs for a solo career in Europe. Basing himself in Paris he collaborated with some of the finest African session

musicians and for his hit album Soro he found a blend of talents which helped him lift his music out of the African 'ghetto' of the specialist market place.

For some aficionados, Keita went too far in blending sophisticated orchestration and highly Westernised arrangements with his electro-griot delivery.

It was a lavish fusion, produced in a 48-track digital studio, with several ingredients guaranteed to please the casual listener. The overall sound was urban, urbane even, with a rock hard kit drummer and a guitarist veering in that direction, a synthesizer player with three keyboards to programme and a horn section leaning towards big band jazz.

During five years absence from the recording studio, Keita had obviously thought hard about his strategy for dealing with the changing demands of the international music scene and the growing Western audience. Production was by Ibrahima Sylla, the Paris-based Senegalese hot shot who has dressed up several West African artistes in his crisp club-crossover style, scoring some of the biggest regional hits of the late 1980s.

Murmurs from fellow musicians that Salif's music did little to preserve his Manding culture, sounded like envy and did not impress the man, who has always been a musical progressive.

Due no doubt to the hardships of his early life, Keita remained a rebel, composing songs which denounced dishonesty and oppression of all kinds.

His growing international stature had opened new doors at the start of the Nineties. His 1991 album Amen was produced in New York by Joe Zawinul featuring American jazz-rock cohort Wayne Shorter, and Keita's old colleague Kante Manfila sparring with Sixties guitar hero Carlos Santana.

The project sounded very American but Keita claimed to be re-creating the mood of the original Ambassadeurs. He was aiming for the main market and, as he put it: "With African music you have to play the type that people will taste and want to eat more of, not the kind you taste and spit out."

Salif Keita's self-image was boosted by his 1991 collaboration with US artistes

lished the Super Ambassadeurs. He remained alongside Keita for many years contributing jazz-inspired licks on all his albums up to the 1990 release *Koyan*. He has also released several albums of his own.

In Mali, more than any other country, women singers of griot families, the *jalimusolu*, have achieved extraordinary fame and fortune, often earning more at home from generous patrons than bands could make from a European tour or hit record. The greatest singer of independent Mali was reputedly the late Sira Mory Kouyate, who passed on her repertoire and knowledge to her daughter Sanougue, considered a born singer. By the age of sixteen Sanougue's talents had begun to rival the male griots of the region and the established female star, Tata Bamba Kouyate, whose clear, high-ranging voice has brought her riches and the attentions of several influential admirers. Sanougue was introduced to the wider world by Salif Keita, producer of her debut album in 1991.

Manding women's voices do penetrate, and others with a pure, piercing quality include Dienaba Diakhite whose cassette releases inspired a huge merchandising campaign in 1991, Nahawa Doumbia and Djanka Diabate, a cousin of Mory Kante. After releasing two albums Diabate was reported in 1990 to be trying to set up a complete band of women, having been inspired as much by seeing the female instrumentalists backing the American superstar Prince as by the trailblazing Amazones.

Two new names for the Nineties whose music has started to charm international audiences are Ami Koita, a tall splendid figure of a woman, the epitome of a successful griotte, loaded with gold jewellery and decked in expensive fancy cloth, and Oumou Sangare from the Wassoulou region of southern Mali. Sangare made her recording debut on her 21st birthday in 1989. The cassette release she cut in Abidjan was an instant smash, selling hundreds of thousands of copies throughout the region. Sangare's music had a more rootsy, village feel than previous hits, with the *ngoni* guitar and violin prominent, and slightly less of the Islamic inflexion popular with singers of the Sahel. Arranged by the bass player Amadou Ba Guindo, who sadly died soon after, Sangare's 'Wassoulou sound' quickly became the favourite flavour of the moment in Bamako and several other artistes followed her lead.

Out of the Mainstream

It was a stunning sight to see the tall, purposeful figure of Ali Farka Toure striding through the drizzle of a winter's afternoon in London as if it was a desert sandstorm, with his brown, full-length *boubou* pulled over the top of his head. Ali was in London to make his British debut in 1987 amid a flurry of excitement from the 'global village/family tree' enthusiasts who were so excited about the similarities of his guitar playing with the Chicago blues style, in particular John Lee Hooker. Could Ali really be the 'missing link' between Africa and the New World, they wondered. Was American blues simply something that had been passed on in a direct line of inheritance from West Africa?

In many ways Ali takes a different stand from other musicians in Africa. He is not from a griot family, in a region where their role is still crucial, and he said he never intended to play past his 50th birthday. Born into a noble Songhai family in 1939, he grew up in the Timbuktu region, where by the age of ten he had begun to play the *gurkel*, a traditional one-string guitar which he chose because of its spiritual nature, and which he played for certain ceremonies. He also took up the *n'jarka* fiddle for his own amusement. The boy obviously showed promise as he was eventually taken aside by jealous professional griots who 'cured' him temporarily of his interest in music. When the Guinean maestro Keita Fodeba visited Bamako in 1956 Toure was there to see him play and his interest in the guitar was kindled. He took up banjo for a while and even played accordion, but in 1957 he was lent a European acoustic guitar. By now he was playing drums in a group with some friends who delivered a mixture of African and European music for teenage audiences.

After Mali's independence in 1960, cultural troupes were set up in each region, and Toure found a position with the Niatenke district group from his home region, playing, singing, arranging and choreographing. While setting the troupe up to be the country's finest, Toure was also amusing himself with American soul and R&B music, an interest stimulated by the slow trickle of American records which made it to the landlocked country. His particular favourites were Otis Redding, Albert King and, most importantly John Lee Hooker. In 1968 Toure made his first voyage outside Africa when he travelled through Eastern Europe before arriving in Paris.

Back in Bamako, Toure was employed as director of the national radio orchestra, which used a mixture of traditional instruments like kora and balafon with western band instruments. He was also learning the trade of radio engineer. But when the orchestra, of which he was extremely proud, was disbanded by the ministry of culture in 1973, Toure became disillusioned with collective activity and decided to work on his own. Following a short spell with Orchestra Kulikoro, he set out on a solo career progressing at his own pace. A strong-willed, independent man, Toure had his farm and his nobility to keep him going, and he has long been aware that people now need him more than he needs them. His travels brought mixed blessings. He met up with his guitar hero John Lee Hooker in Paris in the early Seventies and they played together, after which Hooker nominated Toure as the rightful successor to his style. He recorded several albums in Paris during the 1980s, but relations with French record companies turned sour. He later found more satisfaction with World Circuit, an independent British label.

At the start of the Nineties, Toure claimed he was ready to hang

Zani Diabate and the Super Djata Band

Malian 'jalimusolu', Sanougue Kouyate: one of a phalanx of female artistes

up his guitar. In fact he formed a group with whom he played some big shows in Mali before arranging another foreign tour and discussing a collaboration with American guitarist Ry Cooder. At home his exploits had made him a superhero, none more so than when he brought the first video to his desert village in 1991. For many villagers the first sight of a television was a video of James Brown, which Toure played them all night.

Theatrical content and dramatic presentation augmented the lively music of Zani Diabate, who formed the Super Djata band in 1969 in Bamako. A griot who had polished his theatrical skills during six years with the national ballet, Diabate developed his repertoire around the rhythms and dances of Bambara fishermen and hunters. But he varied the acoustic delivery of the traditional music with highly charged electric ingredients including his own psychedelic guitar style, reminiscent of early blues rockers like Hendrix or Freddie King.

Also outside the mainstream of Malian music is Sorry Bamba, one of the Dogon people, who resisted the imposition of Islam for several centuries and retreated to their mountainous enclave in northern Mali, where they consider they have preserved the original Manding culture. Sorry Bamba began his musical career in Mopti, the Venice of Africa on the Niger river, and in 1960, the year of independence, he formed his first band, Bonijazz, with whom he toured and recorded successfully throughout the Sixties. In 1969 he created Orchestre Kananga which later became a national orchestra after winning prizes regularly at the biennial festival of culture. Bamba's music is more apparently 'African' than the Islamic inflected Manding swing, with a greater reliance on drums and passionate expression. The styles he plays have more in common with music of the street kids, heard from Bamako to Abidjan, than the ancient days of Empire.

Senegal's Family of 'Stars'

All the French West African territories had become independent in 1960 and throughout the region the mood of optimism stimulated confidence and pride in indigenous culture. At Senegal's independence party a musical dynasty was founded with the formation of the Star Band de Dakar, which was to become the training school for several of the country's top artistes, including Youssou N'Dour. The Star Band was established by the photographer, nightclub owner and entrepreneur, Ibra Kasse, who recruited saxophone players Mady Konate and the Nigerian Dexter Johnson, already based in the city with the Guinea Band de Dakar. Other musicians came from Star Jazz de Senui, an electric guitar band formed in the mid-1950s by Pape Samba Diop (Ali Mba), another saxophone player and seminal figure whose praises Youssou sang on his first hit *Mba*. Eventually the Star Band fathered a whole family of popular dance bands. The first offshoot was Dexter Johnson's Super Star Band, followed later by Orchestre Baobab set up by Mady Konate, Star Number One, Orchestre Number One and later a generation of Etoiles.

Rumba music was more than just an influence at the time, it was a living reality. Since the early Fifties Cuban musicians had been coming ashore from the cruise ships and Cuban record releases on the GV label had become universally popular. Seeing the Black musicians from the ships' bands inspired many Senegalese to set up rumba orchestras in Dakar and St Louis which were soon competing in band contests. An influential 'salsa' singer of the period was Laba Sosseh, the leader of Vedette de Dakar. Imitating, or approximating the sound of Spanish lyrics in nonsensical Wolof, his music was enjoyed because it was 'lively and legal'. Sosseh travelled widely as far as the Congo before eventually moving to the USA. There was also an important Congolese ingredient picked up first hand. Following Congolese

Blues from Timbuktu: Ali Farka Toure stunned European guitar fans with his Chicago blues style

Ifang Bondi, ex-Super Eagles of Banjul: pioneers of Senegambian electric dance music

independence in 1960 a group called Ryco Jazz had set out from Kinshasa on an odyssey which brought Congolese rumba to the doors of many West Africans. Touring from a base in Sierra Leone, they put Congolese seasoning on the menu in Senegal as well.

A fertile outfit which produced its own laconic fusion of rumba with softer elements of the local dance rhythms was Orchestre Baobab, formed in 1970, originally to play at the opening of a club with that name. Many Baobab members came from the Star Band with a brief to experiment, and in this cooperative orchestra Wolof and Mandinka music was combined with input from Guinea Bissau and Togo, and more nonsensical Spanish/Wolof. Among the original singers were Sosseh, Thione Seck, and Pape Seck. Throughout the 1970s their mellow, unhurried music made them one of the country's top bands, often only challenged by the Star Band. After suffering deaths and departures the orchestra was kept alive through the Eighties by the singer and timbalist Balla Sidibe, his accompanist Rudy Gomez and sax player Issa Cissako. Thione Seck who played folklore music before joining Daobab, later formed his own band, Ram Daan, with his brother Mapenda. His slow melodious songs, delivered in a melancholic voice, maintained the groove with an up-dated, bass-heavy mix of mbalax with salsa and reggae.

There was also a popular music movement developing in The Gambia, the tiny anglophone enclave surrounded by French-speaking Senegal. The first dance band was set up by a business-man who gathered a collection of 'floating' musicians into a group he named African Jazz. Realising the name was already in use by the top Congolese band of the 1950s, they changed it to the Eagles of Banjul when they became fully professional. Once they had further evolved into the Super Eagles the band toured Ghana and in 1969 they visited Europe and made two records in Britain.

Three brothers: original Toure Kunda members Ismaila, Sixu and Ousamane Toure

Masters of mbalax: Youssou N'Dour with essential accompaniment from tama player Assane Thiam

The Eagles were pioneers of Senegambian music, adapting the historic song content of the griots, and inventing an Afro-Manding sound which combined elements of Mandinka, Wolof, Jola, Fula and Creole culture. They were one of the first groups to bring the popular folk style of 'dirty dancing' known as *ndagga* out of the compound and on to the stage. In 1976 the musicians bought out their contract with the group's manager, and took on the authentic name Ifang Bondi. They moved to Holland soon after but stayed away from home too long to capitalise on their status as pioneers of the mbalax sound, which Youssou N'Dour later made famous.

In Dakar the importance of the traditional heritage was upheld by several griots with recording contracts such as Lamine Konte, but a significant boost was given to the folklore music by Xalam, founded in 1969 by Prosper Niang, and combining traditional and modern instruments. Every succeeding artiste appeared to be consciously re-Africanising the music but it was not until the mid-Seventies that the disinctive *tama* talking drum became a prominent solo instrument and a format for dialogue between drummers, voices, horns and guitars was established.

Any semblance of a music business was late coming to Dakar. Distribution was controlled by the French major labels and only a few folklore artistes had been privileged to record in Paris. Local recording was limited to the radio station and informal club studios, like the Sangoma nightclub in Thies, near Dakar. In 1976 the country's first 16-track studio was opened at the Golden Baobab. Recordings were released in cassette format only; records were not on the agenda. As well as the growing folklore movement there were several other paths being opened up by young Senegalese, including Toure Kunda's Afro-rock and the Star Band's mbalax. By a macabre coincidence crucial members of Xalam and Toure Kunda died during the 1980s, depleting the bands' energies and interrupting their momentum.

Toure Kunda started opening up adolescent French ears to Africa when they moved to Paris in 1979. Playing Afro-rock reminiscent of the Ghanaian band Osibisa some ten years before, they offered a brash, multi-dimensional music developed from Manding and Soninke tradition. A rare understanding of production methods enabled the Toure brothers to pitch their music at French mainstream record buyers, who lacked exciting alternatives, and they became part of the Paris scene.

Talk of the Tama

But it was mbalax which finally made the big time. Mbalax is a Wolof music based on the bursting rhythms of sabar and bugarabu drums which rattle out conversations, punctuated by short pithy phrases from the solo voice of the tama talking drum. At first these rhythms sounded extremely complex to uninitiated Western ears, with a rather lumpy cycle of repeats and sudden changes of emphasis. But this 'exoticism' undoubtedly helped provide a curiosity interest to attract casual listeners to the music, and mbalax has become a familiar sound in 'world music' circles. In Senegambia it is by now a cultural fixture.

Mbalax was developed by the Star Band in the late Seventies. In 1975 the band had several singers including a precocious young attraction called Pape Djibril, aka 'Cheri Coco', a small boy with a piercing voice, who can be seen and heard performing for the wedding reception in Ousmane Sembene's feature film *Xala*. Many believe it must be Youssou singing but he himself denied it. He did join the band around that time, but it was only when Pape left that people noticed the similarity, that they were "getting the same thing, the same voice". They also looked remarkably similar. In 1978 with the Star Band, Youssou took part in his first recording session.

A year later Youssou and some other members, including tama player Assane Thiam, bassist and arranger Habib Faye and most of the rhythm section, broke off to form their own group. They simply translated 'Star' into French and launched Etoile de Dakar. They played around the capital until 1981 when they made their first visit to Paris. Many ex-Etoile musicians were to set up groups of their own and almost all the Senegalese pop bands had some familial connection. Xalam, Super Diamono, Number One, and Baobab are some of the orchestras containing ex-Etoile members. Following a reorganisation in 1981 Youssou's band became known as Super Etoile de Dakar, while breakaway singers Eric Mbacke Ndoye and El Hadj Faye formed Etoile 2000.

From then on, Youssou's name was billed above the band's. He began to grow rich not just from his recordings, which were usually pirated in massive numbers, but also from the presents and donations of the Senegalese women who adore him. Youssou's shows on his home ground drive audiences wild with delight, inspiring the spectacular *ventilateur* dance at which the

Orchestre Baobab: lazy rumba rhythms and nonsense songs

Youssou at his Dakar headquarters in 1983, prior to his global adventures

elegantly robed Wolof women excel. At home his success was often attributed to his *marabout,* Abdul Ahad Mbacke, leader of an Africanised Muslim sect called the Mourides, and recognised as one of the most powerful spiritual leaders in Senegal. As the riches rolled in, however, it was openly said on the steets of Dakar that much of the financial reward was donated to Mbacke. If so, Youssou paid heavily for his initial success.

In the past much of the spectacular stage action came from Youssou's close friend, Allah Seck, a thin, dreadlocked rapper and dancer who could outstep anyone. Following Seck's untimely death from typhoid in 1987, Youssou took on more of the 'animation' himself. While the personnel changed around them, the crucial tama player, Thiam, and the bassist, Faye, remained by his side. As much of Youssou's popularity in the West has undoubtedly come from the 'exotic' elements of mbalax music as from the remarkable quality of his voice.

All The World's a Stage for Youssou N'Dour

A genuine superstar in his home country since the early 1980s, when his name was already painted on fishing boats, taxis and walls, the still youthful Youssou was Africa's representative on the 1988 Amnesty International 'Human Rights Now' World tour which visited North and South America, Asia, Australia and Europe as well as Africa. Both accompanying Peter Gabriel and alone with Super Etoile he has made festival and concert appearances throughout America, Europe and Africa.

The obvious word to describe Youssou's early success on the world stage is 'phenomenal' but that is a label he was not keen to bear. "I don't wish to be seen as a phenomenon," he once said, "I would rather sustain a reputation for good music."

That reputation has been built on Youssou's soaring, clear-toned, almost feminine voice which is a truly impressive instrument. Since his first overseas tour with Super Etoile in the early 1980s, Youssou has attracted a cult following in Europe and fanatical enthusiasm in other West Africa states for the slightly elliptical percussion-powered mbalax music which he pioneered.

Although steeped in traditional culture, Youssou has always preferred to look forward, singing about contemporary issues like immigration, urbanisation, apartheid, feminism and the African environment rather than the historical subject matter of his predecessors. His musical tastes are just as worldly, ranging from Elton John to Prince, and although mbalax is based on traditional rhythmic patterns, it is a contemporary fusion which has also adapted non-traditional elements, particularly Western hardware and the way it is put to use. It is no more 'pure' than the rumba music played by the Sine Dramatic group which Youssou joined as a twelve-year-

old prodigy, back in the early 1970s.

Youssou was born in 1959 in Dakar to a Wolof father and Tukulor mother, Ndeye Sokhna Mboup, a celebrated griot and composer, who it is said contributed many of Youssou's early songs. He started singing publicly at twelve years of age with Sine Dramatic. When he appeared in a national radio talent contest Youssou was quickly spotted by promoters and club owners and at fourteen he was performing to large audiences.

The public response to the small boy with the soulful voice was immediate. He joined Charles Diop and the original Super Diamono and at fifteen he was a star. Two years later he was contracted to join the Star Band at the Miami nightclub in Dakar.

By 1983 he had his own nightclub in the capital, the Thiosanne, where he would appear six nights a week, usually taking the stage well after midnight. While prices there were pitched at the well-to-do, Youssou never neglected the poorer people who provided the bulk of his support and he played regularly at less exclusive venues.

Youssou always had ambitions to find a wider, even global, audience. In 1983 in Dakar, before he had ever played in an

anglophone country, Youssou said he wanted to be "as popular as Elton John. But I don't want to just earn money and find the good life and enjoy it. No way. I want to play for my culture. It's my family tradition and my sons and grandsons will want to know what I have done for my country. I could play reggae and make money if I wanted, but reggae is for Jamaica. Mbalax is for Oonagal. It is authentic music and we want to export only African music. We do not play other music. We play our music for others to hear that African music is good. In the past the musical world was concentrated in America and Europe, and now we want the musical world to be concentrated in Africa."

Youssou's hopes for his own progress in the Eighties were pretty well realised although he concentrated more outside Africa. In 1986, following a marathon, sponsored tour of seven West African countries in three weeks, Youssou played around the Senegal regions before heading back for Europe, Japan and the States.

Judging by his two albums for the Virgin record label, Youssou appeared to have got as much as he had given from the extended foray into Western 'stadium' rock, during which he played with and alongside people like Gabriel, Sting, Bruce Springsteen and Stevie Wonder.

At the risk of upsetting many of his followers, he aimed these Westernised albums squarely at the mainstream pop market. Not for the first time Youssou sang some lines in English as well as his native Wolof. Shaking the Tree reflected Youssou's 'progressive' attitude, dealing with women's rights -- a contentious issue in the largely polygamous, Islamic society of Senegal. For the domestic market he continued with more 'rootsy' home-style cassette releases.

The growing technological sophistication which became noticeable in the 1986 record *Nelson Mandela* has not always appealed to those listeners who like to take their musical vacations in what they erroneously believe to be unspoilt, even undiscovered territories. *The Lion* album blended different moods and musical attitudes into a slick, internationalised package which had little appeal for those aficionados. But 'world music' is supposed to be about cultural exchange, and while the West had discovered Youssou N'Dour, he had also discovered the West. In the Arizona town of Old Tucson he was inspired to write a song about the wonderful day when he found himself in the real world of the Western movies. Beneath his broad weave Senegalese peasant outfit, Youssou N'Dour was wearing cowboy boots.

In 1990, however, he returned the criticism of his cosy relationship with the West with a song about the deadly serious subject of toxic waste from industrialised countries being dumped in Africa. The album *Set* was well received in the States but, despite the support given by Peter Gabriel who had taken Youssou around the world and onto countless television screens and magazine covers, he soon went the way of many other African artistes. The Virgin label dropped him after two albums.

Super Diamono have been described as a young man's band, said to appeal more to male youths than to the females who follow Youssou. Formed at the end of 1975 and named after a famous group from the previous generation, Diamono originally played Cuban rumbas and sang in Spanish for the dance crowds. The motivating forces were singer Omar Pene and guitarist Ismael Lo. A sponsor paid to record their debut cassette release which made them enough money to equip themselves and consolidate their own style of 'Afro feeling' music or *jahazz* with its distinctive reggae feel, before bringing in the more complex mbalax. With songs about social isues like corruption, poverty and Black awareness, Super Diamono have taken a militant stance typical of reggae musicians. In 1985 they were joined by the the Gambian 'rasta' singer Musa N'gom, from Guelewars of Banjul.

Ismael Lo, who had left the group in 1984, began to plough his own successful furrow through the Paris scene. With an ear for progressive sounds, a rugged voice and a sensitive guitar style, Lo became one of the first solo recording artistes from the region. He was actually born in Niger but grew up near the Senegalese capital. By the age of fifteen he was 'discovered' by a television technician playing harmonica and guitar and soon made his television debut. Lo was already developing his own fusion of traditional and contemporary music, which led him to join Super Diamono in 1979. A trained painter as well as musician, Lo spent the early 1980s studying art in Spain before returning home with his solo projects crystallised. He quit Super Diamono in 1984 and began the solo recording career which saw him release four albums in five years.

Baaba Maal (aka the Nightingale) who came to prominence in the West at the end of the 1980s is championed as a spokesman for the Pulaar-speaking Tukulor people of northern Senegal, challenging the Wolof hegemony and launching a sophisticated fusion of minority folklore music with contemporary international arrangement and presentation techniques. Baaba's lyrics appealed to progressive young Senegalese, particularly those seeking an alternative to Youssou's dominance, and his music presented a slicker, less lumpy sound than mbalax. Reggae, soul and electro ingredients made it easily accessible to outsiders. But he denied imitation: the reggae type rhythms were, he claimed, based

Omar Pene: vocalist and founder of Super Diamono

Baaba Maal: music intellectual, showman and spokesman for the Pulaar people

on the *yella* music which takes its beat from the pounding of the women's pestles.

According to cultural practice Baaba, who was not born into a griot family, strictly had no right to become a musician. An enlightened teacher at his primary school, however, gave pupils the chance to study music and he learned the basics of kora, and other traditional stringed instruments before taking up the guitar. His mother was an accomplished amateur singer who actively encouraged Baaba with his music, teaching him much of the repertoire of dances and folk songs. A high achiever at school, Baaba won a scholarship to the school of arts in Dakar. In the capital he joined up with the 70-piece cultural troupe, Asly Fouta, comprised mostly of young people from his home region of Fouta. With them he developed his performing skills, before setting out to research the cultural background of the Pulaar (Fulani) speaking people. His repertoire eventually included worksongs from many of the regions, for which Baaba adapted appropriate dances. He launched his own band Dande Lenol (Voice of the People) in 1985 with a powerful stage show, spectacular virtuoso dancers and dynamic, somewhat contrived arrangements, powered by an extraordinary tama player, Masamba Diop, who batters some of the hardest cracking rhythms from the smallest, snakeskin-headed instrument.

Baaba is a progressive, who questions the traditional attitudes which hinder social or personal development. His lyrics reflect this awareness of contemporary issues as he sings of the dangers of bush abortions or the injustices of class and caste. "It's not enough to have just a good voice," he has said. "You need to have a message and you need the freedom to sing what you want." A small, serious, even pious young man, Baaba's comportment suits his reputation as one of the intellectuals of Senegalese music.

Treichville Rock

The Ivorian capital of Abidjan is one of the main commercial centres of West Africa, with a thriving port and cosmopolitan society divided between the rich and middle-class districts such as Plateau and the animated, music-packed 'quartier' of Treichville. The city has hosted numerous visiting musicians from other parts of Africa, many making it a stepping stone to Europe or the States, yet few Ivorian artistes have made their mark. Those who have include Ernesto Djedje, populariser of the frenetic *ziglibithy* dance of the 1970s, Jimmy Hyacinthe and Daouda. Hyacinthe was a member of the Bozambo group featuring the Burkinabe Georges Ouedrago and J-P Coco, who went on to play with Manu Dibango when he was called in to organise a national orchestra in 1975. Female singers such as Nyanka Bell, Aicha Kone and Dianne Solo have tasted fame with pan-African pop hybrids, but the lack of a national musical identity has not helped them.

Ironically, Abidjan has had better studio facilities than any of its neighbours and musicians from Mali, Guinea, Senegal and Burkina as well as Ghana, Zaire, Cameroon and Nigeria have launched recording careers from there. When Sam Mangwana broke away from the Zairean bandleader Tabu Ley Rochereau in the 1970s, his African All-Stars made their base in Abidjan. Bibi Dens Tshibayi arrived with The Best, had a minor smash with *The Best Ambience* and settled into a residency at the Intercontinental hotel. He also collaborated with fellow Zairean Tshala Mwana on her debut recording.

The first Ivorian voice to be heard across the globe was Alpha Blondy's. Originally known as Seydou Kone, Blondy was born in 1953 in the central region of Cote d'Ivoire. He formed his first group, Atomic Vibrations, while at school, before moving to Liberia, where he made strong anglophone connnections. He then travelled to the USA to study trade and English at Columbia Uni-

Cultures collide in Ouagadougou: the youthful Ivorian pop band Woya electrify the desert night

Roots rocker from Abidjan: Alpha Blondy became Africa's first reggae star

versity in 1976. Simultaneous with his studies Blondy was working on his music, at one stage singing Mandinka lyrics with a New York reggae band called Monyaka. A Jamaican producer recorded six of his songs but vanished with the tapes. More than disillusioned, Blondy suffered a nervous breakdown and on his return to Abidjan his parents had him committed to a psychiatric hospital for two years, as he believed, to dissuade him from becoming a musician. It is the kind of response many parents might think appropriate, but in Blondy's case it did not work.

On his release Blondy took a job with the Ivorian TV station. In his own time he was hanging out with Ghanaian friends, playing reggae. The Ghanaians, he said, had the reggae spirit and with perseverence they managed to record a demo cassette, which eventually landed with a talent show producer who gave him his first break. He was quickly offered the chance to make an album. *Jah Glory*, recorded in the broadcasting station's eight-track studio, and released in 1982, became one of the country's biggest sellers. It received the full commercial treatment with videos, T-shirts and badges promoting the cassette sales across francophone Africa. Within a year it was a triple-gold seller.

His carefree rasta image and straightforward, socially aware lyrics in Dioula mixed with French and a little English, appealed to the youth. His use of African proverbs even endeared him to older listeners, although the contradiction of being a Muslim and a rasta member of the Twelve Tribes of Juda, a 'falasha', confused some people. The ministry of education organised free concerts and he appeared on TV throughout the region. His second album released in 1984 was supported with a tour of West Africa. With his band Solar System he visited Europe in 1985 to make his debut at the Zenith stadium in Paris.

The next albums *Cocody Rock*, with surviving members of Bob Marley's Wailers, and *Apartheid is Nazism*, were even bigger successes, licensed by record labels in Britain and the USA. The follow-up album *Jerusalem*, was recorded at Marley's Tuff Gong studio in Jamaica. A string of Ivorian reggae artistes, notably Jah Solo Gunt, have followed in Blondy's steps, and he has inspired the first generation of reggae musicians across Africa.

Band bus of F. Kenya, a highlife bandleader who often plays over the border in Ghana

Small is Beautiful

The smaller countries of francophone West Africa are unable to compete with the big bands or musical productivity of their larger neighbours but they have quietly been providing talented solo musicians and arrangers who are forced to develop outside their own borders, most often in Paris.

Benin, neighbour to the mighty Nigeria, has cultural affinities with its francophone neighbours of the Sahel as well as the anglophone countries, and has also been home to the Satel studio favoured by musicians from other countries including Cote d'Ivoire and Cameroon. In the 1970s Cameroonian makossa and mangambe were reputedly better known in Benin than in Nigeria, with artistes such as Pierre Tchana and Sam Fan Thomas recording there.

Apart from the fabled Orchestre Poly-rhythmo, led by guitarist Papillon, and Ignace de Souza who played highlife in Ghana, few musicians made their mark internationally until Wally Badarou, a keyboard player who moved in the exalted circles of rock recording sessions during the late 1970s and early Eighties.

As a member of Island Records' Compass Point All-Stars, Badarou played and arranged on recording sessions for the Gibson Brothers, Grace Jones and the British group Level 42, who had six UK Top Ten hits during the 1980s, as well as composing the music for the Countryman film. He has released two solo albums, and scored a British Top 50 hit of his own in 1985 with Chief Inspector.

Another Beninois, Jimmy Houetinou, made his way in the music business as producer of the Paris-based Zairean super-group, Loketo.

At the start of the 1990s the new voice of Angelique Kidjo was being heard in Europe. In fact Kidjo (above) had been singing folklore and variety with her brothers since childhood in the Kidjo Brothers Band, and recording for more than ten years, first for Benin radio.

In 1979 she recorded her first local hits and toured in Cote d'Ivoire. In 1980, at the suggestion of the Cameroonian composer and arranger Ekambi Bril-lant, she travelled to Paris, where she worked with a band called Pili Pili, recording two albums.

Her debut solo album, Parakou, made in 1990 in collaboration with keyboard player Jean Hebrail, reflected the pan-African Parisien milieu, with makossa, soukous, reggae and zouk rhythms carrying her adaptions of folklore from Benin and West Africa.

The name 'Par-akou' refers to a town in central Benin which is a cultural cross-roads between the Sahel and the coastal peoples.

To the north, the landlocked country of Burkina Faso has become known as the cultural home of Africa's burgeoning cinema industry, and little is heard of its music. Hamidou Ouedraogo, who originally played accordion, is probably the best known Burkinabe musician. The late president Thomas Sankara was a keen guitar player.

The even smaller country of Togo has a similar profile to Benin as a service facility for pan-African music -- a hi-tech studio in Lome, Africa New Sound, which was used frequently in the 1980s by Nigerian and Zairean musicians -- and a memorable solo artiste, the late Bella Bellow who made her one and only album with Manu Dibango, and whose composition Blewu was one of the songs interpreted by Angelique Kidjo.

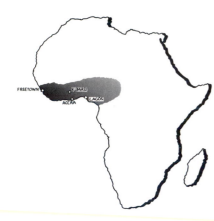

The Highlife Zone

The name 'highlife' just about sums up the aspirations and emotions of most African popular music (and indeed other types of pop the world over). It conjures images of fancy nightclubs, shiny dancefloors, champagne, fine clothes, sophistication and the yearning for a good time which echoes down through the scale of indulgences to a spare 100 cedis for beer money. Appropriately highlife was the name eventually given to West Africa's seminal popular music and by which it is now known throughout the continent. To many anglophones the name is used generically for any African guitar pop. Many completely different styles from far corners of Africa are referred to as one or another kind of 'highlife', and the credit is not far wrong. From the start highlife was a synthesised music which mimicked European dance band trends as soon as the first brass instruments arrived on the West Coast before 1900. It is primarily an anglophone music, from the territories of the old British West Africa, which has remained the most prominent style in Ghana, and has enjoyed widespread but fluctuating popularity in Nigeria, Sierra Leone and Liberia, and in the French-speaking countries of Benin and Togo.

The flavour of highlife has also been used to spice up some of Africa's other great musics. The pioneers of Zairean *soukous*, Cameroonian *makossa* and Manding swing were all inspired by early highlife, while almost all the popular music in anglophone West Africa, including Nigerian juju and Afrobeat, has descended directly from highlife re-infused with indigenous or foreign music. The heyday of highlife was during the Fifties and Sixties, but at the start of the 1990s the guitar form is still alive in Ghana, and at a lower level in Nigeria, where forecasts of a 'highlife revival' are announced almost annually.

In the 1920s when highlife took off on the West Coast, the sophisticated image suggested by the name was exploited mercilessly. In the dance bars and hotels, champagne was on sale, tickets cost about a week's wages, and the bourgeois elite who turned out to dance attracted their own audience. Yebuah Mensah, brother of E.T. Mensah and a co-founder of dance band highlife, told the writer John Collins how the name caught on in Accra. "The term highlife was created by the people who gathered around the dancing clubs such as the Roger Club, to watch and listen to the couples enjoying themselves. Highlife started as a catchy name for the indigenous songs played at these clubs by such early dance bands as the Jazz Kings, the Cape Coast Sugar Babies and later the Accra Orchestra. The people outside called it highlife as they did not reach the class of the couples going inside, who not only had to pay a relatively high entrance fee of about seven shillings and sixpence, but also had to wear full evening dress, including top hats if they could afford it."

Highlife was one of the first examples of a fusion between the old world and the new, and a prototype for all African pop. It probably began the moment Africans in the Gold Coast and Sierra Leone first heard Black music from the Americas. Army bands, often containing a mix of races, created their own blend of the ragtime music arriving from America, mixed up with the more common European foxtrots, waltzes and polkas, interpreted with African characteristics in the phrasing and in the rhythms. Caribbean soldiers who were stationed in the region around the turn of the century had contributed some of their pre-Calypso *kaiso* music; and many of the middle-class elite who effectively

Rhythm machines: drum maker Kofi Donkor with his wife and a newly made pair of adowa drums in Akumadan, Ghana

Highlife guitar maestro Nana Ampadu: leader of the African Brothers Band, favourites in Ghana since the 1960s

ran the colony had also been recruited from West Indian professionals. Army, police and evangelical marching bands acquired the first brass wind instruments on the continent. Soon civilian brass bands were heard throughout the Gold Coast and every small rural town had to have its own formation of musicians for ceremonial occasions. After a while this music became seen as far too 'colonial', but some of the instruments were carried over into the burgeoning popular dance scene.

The piano had become a fashionable prop of the Christian middle class by the Thirties. Along with the instruments, which were shipped in to the west coast in surprisingly large numbers, came contemporary sheet music, introducing popular American ragtimes and later jazz and dance band arrangements, still current and fresh in the New World. New dances, songs and improved instruments were available on the West African coast

Kwaa Mensah: early palm-wine stylist and nephew of Sam Asare, Ghana's first recording artiste

almost as soon as they had been launched in America. There were also occasional visits by American vaudeville artistes, who helped inspire a modern theatrical tradition in Sierra Leone and led to the development of one of Ghana's cultural assets, the concert party. Meanwhile sailors, dockers and artisans along the busy West African waterfronts popularised the harmonica, button accordion and guitar.

At the dawn of the highlife era, people who had no money for band instruments, let alone champagne and top hats, made their own box guitars, either to traditional or foreign design, and sat down with a bowl of sweet, strong palm wine to pick out versions of the music they could hear drifting out of the swanky hotels. This lower class 'street' entertainment, known as 'palm-wine' music, relied on percussion and traditional drums to support the guitarist/singer. The guitar picking style is believed to have originated with Liberian 'Kru men' who, due to their reputation as fine seamen, were often recruited on to European ships and could be found right along the coastal regions of West Africa down as far as Congo. They were renowned guitarists and undoubtedly at the root of what turned into Africa's original pop music. But no Liberians ever made the highlife big-time and within Liberia the craze for dance band highlife did not catch on. Eventually the palm-wine style was consolidated in Ghana by the guitarist Kwame Asare, followed by Kwaa Mensah and Koo Nimo. Similar forms also evolved in Nigeria and Sierra Leone.

Palm wine was actually the first type of Ghanaian music to be recorded when 'Sam' Kwame Asare was invited to London in 1926 to record for the Zonophone label. Known as the 'father' of palm-wine music, Asare soon passed on his skills to his nephew Kwaa Mensah who began playing in the waterfront bars, before joining an *adaha* band as a drummer, and bringing guitar into that percussion-based folk music. In 1951 Kwaa Mensah formed his own guitar band and began a prolific recording career. Following in the steps of E.K. Nyame, he also combined music performance with comic theatre and toured with a concert party almost up to his death in February, 1991. In later years Koo Nimo had become the 'curator' of the palm-wine style. A graduate who maintained a career at the university in Kumasi, Koo Nimo's musical experience goes back to the late 1940s. He has played pop and highlife music and eventually studied Spanish and classical guitar before concentrating on the preservation of the palm-wine idiom.

While dance band music was becoming fashionable in the Gold Coast towns of Accra, Cape Coast and Takoradi, the tastes of the rural people in the interior were less cosmopolitan. In the towns and villages of the Ashanti region, another form of highlife played by guitar bands started in the Thirties which continues today. More formal than palm-wine, guitar-band highlife was intended as ticket-selling entertainment and over 50 years later it brings a steady living for some of Ghana's top musicians. The Ghanaian papers regularly publish the touring dates of guitar bands including the country's favourite group, Nana Ampadu's African Brothers Band, who play nightly in rural towns with weekends in the Accra area.

In Sierra Leone, the ragtime bands formed in the Twenties gave way to ballroom dance bands whose titles gave some idea of their orientation, from the Cuban Swing Band to the Mayfair Dance Band. Many of these were orginally school groups formed by Old Boys assocations, which still provide a context for Sierra Leonean social life. By the 1940s Freetown, which was an assembly point for war-time Atlantic convoys, had become one of the busiest ports in the world but, despite the cross-cultural exchanges, Sierra Leone never matched the national cohesion of the richer Gold Coast which gave dance band highlife its impetus. Ragtime piano bands and comic theatrical shows monopolised the live music scene, and during the Thirties there was a thriving business in local recorded music. When the Freetown Rediffusion Service was launched in 1934, popular music was given air time and when expanded into a proper radio service twenty years later there was a full spectrum of indigenous music styles being released on 78rpm records. The form which proved most popular until the Sixties was *maringa,* a close relative of 'merengue'. The top selling artistes were Ebenezer Callender and S.E. Rogie who both combined this Caribbean idiom with highlife and palm wine. Another local style of street music was 'Milo Jazz', based on the rhythm of a frame drum combined with guitar and percussion instruments, including a Milo milk can filled with pebbles and used as a shaker.

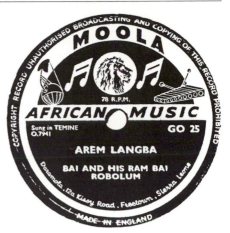

Sooliman Ernest Rogie, born in the 1920s, took up guitar at a young age but did not release his first disc until 1961. *My Lovely Elizabeth* displayed his own blend of palm-wine with American rock and twist and a dash of calypso. At the time Rogie was a hot, progressive artiste who launched a string of hits. After releasing nearly 50 singles he moved to America, where the music business passed him by, until the late Eighties when he released an album of his old favourites. Rogie made a remarkable comeback and reached a level of international fame he never achieved during his active musical career.

During the early Sixties the Congolese group Ryco Jazz based themselves in Sierra Leone, touring the region and influencing local musicians. Among those who favoured a Congolese touch were the Cisco Kids, the Ticklers, Afro Nationale and Super Combo. Later in the decade American soul music had a powerful effect throughout Africa, not least in Freetown where Gerald Pine, an electric guitarist and radio technician, was particularly inspired by James Brown. Pine, who later performed under the more exotic name of Geraldo Pino and the Heartbeats, had an effect which outlived his own brief moment of fame. For Pino is widely credited with having a major influence on Fela Kuti's Afrobeat sound. Another 'internationaliser' was Bunny Mack who had a hit in 1981 with *Let me Love You*. A Freetown boy, he played whistle, harmonica and banjo before joining the Soundcasters as lead guitarist and singer. The band's Afro-tinged soul attracted a mod following on the British R&B scene in the mid-1960s. They cut their first record in 1967 and worked on the European continent for a few more years. In 1970 they teamed up with producer Akie Deen of Afrodisc, and Mack recorded his first hit *Discocalypso*.

Koo Nimo: the 'curator' of palm-wine music, playing at Legon University, Accra in 1971

Dance Band Days

Since the turn of the century, dance bands playing on the Gold Coast had catered as much for the Black elite who administered the country as for the few Whites. The first proto-highlife band was, Frank Torto's Excelsior Orchestra formed in 1914. By the Twenties the Jazz Kings and the Cape Coast Sugar Babies were also on the scene, and they were followed later in the decade by the Winneba Orchestra, Sekondi Nanshamang, Ashanti Nkrame and others. The Jazz Kings, a typical band of the time, played a variety of ballroom, ragtime and their own version of highlife at formal dances and vaudeville shows. Among the original band was a

Boys' fife-and-drum band, *circa* 1930: 'Teacher' Joe Lamptey with proteges including, somewhere, the young E.T. Mensah

The *seprewa* traditional stringed instrument in the hands of Little Moses

character who opened up the music scene for the next generation, and became the founding father of dance band highlife.

'Teacher' Joe Lamptey was a schoolmaster at Accra Government School with a special interest in football, and music. Lamptey had earlier formed a mass fife (metal whistle) and drum band of junior school pupils, and in 1927 he quit the Jazz Kings, withdrew his life's savings and bought a collection of instruments to set up a proper school band. By 1932 this had evolved into the Accra Orchestra, with members selected from Lamptey's pupils. A short while later a young piccolo player named E.T. Mensah joined up. As E.T. remembered, the band was huge and not limited in number of players or instruments. The line-up included a complete set of brass, from cornet to sousaphone and tuba, a full woodwind section, jazz drums and various percussion, violins, violas, cello, acoustic guitar and novelty sound effects. At the time there was no amplification. The repertoire was rumba, swing, ragtime and ballroom. Although they quickly made a name and were called to play frequently, the band broke up in 1936 because of the sort of 'money palaver' that has become familiar throughout Africa where music is played 'commercially'.

E.T. was by now playing sax and in his last years at high school had also taken up the organ. He finished school around the time the Accra Orchestra broke up, and joined his brother Yebuah in the reassembled ensemble now known as the Accra Rhythmic Orchestra. This new band, which included the drummer Guy Warren (Kofi Ghanaba), had a big fifteen-piece line-up with five saxophones. Horns were very much the preferred solo instruments at the time and almost all the future dance bandleaders were trumpet or saxophone specialists. Guitars played a background role as part of the rhythm section; the subtly changing inflexions of those rhythms, however, gave highlife its character.

"What happened was that, in those days we urgently wanted an indigenous rhythm to replace the fading foreign music of waltz, rumba, etc.", recalled Mensah. "We evolved a music type thereafter relying on basic African rhythms. A criss-cross African cultural sound so to speak. No one really can lay claim to its creation. It had always been there, entrenched in West African culture. What I did was give highlife world acceptance." E.T. was not working single-handed, however. Sitting at the drum kit busily weaving those rhythms through the melodies was Warren, the drummer who was at the core of the new fusion.

Among the indigenous roots rhythms which lent themselves to this exciting hybrid were *osibisiba, gome, ashiko* and *dagomba,* a rhythm from the north of Ghana, with fleeting undertones of the Sahel. Related rhythms can be heard right across the semi-desert regions of northern Nigeria, Cameroon, and Chad. Another form of music was *adaha* which evolved from experiments by the choral sections of the military brass bands. The later *konkomba* percussion style maintained the connection but the music had moved a long way from brass bands.

By 1940, E.T. Mensah was also playing in another band led by a saxophone-playing Scottish soldier, Sergeant Jack Leopard and his Black and White Spots. Mensah acknowledged that he learnt a lot technically from Leopard who had been in a professional dance band in London, and he made a deal more money in Leopard's band, who played for mainly White audiences. During World War Two British and American musicians had helped to open Ghanaian ears to new developments in dance music. After the war, the fresh influence from the States was Afro-Cuban music, a languid style more suited to small combos than big bands, which made creative and economic sense for bandleaders and club owners alike. In 1947 E.T. and Guy Warren joined up as members of the first Tempos led by Joe Kelly. Warren went briefly to America and Britain to play with the influential saxophonist Kenny Graham, whose Afro-Cubists were infusing some long-lost Latin elements into post-war jazz, and he returned from New York with Cuban and calypso ingredients to add to the new blend.

In 1949 the Tempos travelled to Nigeria to introduce their dance band highlife. The bandleader Bobby Benson, who was then playing straight swing, was immediately converted. The cross-pollination between the music of the two countries was helped by several Nigerian musicians. Trumpeters Zeal Onyia and Victor Olaiya, who were both playing with Benson at the time, later joined Mensah. Following a split between the musicians, E.T. took over the leadership of the reorganised Tempos. One of the first recruits to the new outfit was the young sax player, Jerry Hansen, who eventually went on to lead the Ramblers, the top dance band in later decades.

Members of the original Tempos: multi-instrumentalists J.A. Mallet (left) and future bandleader E.T. Mensah in 1937

The dance band scene was thriving in the early Fifties, and as opportunities arose it was natural that some of the Tempos regulars would be tempted to break out. In 1952 King Bruce left to form the Black Beats, followed the next year by Joe Kelly who set up the Red Spots, but none were in the same league as the Tempos which had now become the first fully professional band in Ghana. For a while the Tempos musicians were making good money. In 1954, under the threat of competition from newly-formed bands including the Rhythm Aces, a second team called the Star Rockets was set up to look after Ghanaian business while the Tempos were away in Nigeria. In the mid-1950s there were plenty of clubs opening in Accra, money was flowing and the mood was light. Many bands established themselves including the Hot

The King of Highlife

The undisputed King of Highlife music, who started playing in the early 1930s, E.T. Mensah was still active in the late 1980s. His is probably the longest career span in African music. Born in 1919 in Accra, Mensah grew up in the formative years of the highlife style.

On leaving school he studied to become a pharmacist, the profession he was to fall back on several times during his career. In 1943 he qualified and was stationed in the north of the country but when he returned to Accra in 1947, he joined the original Tempos Band with leader Joe Kelly and Guy Warren (Kofi Ghanaba) on drums.

Mensah broke away in 1948 to start his own pharmacy and his own band, still called the Tempos, which offered a blend of highlife and jive that appealed to both Africans and Europeans alike. Continually plagued by the departures and squabbles of his musicans, E.T. developed a new style of playing, which was less dependent on Western dance band techniques or the popular American and English renditions.

Considering his musicians in the 1952 line-up not to be proficient in these formal styles, Mensah augmented the percussion section and turned his ear more toward the tropical rhythms of South America, the Caribbean and of course, Africa. He had also taken up trumpet in addition to his alto sax because he could not always rely on finding a suitable sideman.

E.T.'s relaxed, natural style proved immediately popular in Accra and when he recorded his first 78rpm discs in 1952 he was quickly proclaimed the King of Highlife. The first recordings from the golden era of highlife were sung in the main Ghanaian languages, Twi, Fanti and Ga, as well as in English. The records were frequently backed with calypso numbers. In 1953 the Tempos were the only professional band in the then Gold Coast, a status they could only

maintain by frequent and lucrative tours of Nigeria. That year E.T. also made his first solo trip to England where he performed with many jazz regulars and caught the eye of the British press.

One of the biggest moments of his career, and a great morale booster to the emerging independent state of Ghana, was the visit in 1956 of Louis Armstrong. As the country's top trumpet player, E.T. was invited to meet and play with Satchmo in front of enormous crowds.

Independence in 1957 found Mensah proprietor of his own club, the Paramount, but economic problems soon forced him to shut down and he set out on a tour of West Africa. His early popularity in Nigeria was largely uncontested, as there were few local groups playing highlife at the time and his records were well known. In 1958 he spread his message even further with a tour of the region, during which he played for several heads of state.

E.T. was often thwarted in his commercial ambitions and by the 1960s he was practising pharmacy again. He was quite content to be a semi-professional musician, saying that he had never expected to make a living out of it. In 1969, however, at the age of 50 he took a new Tempos line-up to Europe for three months. The repertoire now included elements of Congolese rumba, soul, pop and calypso as well as a dash of reggae which he knew had become the dominant Black music in London.

In 1986 a show was given in his honour in Lagos and he joined his old colleagues Victor Uwaifo and Victor Olaiya on stage. Later in the year some of his earliest recordings were re-released by the London-based RetroAfric label. Despite failing health which meant he could barely walk, E.T. took the stage again at the Africa Centre in London, and for a short time his music evoked those optimistic days of the golden age.

In 1989, he was formally honoured by the Ghanaian government for his contribution to the country's culture.

Shots, the Top Spotters and the Havana Delta Dandies.

In 1957 Ghana became the first West African nation to achieve independence, under Kwame Nkrumah. That alone was a great boost to the country's culture. E.T. Mensah went on a voyage round West Africa and spread the music into Cote d'Ivoire, Guinea and Sierra Leone. Highlife was now the national music, an aural equivalent of the *kente* cloth worn by Ashanti noblemen and the new President. Nkrumah poured resources into the arts and provided government incentives to boost Ghanaian culture which included the importation of musical instruments and PA equipment and the setting up of state-sponsored bands.

E.K. Nyame's band in 1952: pioneers of the concert party combining music with slapstick comedy

The newly nationalised corporations like the Builders and Workers' Brigade, the Black Star shipping line, the Cocoa Marketing Board, as well as the police and army regiments established their own employees' bands. Nkrumah set up training schemes for musicians to learn traditional idioms, and made the study of African music compulsory in schools. When the President travelled he was always accompanied by a top highlife band. E.T. Mensah, E.K. Nyame, Uhuru Dance Band and the Ramblers were called at various times for presidential journeys. In 1959 there were attempts as part of Nkrumah's Africanisation policy to change the music's name from the English 'highlife' to an authentic African name. The name of a local rhythm, *osibisiba,* was believed to be the presidential favourite, but was never officially imposed.

The Sixties was a boom time for highlife. The economy was healthy and record production was able to supply public demand. Three multinational record companies, Decca, EMI and Philips, had studios and pressing plants in Ghana, and outside the country the music was creating a market for itself throughout West and Central Africa, as far east as Kenya. Ghana had a relatively efficient electricity supply and there were enough record players available for people to be able to listen to the new 45rpm singles. Nightlife flourished, and dance bands such as Broadway, the Stargazers, Messengers, Melody Aces, Rhythm Aces, Globemasters, Red Spots and the Modernaires were riding high.

Highlife dance bands chugged through the decade with Jerry Hansen's Ramblers, set up in 1961, proving the most consistently popular. The Ramblers played a more soulful contemporary highlife and they became popular enough for Hansen to later claim that his was the first West African band to tour Britain. They also covered some eighteen African countries. Along with Bobby Benson in Lagos, Hansen became the first West African musician to be paid for endorsing an instrument maker, the saxophone and brass manufacturers Selmer, and both bandleaders became sales representatives for the company. Later Hansen moved to the USA but when the 1968 collection *Hit Songs of the Ramblers* was re-released in 1990 his son, Jerry Hansen Junior, reactivated the band.

The Guitar Bands

In the early years the dance bands had provided the main thrust of highlife, but that was not the only form to adapt local rhythms into a popular fusion. The distinction was formally recognised in 1960 when two musicians' unions were set up in Ghana, one for dance band musicians and one for guitar bands.

The parallel guitar-band highlife was a rural style originated by E.K. Nyame and Kwaa Mensah (no relation to E.T.) which had poorer but intensely loyal audiences in the interior of the country.

By the 1940s Kumasi, the Ashanti capital, had become a centre for this new form, with dozens of guitar bands following the lead of the Kumasi Trio who had been the first to be recorded on the Zonophone label.

E.K. Nyame, who died in 1977 aged 50, was one of the most popular musicians of his generation. He started out with the Appiah Adjekum Band which used guitar, concertina and percussion, before forming the Akan Trio, for which he brought in double bass and Western 'jazz' drums. By 1952 he had expanded the line-up and developed his show into a musical comedy review incorporating slapstick, which immediately established a new tradition, the theatrical concert party. The shows were originally delivered in English but gradually the Ashanti language, Twi, took prominence. Nyame released over 400 records, starting with the 1951 hit, *Small Boy Nye Me Bra.* He remained at the top until his sudden death when he was given a state funeral attended by tens of thousands of his fans.

Guitar bands and the associated concert parties quickly became the pop music of the ordinary rural or urban people. The most influential and long-lasting proved to be the African Brothers, formed by the guitarist, singer and showman Nana Kwame Ampadu in 1963. Ampadu broadened the music's base, introducing numerous African roots rhythms, some of which came from outside the country. The style quickly spread and soon there were dozens of guitar bands, the most notable being Akwaboah's, Kakaiku's, the City Boys, Okukuseku, F.Kenya, the Ashanti Brothers, K.Gyasi's Noble Kings and Cubana Fiestas.

Unlike his predecessors, whose lyrics were often about the past and absent friends, Ampadu sang about contemporary issues of a social, personal or spiritual nature. The use of proverbs and allegory to help illustrate the morality tales was taken up by other bandleaders and song content became as important as dance entertainment. "When I became a musician, I was most concerned with the role of the musician in society," Ampadu said of the early days. "I found out that music can change the lifestyles of a people. Music is one's culture. So I tried to embody our culture, our way of living, in the lyrics of my music so that my people will become what they are rather than adopting foreign tactics in their cultural deliberations."

Ampadu is renowned as a composer, guitarist and leader of one of the most energetic and versatile bands. Since the African Brothers made their first recording in 1966 they have released over 60 albums and twice as many singles. The band has been an informal academy for musicians such as Eddie Donkor and Osei Kofi who have gone on to their own successes. Ampadu claims to have created at least ten 'new rhythms', including the Afrohili system which came in highlife and reggae versions.

The African Brothers Band: introduced roots rhythms and inspired a generation of musicians

His lyrics are a repository of natural wisdom and home-spun philosophy appealing to his largely rural audiences, who also admire him for his professionalism. "I have great enthusiasm for the profession and I have never toyed with my job," he said in 1991, after nearly 30 years of success. "My music is a direct talent from God which means that I have no difficulty with lyrics and tunes. I have composed with most rhythms of the world, with the exception of Asian and Arabic rhythms. Talk about jazz, *adowa* is jazz; talk about Caribbean, Latin, Congo and Nigerian rhythms, I have done it. At times I get a tune, I don't know where it comes from. I also try to humble myself with the public, the society, because it is them that will give you the encouragement and the support. In Ghana when you try to be proud or mean, the society

Osibisa's Rhythms of Happiness

In 1970 a new style, known as Afro-rock, burst into international prominence with the launch in London of Osibisa, formed by three Ghanaians - sax player Teddy Osei, trumpeter Mac Tontoh and drummer Sol Amarfio.

Osei, who also sings and plays drums, was already in London studying music when he called his brother Tontoh and Amarfio to set up the band.

In London they recruited Nigerians Loughty Amaoh on sax and the drummer Remi Kabaka, and West Indians Spartacus R, Robert Bailey and Wendell Richardson. They created a fusion of 'criss-cross' osibisiba rhythms and Ghanaian melodies with Caribbean, soul and rock techniques which found a keen audience in Britain and throughout the world.

Their debut album became a platinum hit, with sales in excess of one million. After breaking through into the British singles charts in 1976

and gaining full exposure by touring in Europe, the band

consolidated with further albums throughout the Seventies, but their prime audience later proved to be in Africa and the Third World.

The impact of Osibisa's fusion was felt throughout a generation of African musicians, particularly those who were teenagers during the time of the Beatles and Rolling Stones.

Several original musicians quit during the 1970s leaving a core of Ghanaians including newcomers Alfred Bannerman, Herman Asafo-Agyei and Kofi Adu.

Osibisa provided the hard, modern excitement and the power of a Western rock band with an 'Afro' feeling that was recognised far from Ghana. Their tours of West and East Africa inspired many musicians to copy their style, although no other Afro-rock bands have managed to emulate their success.

In 1980 they played at Zimbabwe's independence party and later became the first 'Western' band to tour India, where they had also accrued sales of over one million albums.

will reject you, whether you sing the most beautiful song. They just won't accept you as a good musician."

As leader of the musicians' union in 1991, Ampadu felt a responsibility to develop young talent, and make up the shortage of women in Ghanaian music. "We found out our female counterparts are missing in music circles. One would periodically rise, and then get lost to marriage or something else. I want to correct this, so that is why I am starting with Akosua Ageypong and Abena Nyanteh, daughter of Senior Eddie Donkor. I want to come up with eight of them, and I hope they will stay in the business."

The early guitar bands had a sound constructed around two or three guitars and, following the lead of Dr K. Gyasi, electric organ was added to the line-up of many bands, including Ampadu's. Gyasi's Noble Kings had a long career as innovators and hit-makers, famous for their *sikyi* system in which trumpets and saxophones appeared, making fresh contact with highlife's instrumental roots. Meanwhile another strain developed using only one guitar. C.K. Mann showed that more traditional, cultural dance music could also be popular throughout the highlife zone. His single guitar was accompanied by African percussion including frame drum bass.

C.K. Mann gew up in a fishing community in the western region of Ghana and went to sea as a merchant sailor. He started playing music in the Sixties with Kakaiku's Guitar Band before forming the Carousel 7, playing a contemporary form of guitar highlife. In the 1970s, when Ghanaian musicians began leaving home to avoid sinking with the ailing music industry, C.K. did not succumb but rather retraced his steps and revitalised a traditional dance rhythm, the *osode* beat. In collaboration with the

Ampadu: 'I tried to embody our culture, our way of living, in the lyrics of my music'

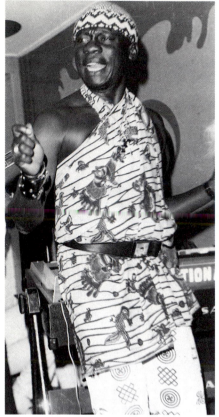

'Senior' Eddie Donkor: graduate of the
African Brothers band

singer Papa Kofi Yankson he made several best-selling albums in
the 1970s for the Essiebons label, one of the few Ghanaian record
companies to survive the industry's virtual collape. In the late
Eighties Mann revived his career with a new version of *Adwoa
Yankee* that became a solid favourite.

Alex Konadu, 'One Man Thousand' is another guitar highlife
stalwart who stayed on in Ghana, cutting records during the hard
times. While others headed for the lure of the big cities in Germany
and Canada, Konadu retained his roots feeling, moving the music
forward with its own inherent energy rather than with technological power. His up-beat guitar highlife numbers bounce along over
an organ sound that serves as a soft mattress, contributing to the
overall dreamy quality of the shuffling highlife.

One of the 'works bands' set up by nationalised companies in
the Sixties was the El Dorados, contracted to a glass factory which
they promoted throughout the country. Among the band was the
singer A.B. Crentsil who went on to help found another little
highlife dynasty. With a nose for a good commercial deal Crentsil
along with J.Y. Thorty, quit to form a group sponsored by a hotel,
before settling at the Talk of the Town nightclub, where they
coined the name Sweet Talks, in 1975.

Alongside Crentsil was guitarist and singer Smart Nkansah,
with two long-time members of Dr K. Gyasi's Noble Kings, drummer Thomas Frempong and guitarist Eric Agyeman. Sweet Talks
had a short but influential career which saw them rise to national
fame. They played for the head of state, released hit records and
travelled to the USA where they recorded. On their return from the
States, however, the band broke up. Nkansah moved on to found
the Black Hustlers, while Crentsil, Frempong and Agyeman set
out on solo careers.

Also in the Sweet Talks line-up had been Eugenia 'Lady'
Asabia Cropper, a singer who went on to become an accomplished
instrumentalist. Asabia had taken up music at the age of eighteen, singing with various groups in Accra, before becoming a
protege of Koo Nimo who encouraged her to develop her own
songwriting rather than sing 'copyrights'. She also took up saxophone. She was a member of Sweet Talks for two years during
which she made her first visit to Abidjan. After the band split up
she stayed alongside Smart Nkansah in the Black Hustlers where
her brother Eugene also played bass. She later returned to Cote
d'Ivoire where she made an album featuring her saxophone
playing and singing, and also recorded with Sam Mangwana and
Jimmy Hyacinthe. Asabia made several celebrated return visits to
Ghana, including a supporting spot at a festival in 1986 at the Independence Stadium where she virtually stole the show.

By the Seventies Ghana's dance band highlife had begun to
suffer commercially from competition with music from America
and from other parts of Africa. Amid a general loss of confidence
among highlife musicans, people started dancing to Congolese
music, and after Osibisa's British debut in 1970, Afro-rock had its
moment of glory. At the same time, straight Western pop and even
middle of the road American country and western were catching
on with the more outward looking Ghanaians. The biggest shock
stemmed from the memorable 'Soul to Soul' festival in 1971,
which brought Wilson Pickett, Ike and Tina Turner, the Staples
Singers, Roberta Flack, Carlos Santana and others to Accra for
one of the country's biggest parties. The eventual effect was that
imported records played in discos became more popular than live
bands, many of which broke up. Stan Plange, leader of the Uhuru
Professional Dance Band, blamed the demise of the dance bands

on the invasion of soul and funk. "The kids who should be digging our music don't want to know. They just want the disco stuff," said Plange.

There had been some earlier attempts to maintain the credibility of roots music, and help it expand outside Africa. In 1973 the businessman, producer and owner of Accra's Napoleon club, Faisal Helwani had financed the formation of a band called Hedzolleh Soundz to play a new kind of roots highlife fusion with traditional and modern instruments. Helwani took them to record in Nigeria where they impressed Fela Kuti and met and played with the South African trumpeter Hugh Masekela, who arranged for them to visit the USA. In the Eighties, Helwani befriended and recorded a blind street musician called Onipanua, who by the time of his death in 1990 had become the country's best loved traditional musician, playing a sardine can thumb piano and singing in Hausa. Another roots movement was initiated by the vocal group Wulomei, who performed a contemporary folk music, singing popular 'street' songs in the Ga language accompanied by acoustic Western instruments and traditional percussion, and setting a trend followed by dozens of Ga folk groups during the late Seventies.

Nii Amponah of Hedzolleh Soundz: the band impressed fellow musicians and producers in the early 1970s

As everywhere in Africa, Congolese music was popular on record, with releases by major artistes such as OK Jazz and Dr Nico coming out of the Ghanaian and Nigerian pressing plants under licence. In Accra live experience of Congolese music had been provided by Ryco Jazz, whose founder, Henri Bowane, settled in Ghana and Togo for nearly 30 years, after leaving Kinshasa in 1960. In the mid-1970s Orchestre Veve passed through, and the pioneers of Kinshasa's new wave, Zaiko Langa Langa, stopped off for several months with a residency at the Caprice club. They also cut an album for the Essiebons label, with sessions set up by Bowane who added local horn players on the final mix.

Throughout the Sixties the Ghanaian music industry had enjoyed a continuing boom, with a variety of labels in business, including HMV, Queenophone, Skanophone and Parlophone, in addition to the big three majors. But during the Seventies first the majors pulled out, then many of the smaller labels went under. The Philips/Polygram pressing plant was sold to Essiebons, who managed to keep pressing discs until the late Seventies' oil crisis affected the supply of vinyl. The two recording studios still active in 1980, Ghana Films in Accra, and Ambassador in Kumasi, were restricted by the difficulties of importing blank master tapes, spare parts and new equipment. It was the beginning of the end for vinyl. Records now had to be manufactured abroad and imported with tax penalties added to transport and foreign exchange costs. The vacuum was filled by the cheaper and more practical cassettes.

Faisal Helwani opened an eight-track studio and began releas-

Ghanaian musicians union on strike in 1979: 'We are musicians not band boys'

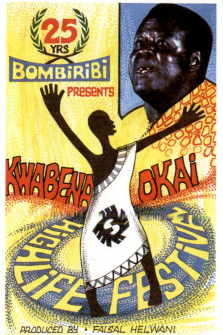

Cover artwork for cassette release by Kwabenah Okai, a product of Faisal Helwani's studio

ing local and foreign music under licence. The musicologist and writer John Collins opened the Bokoor 'mini-studio' outside Accra which hosted hundreds of religious, cultural and highlife musicians recording cassette releases for the domestic market. Collins also released two volumes of a compilation, *The Guitar and the Gun*, in Britain. But it was also the era of the tape bootleggers who at their peak in the mid-1980s accounted for some 90 per cent of music sales with pirated imports. Live music suffered too, not just through lack of equipment but the more general problems of political uncertainty, coups, food shortages and curfews, which all but destroyed nightlife.

With the lifting of the curfew in 1983, restaurants, video cinemas and nightclubs wakened to the promise of a new business revival. But the music industry which should have been bringing on new talent and providing regular sustenance for masters of the trade, was in a double bind. It had become virtually moribund. Cultural (traditional) and church music apart, Ghana's pop culture, which was once so influential on African styles had been overtaken by imported pop. Guitar bands continued to circulate and some managed to prosper, but the biggest internal revival was set to come from reggae music.

During the Eighties many musicians were obliged to quit Ghana in search of live work and recording facilities. Their main destinations were Lagos and Onitsha in eastern Nigeria, where the Canadoes, Opambua and Sammy Kofi's Okukuseku successfully played the Ibo highlife circuit, and the capitals of Cote d'Ivoire, Togo and Benin, which all had modern studio facilities. Others reached farther afield through London and on to New York and Toronto. But the most productive musical base was in the unlikely setting of Hamburg, Germany.

Boogy with the Burghers

The European gateway had been opened up by Pat Thomas, another ex-Sweet Talks singer, who recorded his album titled *1980* in Hamburg. The hi-tech production, synthesizers and mechanical disco beat fired the imagination of some of Thomas' musicians who stayed on in Germany. The biggest success came to his guitarist, George Darko, first with a Ghanaian hit album *Friends,* followed by the record which brought international fame, *Highlife Time.* Darko always had a preference for Western music. He started in Accra with the Avengers, playing Beatle-style pop in the 1960s, followed by a spell in the Soul Believers with a more adventurous repertoire of Jimmy Hendrix, Booker T and Santana covers. In 1972 he joined the military group, Fourth Dimension, at the same time as studying guitar with Koo Nimo, the master of palm-wine picking.

Darko travelled in 1977 to West Berlin, where he formed Sikadwa, later known as Fire Connection. Unable to chose between a repertoire of highlife or funk, he eventually combined the two in the group Bus Stop, which featured Lee Doudou on vocals. Their first album with the song *Akoo Te Brofo* was a smash hit back home in Ghana, and inspired the phrase 'Burgher highlife' to denote its hi-tech German origins. The album sold steadily in Germany, France, Britain and America and, although it was not a massive hit, it established Darko's reputation.

Following the break up of his band in 1984, Darko took up singing for his third album, *Money Palaver.* He returned home to Ghana in the late Eighties and in 1991 was recording an album at the newly-opened, 48-track Overdrive studio in Accra. His fusion

Highlife time: George Darko blended funk with his national music from a base in Berlin

music has often been seen as too progressive by the many nostalgists who hate to see their beloved highlife go through changes. "No music stays the same for ever," Darko told *West Africa* magazine in March, 1991. "Highlife music must also move ahead. We can't have it like the Kakaikus and Uhuru played it all the time. Look at rap music today. Even giants like Quincy Jones are with it. It's time for the so-called purists to shut up and move abreast of me."

Pat Thomas, meanwhile, had moved on to Canada where he released several records and was working out of Toronto with Herman Asafo-Agyei's Native Spirit, including several itinerant musicians such as stalwart highlife and jazz drummer, Kofi Adu, and guitarist Alfred Bannerman. Other highlifers who have made their mark outside Ghana since the Eighties include Charles Amoah, Eric Ageyman, George Lee, Ben Brako, Rex Gyamfi, Sir Roberto, Obo Addy, Kumbi Saleh, Jon K. and Kwadwo Ahoi. Among the more recent bands to break through are the Lumba Brothers, also based in Germany, who have introduced hip-hop and rap elements to bring their highlife into the modern age.

Setting a different course through the murky waters of international music, Kojo Antwi has helped to pioneer the Ghanaian style of reggae, a rhythm claimed by musicians throughout Africa as 'one of theirs'. As the front man with Ghana's first popular roots reggae band, Classique Vibes, he played in Cote d'Ivoire, where the band had a major influence on Alpha Blondy. They later moved to Denmark from where they toured Europe with reggae superstars Peter Tosh, Burning Spear, Steel Pulse and Gregory Isaacs. Back in Ghana, Antwi developed a fresh dance style one step removed from the early roots variations, and started the Nineties with a couple of big hit albums. Other artistes bringing a mature, developed reggae out of Ghana include K.K. Kabowo with his 'skanking' style and the pure reggae of Roots Anabo, who have developed a distinctive sound called 'sunlife' music. Roots Anabo, formed in 1982, was the first African reggae band to be invited to play at Jamaica's Reggae Sunsplash festival two years later.

In Accra, the major superstar of the new decade, who blends classic guitar band highlife with its reggae cousin, is Daniel Amakye Dede. With his Apollo High Kings, Dede had won the national equivalent of an Oscar for Best Band four years running since 1987. Amakye Dede started out as a teenage singer/songwriter with the Kumapim Royals, a successful guitar band led by Akwasi Ampofo Adjei, also known as 'AAA'. In 1980 he formed the Apollo High Kings and travelled to eastern Nigeria where they set up base in Onitsha, making enough money to earn their independence by paying off the loans on their instruments. One of the songs they recorded in pidgin English, *Jealousy* became an enduring favourite. Back in Ghana he scored his first major success in 1986 with *Kuse Kuse*. Subsequent hits showed it was no fluke and his fame has only increased. He made his first visit to Europe in 1990.

Amakye Dede's followers identify strongly with their hero's lyrics on the perennial themes of life, love and the problems they bring. Like Ampadu he gives potted advice full of common sense, hope and positive images. A true superstar, he gets mobbed regularly in Accra and has been dubbed 'Expensive Boy' by his fans. Although a naturally humble man, Dede takes care to preserve his image and, as he puts it, "I give respect to my dress, so my expensive will be more expensive." In Ghana the fashion for torn, faded jeans was named 'Amakye Dede'.

Roots Anabo; 'Sunlife' reggae artistes from Accra visited Jamaica in 1984

Expensive Boy: Amakye Dede, a national hero for the 1990s

Home-made music from Nigeria

Featuring:
APALA
JUJU
SAKARA
WAKA

PHILIPS

Big Sounds of a Big Country

Nigeria, the busiest and most highly populated country in Black Africa, is both a treasury of tradition and a market place for commercial contemporary music. But since the golden era of highlife the country has offered little to the development of African music apart from the iconoclastic Fela Anikulapo Kuti, whose fascination lies in more than just his music, and the juju superstars who briefly stood in the international limelight. The lack of a cohesive Nigerian sound to be known and enjoyed elsewhere in Africa is surprising but the country has come a long way since World War Two when it was considered the poor relation of the Gold Coast (Ghana).

The main ethnic groups, the Yoruba, Ibo and Hausa centred on homeland territories in the West, East and North, preserve markedly different cultures and there are scores of minority groups still predominantly 'tribal' in cultural matters. The ethnic groups retain their own separate languages, supported by all kinds of media, and following highlife there were very few cross-over success until the Eighties pop generation fluttered into prominence behind people like Chris Okoti, Christie Essiens, Onyeka and Majek Fashek.

Outside Nigeria, Yoruba musicians have made the biggest noise in recent years with Fela's Afrobeat hitting a pan-African nerve during the Seventies and the juju superstars making their international breakthrough a decade later. Juju began to develop around the end of World War Two when the accordion player and band leader I.K. Dairo brought in double bass and amplifiers, but its origins go way back to a late nineteenth-century idiom associated with the Aladura churches of returned slaves from Brazil. Irewolede Denge, the 'grandfather' of juju, recorded for Zonophone in 1929, and in 1932 Babatunde King, who was playing a variant of palm-wine guitar styles, called the name 'juju' on disc for the first time. The distinctive talking drum only came in after World War Two, at around the same time as amplifiers. Another Yoruba dance rhythm popular since before the war was *agidigbo* named after the thumb piano which powered the music.

The Ibos also had a variety of social music including the palm-wine guitar style of the 'Ibo minstrels', which evolved in a different direction, via Ibo blues, to guitar highlife. The Hausas who live in the arid, semi-desert North, have more in common culturally with their relatives in Niger, Chad and even Sudan than with southern Nigeria. Their music reflects Hausaland's geographical and historical isolation. Just as the landscape is barren and bereft of variety so there are few traditional instruments, apart from simple lutes, fiddles, drums and some wind instruments. The flavour of their music echoes the sparse environment and their Islamic culture. Traditional court music survives in the ceremonial functions of the ruling *emirs* but while music is enjoyed there is no significant place for it in daily life, which in the northern regions is markedly different from the south.

In Lagos, a radio service was launched in 1939 when transmissions from the Nigerian Broadcasting Service were piped through fixed wiring to 'rediffusion' sets which could not be tuned to other frequencies. Genuine 'wireless' radio arrived in 1951, but the most popular broadcasts were from the powerful 50kw Congo-Brazzaville station which could be heard across the region, and by the late Fifties Congolese music was being enjoyed and danced to throughout southern Nigeria. Equally popular since the end of World War Two had been the American and European music

Bandleader Bobby Benson livened up Nigeria's ballroom dance scene in the 1950s, following the influence of E.T. Mensah

brought home by returning troops, and there was a growing jazz scene nurtured by such musicians as sax player Babyface Paul Osamade and trumpeter Mike Falana.

One of the most influential of the early bands was the West African Rhythm Band, formed by Ambrose Campbell in 1947 with a group of ex-servicemen and students specifically to create a new 'Africanised' dance music in response to the smooth Western big bands. With an instrumental line-up including *shekere* (shaker), *gongong* (talking drum) and mandolin to accompany Campbell's drums and guitar, they brought a 'diversity of indigenous folk music into the spotlight as a measure of our culture, of our beliefs'. The Rhythm Band became one of Nigeria's early highlife champions, but in the early 1950s Campbell travelled to England, where he made a new career, re-interpreting his *abalabi* rhythms and developing multi-cultural fusions with musicians from various parts of the world. At the time there were half a dozen African clubs in London's Soho district where musicians could link up with brothers from the Caribbean, America and Europe. Campbell settled into a residency at the Club Afrique and backed up his live work with regular releases on the Melodisc label.

Highlife Heroes

Back in Nigeria the real action was being generated by a contemporary of Campbell's who capitalised on his own London experience. Bobby Benson was one of African music's larger than life characters, a joker, showman and musician with a colourful early background. Born in 1921 in western Nigeria, Benson followed his secondary schooling with training as a tailor, but he was soon overtaken by the urge for adventure and briefly worked as a boxer, before leaving for new horizons as a sailor in the British Merchant Navy. In 1944 his ship was torpedoed and he was adrift at sea for 32 days before being rescued and taken on to London. There he made his entertainment debut with the Negro Ballet, with which he toured the European capitals. In 1947 he returned to Lagos with the wife he had met in Britain, and established his first band with her, the Bobby Benson and Cassandra Theatrical Party, in which he played guitar and saxophone and she danced. This was followed by the Bobby Benson Jam Session Band.

The Benson band started out playing regular ballroom dance and swing music spiced with jive, sambas and calypsos. Dance

The Emir of Kano, northern Nigeria, with entourage and ceremonial horn players at Sallah Festival procession

bands faced some competition from *kokoma* groups and the early juju outfits but although Benson inserted African numbers into his repertoire they were not so popular with the internationally minded Lagosians. Ballroom dancing was the big craze at the time with studios all over Lagos offering lessons in the latest imported styles. In the early 1950s, following E.T. Mensah's visit to Nigeria, and the subsequent release of Tempos' highlife records which caught on with the radio, Nigerians showed they were now ready for highlife and Benson changed the direction of his band.

His eleven-piece outfit included an important trumpet section which featured, at various times, Victor Olaiya, Zeal Onyia, Roy Chicago, Chief Bill Friday and Eddie Okunta. One of the Benson band's best known hits was the classic song *Taxi Driver,* covered by countless other artistes including the Delta Dandies who called their treatment *Motor Driver.* Benson became the first president of the Nigerian Musicians Union when it was formed in 1960. He continued playing highlife until he died in 1983, one year after the death of his old associate Bill Friday, composer of *Bonsue,* which had been a great hit for the band back in the heyday of highlife.

Victor Olaiya put the final polish on his talents in the Benson band before setting up his own group the Cool Cats. By Nigeria's independence in 1960 his was probably the top band in the country, with musicians like Victor Uwaifo playing guitar, and the young Tony Allen on kit drums. Olaiya was born in 1931, the twentieth child of a 'modest family' in Calabar. He discovered a taste for music with his school's brass band, playing a 'bombadine', French horn and cornet. In 1946 he led the band at the Empire Day celebrations, which he 'remembered with joy'. The following year he left school and started playing in Lagos with the Ekpo Band, a street band with three brass instruments, two drummers and six 'stick players'. "I learnt a lot in this band," Olaiya once said. "But the one thing I detested most was the poor payment system, which included non-stop perambulating of the proprietor's residence."

Olaiya then filled a vacancy in Sammy Akpabot's Sextet as assistant bandleader and lead trumpeter. He also took up saxophone and spent two years learning the trade with Akpabot, before moving on through the Lagos City Orchestra and City Tempo Orchestra. By 1952 Olaiya was leader of Benson's second band, Alfa's Carnival Group, which played daily at carnival shows and nightclubs. In 1954 he launched his own band, the Cool Cats, at the West End cafe in Lagos. He soon progressed to more fanciful engagements, picking as career highlights the 1955 state ball for Queen Elizabeth II, and the 1957 gala for the Miss Nigeria competition. His own crowning achievement came when he was chosen to play with his new band, the All-Stars, at Nigeria's independence celebrations.

Another Victor in the All-Stars, who also became a contemporary bandleader, was Victor Uwaifo, who hailed from Benin city, where he was born in 1941. An all-rounder who shone at sports and practical subjects, Uwaifo was still at secondary school when he started his musical career with the All-Stars. In 1962 he enrolled on a graphic design course but continued his musical work playing nightly with E.C. Arinze's highlife band. Uwaifo maintained the busy schedule until he graduated and took a job with the Nigerian Television Service, which included preparing a weekly programme on Bini (or Benin) people's folk music.

Uwaifo's long-held vision of running his own band came together with the inauguration of the Melody Maestros in 1965. Their recording of *Joromi*, a morality tale about a great wrestler who takes on the monsters in hell, became a hit and continued to sell well for several years, even inspiring a popular design of printed cloth. In 1969 Phonogram presented Uwaifo with a gold disc for selling over 100,000 copies, which he claimed was the first to be given for an African record. Students at Nsukka University awarded him an unofficial knighthood and he started to advertise himself as 'Sir' Victor Uwaifo.

In 1969 Uwaifo represented Nigeria at the Black Arts Festival in Algeria where he won a bronze medal. Later he travelled the world, performing in the USA, Japan, Russia, Eastern and Western Europe. Playing guitar with wa-wa pedal, flute and organ, Uwaifo was a showman, whose stage presentation included a comedy cabaret by two dwarf dancers. Among the musicians who went through his band was Sonny Okosun, whose own days of glory came in the late 1970s.

Uwaifo's art training inspired him to work out a unique, personal theory of music which led him to develop that vital element, his own 'system'. "All my early numbers belonged to my *akwete* sound which I evolved by using colours to represent musical notes. It was at art school that I discovered colours in sound and sound in colours. I carried out some research with colours and was able to transpose them so that 'Do', the strongest note was black. 'Ray' was red. 'Me' was blue, 'Fa' green, 'So' white, as it is a neutral colour and sound. 'La' is yellow and 'Te' Violet. But the whole change came when I transposed the colours of akwete cloth, a hand-woven cloth made in eastern Nigeria. It is a very beautiful cloth and if you see it you will see that different colours recur, creating a moving rhythm of colour. When I interpreted this it gave the sound which I later called 'akwete', and that was the beginning of *Joromi.*"

The Ayinle Omowura Memorial Band, in Abeokuta: they maintain their founder's Apala music, sharing roots and rhythms with fuji

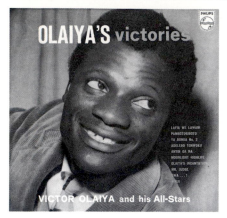

OLAIYA'S victories

PHILIPS

LAFIA WE LAWARI
PAMBOTORIBOTO
YA BONSA No. 2
ADELEBO TONWOKU
ANTOI GA RA
MOONLIGHT HIGHLIFE
OLAITA'S INCANTATION
MR. JUDGE
NWA ...1
ANU

VICTOR OLAIYA and his All-Stars

He maintained the system for three years before introducing the 'shadow', a link between akwete and the twist. "I first derived this dance as I stopped one day and looked at my shadow and likened it to death, man's inevitable destiny. I thought that every movement in a dance casts a peculiar shadow on the ground. As the dance comes to an end the shadow cast by the movement of the dancer fades away, just as the body of a man perishes as he dies". He held on to the shadow for only a year, before evolving a new system called 'Mutaba', followed by 'Ekassa', and 'Sasak-ossa', both with historical roots in Benin culture. By 1980, Uwaifo had invested his profits and skills in a 16-track studio in Benin City from which he continued to release local hits. He also hosted a weekly television show.

The trumpeter Zeal Onyia had joined Bobby Benson in 1947 while still at secondary school. In 1954 he travelled with the band to Ghana, where he quit to link up with the Tempos. After only three months, however, he left for Britain, where he studied music, sat in with British trad jazzers, and for a while joined Ambrose Campbell's band. In 1957 Onyia returned to Nigeria and formed his own band. He was instrumental in setting up the musicians' union and he later became a full-time trade unionist, leaving little time for playing. He often sang about social issues, especially trying to discourage the rush to the cities. The future singing star Stephen Osita Osadebe was also in Onyia's band for some three years, contributing several popular numbers including *Lumumba,* dedicated to the Congo's first elected Prime Minister whom he had met in Ghana. In 1960 Louis Armstrong came to Nigeria. Onyia had already met him in London and, like E.T. Mensah in Ghana, Zeal was part of the welcoming committee at Lagos airport. Later Onyia travelled to the USA where he played with Freddie Hubbard amongst others. Back in Nigeria after the Civil War, he found work as a music programmer and researcher with NBC radio.

Stephen Osadebe, who took up music in 1959, formed his own band, the Sound Makers International, during the early Sixties. With a distinctive 'bluesy' guitar style, Osadebe maintained his own course, without deviation, even when the 'Congolese'-inspired highlife style known as *nkowkrikwo* later became the rage. One of the few musicians not to have awarded himself a spurious title, Osadebe was already a traditional chief. He was still active at the start of the 1990s and remained one of the last surviving highlife bandleaders.

One of the highlife greats whose music survived well past his own lifetime was Rex Lawson, the trumpet player and bandleader whose revived music was filling the bustling streets of Lagos again in 1991. Lawson came from Calabar in the eastern Cross River State, a town which produced several trumpeters including Olaiya, the Efik bandleader Chief Nyang Henshaw, Eddie Okunta, and Eddie Edem who played with Ambrose Campbell in London in the Fifties, and later ran his own bands.

Lawson started his musical career in the late 1940s at the age of twelve as a band boy with the Starlight Melody Orchestra, learning his trumpet technique from Sammy Obot, later the leader of the Uhuru band from Ghana. When the Starlight band played some shows in Lagos, Lawson stayed behind and spent the best part of the Fifties playing with Benson, Olaiya and Roy Chicago. At the time of Nigeria's independence in 1960 Lawson formed his own eleven-piece band which became known as the Mayor's Dance Band. Throughout the Sixties and Seventies, 'Cardinal ' Rex Lawson was one of the most consistent highlife hitmakers.

Star material: Victor Uwaifo, artist and showman

Guitar Pickers and Heartthrobs

As the big band era gradually came to an end it was replaced in eastern Nigeria by a parallel form of guitar highlife developed out of various local 'blues' and palm-wine styles. There were Yoruba variants, although the most flourishing scene was in the eastern Iboland region. Ibo highlife was championed during the post-Civil War years of the Seventies by artistes like Celestine Ukwu, Oliver de Coque, Stephen Osadebe and a string of guitar bands modelled on Congo-Zairean formations with two or three guitars, bass and drums. The rhythms were more agitated than typical highlife with an element of *makossa* creeping in over the border from Cameroon.

Dr 'Sir' Warrior: Ibo highlife champion with the Oriental Brothers International

The main Ibo highlife bands which came to light in the early Seventies were Super Ikengas Stars of Africa, under the direction of Vincent Okoroego, the Peacocks, the Imo Brothers International, African System Orchestra, Sonny Oti's band and the Orientals. Formed by three brothers, Dan Satch Opara, Kabaka and Warrior, the Orientals became the most popular highlife band before suffering several splits as first one brother then another left to form their own outfits, leaving Dan Satch with the original name. First Kabaka formed his International Guitar Band, while some years later Warrior founded the Oriental Brothers International and promoted himself to Dr 'Sir' Warrior. When the mood suited them the brothers would re-group as the Orientals.

One of the last gasps of Nigerian highlife came in 1976 with the huge regional hit *Sweet Mother* by Prince Nico Mbarga and his Rocafil Jazz. Highlife was already considered obsolete by younger audiences and Nico, who played Congolese style guitar and sang in pidgin English, was keen to emphasise the pan-African identity of his music, sometimes known as *panko*. "It is not entirely highlife," he said, "but it is a blend of some Zaire, Cameroon, Nigerian background which means I am trying to bring exactly African culture. For example I can't come to play reggae or pop or disco, which is not our line, not our tradition."

Although he grew up in Cross River State, Nico straddled the border between Nigeria and Cameroon. His father was Cameroonian and during the Nigerian Civil War the family lived in western Cameroon, where Nico took up his musical career with the Melody Orchestra. He had already started playing xylophone and congas at school and now he worked his way through the band's instruments, learning to play kit drums, bass and finally guitar. In 1972 he was back in Nigeria playing at the Plaza Hotel in Onitsha. The following year he released his first hit single and then in 1976 came *Sweet Mother*, the smash success which provided the momentum to see him into the Eighties. In 1983 he became one of the first musicians to introduce African music to a new generation of British listeners, emphasising the connection between his lively pop-style and the traditional roots. "In Nigeria as well as the rest of Africa we have a lot of tradition. In 500,000 years to come our culture will remain the same and it needs to be cultivated. We need to activate our natural resources musically. There is so much." Claiming to have been "cheated, been duped all about" in business matters, Nico decided to set up his own record label but he never repeated the success of *Sweet Mother* and he lapsed into semi-retirement as proprietor of two hotels.

While Nico was at his peak in the mid-Seventies, another singing guitarist was making his charge with a personal Afro-pop-highlife-reggae fusion called *ozzidi*. Sonny Okosun had already been playing for ten years, first with a pop group called the

Yoruba drummers: artwork in wool applique by Kofi Ankobra, one-time student at Oshogbo, the Yoruba cultural capital

Postmen and later in Uwaifo's band. His 1978 hit *Fire in Soweto* brought a flash of international fame and in 1980 Sonny, who delivered militant, socially aware lyrics in English, became the first West African musician to play in independent Zimbabwe.

Throughout the 1970s, Nigeria maintained a healthy record market with several productive studios. In 1980 Phonodisk opened Africa's first 24-track studio at Ijebu Igbo, some 60 miles north east of Lagos. The scheme was hatched by a collaboration of musicians, technicians and businessmen, including Alhadji Ishola, hero of traditional *apala* music. The plant had not only a studio but also metal mastering, pressing and sleeve printing facilities under one roof. The first product out of the Phonodisk factory was a new sound that launched them with a fanfare and sat atop the Lagos music charts for some time. With the album *I Need Someone*, Chris Okoti became a Nigerian heartthrob. His pop highlife style grew out of a career which began with cover versions of James Brown before moving to the softer, more personal format of guitar folk music, in which he tried to emulate Western performers while maintaining a highlife guitar style. The major record label EMI soon followed Phonodisk with a 24-track facility at Ikeja, as did the independent Rogers studio, whose first release on the new equipment was a Prince Nico album.

One-man's fusion

Fela Anikulapo Kuti, the most iconoclastic and provocative of performers, is known throughout the continent of Africa as much for his political and social activities as for his rousing, big band music. Alone among the giants of African music, Fela Kuti has always made use of his time in the spotlight to amplify the radical views he espouses. Unlike other pan-African superstars of his, or any other generation, Fela's compositions are always confrontational, dealing with subjects like injustice, corruption and brutality. His use of pidgin English has made his songs accessible to a wide international audience, and his crusade on behalf of the 'ordinary' African has given him heroic status among Blacks throughout the world. As the innovator of 'Afrobeat' in the late 1960s, Fela has an established popular base. He was a musical pioneer; inventor of a big band sound, which incorporated massed saxophones and trumpets, and choral arrangements based on call-and-response patterns, with a pulsating dance rhythm and stinging anti-establishment lyrics. Fela has seen much of the African dilemma, from colonialism through independence, civil war and bureaucratic corruption to military coups. And these are the subjects about which he has sung since the early 1970s. Among the best known titles of over 50 album releases are *Gentleman* ('I no be gentleman at all-o, I be African man, original'), *Expensive Shit, Confusion, Zombie, Sorrow Tears and Blood, Vagabonds in Power, ITT (International Thief Thief), Black President, Teacher Don't Teach Me Nonsense*.

Many of these songs became anthems for politicised youth and radical intellectuals and Fela has kept a rebelliously high profile in his attacks against successive Nigerian regimes. Frequently his uncompromising stance has brought him trouble. He has been imprisoned several times, deported, and severely beaten by Nigerian soldiers. In 1986 he was released from the notorious Kirikiri prison after serving part of a five-year sentence imposed for allegedly trying to export some US$1600, while on his way to play in America. Once free he caused uproar by claiming the trial judge had apologised to him for imposing a politically motivated sentence. At a press conference following his release, the ever provocative Fela announced he would be running for president when free elections were held. Espousing a doctrine of 'African humanism' he outlined his method for defeating militarism: give everyone a weapon and a rank, then 'everyone is a soldier'. While Fela was in prison the Egypt 80 band had been kept ticking over by his son Femi, who also plays saxophone like a reflection of his father. Understandably Femi was both proud and resentful of the association and strove to create personal expression of Afrobeat, finding an appreciative audience in France, at least.

During the enforced lull in Fela's career, it was refreshing to hear a burst of crisp Afrobeat coming from a different source. For all the sympathy and outrage expressed for Fela in his time of detention, his music had lost its percussive edge during the mid-1980s, and it was not just his injuries that weakened Afrobeat. Part of the problem was that Fela did not have Tony Allen drumming for him anymore. He said as much in London when he

The Ever Feisty Fela

Fela was born in Abeokuta, Nigeria in 1938, to a well-respected Yoruba family. His father, The Reverend I.O. Ransome Kuti was a composer and influential preacher, like his father before him who had been a pioneer of the Yoruba Christian Church. His mother, Funmilayo, was a key figure in the nationalist struggle; a confidante of Kwame Nkrumah, she met Mao Tse Tung in China, and won a Lenin Peace Prize.

Both Fela's parents were fiercely anti-colonial, but Fela became even more so. A rebel from an early age, Fela refused to study law or medicine like his brothers (one of whom, Olikoye, went on to become Minister of Health in the Babangida government) and he made his way to Trinity College of Music in London, where he studied composition and trumpet. After four years in London he returned to Nigeria and formed his first group, Koola Lobitos.

Playing a modern form of highlife-jazz, Fela and the band began to carve their name in both Nigeria and Ghana. Then in 1966, inspired by the soul-flavoured music of Sierra Leonean Geraldo Pino, he started to evolve his own Afrobeat style. With the help of the master kit drummer Tony Allen, Fela was able to synthesise a new dance music which could match James Brown's for rhythmic intensity

and organisation, while remaining totally African.

With his band Africa 70, Fela reflected the mood of the times; his was an African version of Black Power, and throughout the Seventies he projected a volatile mix of heavy Afrobeat music and stark pidgin rhetoric

with confrontational politics and the blatant use of marijuana.

Often his personal life has been as outrageous as his polemical songs. His sexual boasting was well publicised and his polygamous nature inspired the celebrated marriage to 27 women in 1978, although he later modified his hard-line sexism to agree that women had a right to control their own bodies.

His notoriety guaranteed him full houses in Europe and America, with healthy record sales to match. Alone among African musicians he had an international record contract which ensured a world market for his music and everywhere he tours he has been courted by the media.

In Nigeria, however, Fela has 'made his own bed'and it has proved extremely uncomfortable. His particular target has been military governments and they have never been slow to respond.

Undoubtedly the worst incident was the storming of the 'Kalakuta republic', his fortified compound in Lagos, which was 'invaded' in 1977 by several hundred soldiers, who beat Fela, his wives and musicians and threw his 77-year-old mother from an upstairs window, causing injuries from which she died a few weeks later. Fela himself suffered injuries which later affected his capability on trumpet and saxophone.

From the heydays of the early 1970s when he released seventeen albums in three years, Fela's output slowed down, with new releases coming every few years rather than months.

By now he was insisting that Afrobeat was over, that it was insulting to consider his music as mainly for dancing. It was 'African classical' music and people were not expected to dance until they had listened to the lyrics.

Fela (standing on car roof) surrounded by supporters returns from court after a confrontation with the army in 1974, his head and arm in bandage

invited Allen to rejoin the band. Tony said he declined because after some ten years he felt he knew the route too well and it would divert him from his own recording work in London, Nigeria and Paris. Very much a perfectionist, Allen's output is hardly prolific, and although he had recorded material in Nigeria for at least four albums he was never satisfied enough to release them. "Bad production is the reason I stopped recording for five years. I am not able to find a sound," he explained in 1987, adding with typical philosophical insight, "When one road close another one go open. The proverb tells you, if someone goes forward and blocks your path you must reverse and find another way. Maybe the road you find there will be the best road."

Brought up in Lagos, Allen began like so many others playing in his school band. Before linking up with Fela's Koola Lobitos in the late 1960s, he worked his apprenticeship with Victor Olaiya's Cool Cats, Paradise Melody and the Western Toppers. He joined Fela in Ghana in 1968. At the time Fela used to compose on keyboard and transpose lines to tenor guitar. He would write down all the parts which the musicians had to copy, including the drum patterns. But, following a visit to the States in 1970 which inspired a new political and musical radicalism, Fela changed the system.

"At that time we got onto the same wavelength and Fela would ask what type of rhythm I wanted to play. It was complicated at first, too much, but I advised him to keep it simple. It is hard work playing African music. It sounds simple but it is not, especially drumming. No-one else plays Afrobeat. You only hear it in Europe when Fela comes. Basically it is easier for drummers to play highlife. But you can tell a good drummer because we all have four limbs and they are supposed to be playing different things. If I make an electric Afrobeat I might use synthesiser, electronic drums and effects, but I'll be there playing the drums, not a machine. All juju musicians that I know try to take from what Fela has done. Most of the patterns did not come from Yoruba music alone but from other parts of Nigeria and Africa."

From Juju to Fuji

The fluid interplay between talking drums, wailing Hawaiian style electric guitars and call-and-response vocals which characterises juju music heralds one of the most successful of the continent's uni-cultural or 'tribal' musics. Juju is a contemporary social music which also incorporates several cultural functions, including praise singing and worship, or acknowledgement, of both Christian and Yoruba gods.

The idea of gods and juju conjure images of strangeness which would have inspired fear in White breasts a few generations ago. "The name juju music is a name given to the particular music by the colonial people," said Sunny Ade, the so-called King of juju. "In the old days any Black (African) medicine was called 'juju', and any music playing around there, they called it juju music But now it is a different music entirely and we still want the name to remain. Because it is a name which is simple to call, like rock, jazz, reggae, soul, juju, that is the name of the music. The meaning of juju is not connected to Black medicine or magic or anything like that." Traditional Yoruba culture is rich and the predominantly Christian juju does not have a monopoly; in addition to traditional forms, the sparser fuji music sells as many, if not more, records to the many Muslim Yorubas.

A particular Yoruba characteristic is the ability to incorporate new or alien elements into their own culture, and juju has been the musical form to be most spectacularly modernised throughout its history. The roots of juju lie in the traditional drum, percussion and vocal forms, *apala, sakara* and *waka,* but its influences include the ubiquitous Latin music heard throughout West Africa on the GV label. It has a close relation in the Yoruba idiom known as *tchinkoumey* from the neighbouring country of Benin, in which a calabash water drum creates a similar 'bending' effect to a talking drum. The Yoruba cults which survive in Cuba and Brazil, and the elements they contributed through the Lagos community of Brazilian 'returnees', apparently had an effect on the city's popular music in the first half of the century, as did the indigenous Aladura churches. Early exponents who directly influenced today's juju superstars were Tunde King, Ojege Daniel and Tunde Nightingale in the 1940s, and Ayende Bakare and I.K. Dairo in the 1950s. Dairo created the basis of contemporary juju by introducing the accordion (a sound later revived with the synthesizer) and bass, he was also one of the first generation to use amplifiers and electric guitars.

Juju innovator: Ebenezer Obey expanded the guitar section and added a drum kit

One of the links between highlife and the modern juju was 'Toye motion' which flourished briefly in the late 1950s. 'Toye' was a local name for marijuana. Inspired by 'proper' bands like those of Tunde King, Ambrose Campbell and the Jolly Orchestra, toye was developed by Julius Oredola Araba and Joseph Olanrewaju Oyesiku and his Rainbow Quintet. These two educated men were older than most musicians, had careers outside music, and considered themselves a cut above the 'illiterates' playing early juju. Toye used palm-wine styles, blended with international elements similar to highlife but with a juju feel, sometimes using kazoo. A more recent exponent of the idiom is Orland Owoh who continued the marijuana imagery by titling himself 'Dr Ganja'.

By the 1960s Ebenezer Obey had brought in more guitars and Western drumkits, and the transition of the music from a neo-traditional form to an urban social music was complete. "I noticed", said Obey, who made his first record in 1963, "that people like to stick to their own ways, especially old people, they don't want to bend, they don't want to compromise. But the younger ones always want freedom from the old system. They want new things. And knowing that, I modernised the music, and created my own fashion in music, the 'Miliki' system. And I happened to be the one who started the modernisation of juju music. The fathers of juju music only played one guitar. I introduced three guitars and arranged it in such a way that would catch the attention of the youth and cross to the older folk, so as to have both sets of listeners, and it worked." The three guitars are tenor, rhythm and lead: a line-up similar to, and some would say influenced by, the instrumentation of Congolese music, which was gaining popularity in West Africa at the time, although Obey's own style was coloured with blues inflexions. "Tenor for example backs, rhythm supports the tenor, plays the same part, while the lead takes the solo. Combined with my own guitar that is four, and then you have the Hawaiian. The keyboards came later. The drumkit too came along later."

In 1966 Obey's main rival, Sunny Ade, came on the scene, following his induction as a *samba* drummer with the showman and comedian Baba Sala. With his own ten-piece band, The Green Spots, Ade made his first record in 1967, playing the solo guitar parts himself. "We were very lucky. The second year we recorded a single in praise of a football club called Stationery Stores and it was a big hit. All the fans bought it. So I was given a gold disc for the first time and since then we have been doing it happily."

Makossa Movers

The music of Cameroon hit the world stage with a blast of individual power in 1972, with the release of Manu Dibango's *Soul Makossa,* the record which is probably the biggest selling African disc to this day. Manu is a consummate all-round musician, who made his success because he had all the right things going, at the right time and in the right places; although with such a powerful fusion of urban dance and African melody Manu's original hit would probably have struck just as hard if it had been released any time in the twenty years since. His music has the stamp of an innovator, yet it is not coolly detached; the sensuous sound of Manu's saxophone has a warm familiarity. It is the solo voice of a well travelled and tutored musician, which has not evolved in a direct line from some folkloric root, but which has returned frequently to embrace and refresh the popular culture of Africa. The ability to penetrate the closed circles of Western music cliques, from soul to jazz and hip-hop, is what makes Manu's music a pan-African asset.

With the widest range of experience among African musicians, Manu eventually came to resent the typecast image of 'makossa man', but his international career was established at the highest level, and this gave him a unique ambassadorial role as a kind of African diplomat. He became the first Cameroonian to be an international household name and for putting its name on the map his country will be eternally grateful. Manu's transatlantic hit brought a surge of self-respect to Cameroonian musicians. The fact that all of America knew the name and the rhythm of the music was crucial. His own soul version was still years ahead of the home-grown music but Manu had almost single-handedly laid the foundation for what is now a self-contained and successful African pop style. This tall, power-packed figure with his distinctive shaved head, dark glasses and booming laugh has become one of Africa's most recognisable images.

Makossa is slick, urban dance music, based on punchy call-and-response riffs, and it sounds more precise, although more minimal, than musics like Zairean rumba or juju and lacks some of their mystery. It is recognisable by up-beat, funky bass lines, often mixed above the solo guitar parts, and short unaccompanied verses answered by perky female chorus and snappy horns. The presentation has an air-conditioned feel; crisp, fresh and state-of-the-art. It has the requisite high-living associations that helped it prosper in up-market Africa, and in flash Western nightclubs where the ambience precludes anything that is in the least bit 'bush'.

Makossa, invariably sung in the Douala language, is only one of several popular fusions which have evolved in Cameroon since the Fifties. Other forms which have also made the transition from bush to dance floor include the Bassa peoples' *assiko* (similar to a Ghanaian rhythm of the same name) the *mangambe* of the Bamileke, and the *bikoutsi* of the Beti people from Yaounde, which was relaunched on the West in 1990 with the scorching excitement of Les Tetes Brulees. In the early Eighties just as the 'new-look makossa' boom began, Manu introduced his country's rhythms: "The makossa is something from the south, from the Douala people, near the border. Then the mangambe from the west of Cameroon, the bikoutsi from the south central and the assiko, whose people are really the first Cameroonians. We are trying to combine all these and maybe one style will come out of it. The

Cameroon's horn players have tradition behind them: musicians from the Sultan of Bamum's Theatre

CHAPTER SIX

Soulful sax: the master of makossa,
Manu Dibango entertains a young
audience in his home town of Douala

people won't understand the lyrics of all the different musics. But what makes the makossa popular is that every Cameroonian can find himself in the makossa."

The original makossa was not even a rhythm, but a style of expression which grew out of the *kossa,* a children's dance accompanied by handclapping. Since World War Two the contemporary influences which eventually inspired a national popular music came from the neighbouring idioms of Nigerian highlife and Congolese rumba. A trend had also developed for solo artistes performing more lyrical, non-dance folk songs with guitar accompaniment, such as Eko Roosevelt, Francis Bebey, Ebanda Manfred and Eboa Lotin.

While they don't play highlife music anymore, the Cameroonians do know how to live up to the same aspirations. The country has frequently been among the top African importers of champagne, what some people call the Cameroonians' favourite beer, and the young middle classes thrive in the modern high-life atmosphere of glitzy nightclubs where makossa is mixed with zouk and American soul.

Makossa has generated several dance floor hits which spread throughout the francophone world during the late 1980s, but there have been very few opportunities for listeners outside Cameroon to catch a live show. The assumption was that while the records sold well, the star performers were all solo artistes who did not maintain regular touring bands. Many listeners wrongly assumed that makossa was strictly a studio sound. In Paris that may be so; it is rare to see a unified group, rather than a collection of sessioneers supporting a solo singer. But in Cameroon, as throughout Africa, there have been bands for as long as instruments have been around. However, about the only full-size band to have become known outside the country through record

Stars of African jazz in Kisangani, Congo: Manu Dibango (left) with Tabu Ley, Dr Nico, the governor and his chauffeur, Kabasele and Izeidi Roger

Bringing music to the people: artwork for Les Veterans' album, Au Village by Phillipe de Youmsi

releases are Les Veterans, with a repertoire of bikoutsi and Congo-Zairean style rumba.

Recording opportunities fell to singers or solo musicians, but innovators cannot push the music forward in a vacuum, and most developed their sounds in a collective atmosphere. An important pioneer of makossa, Nelle Eyoum, plied his trade with Los Camaroes, alongside Ebanda Manfred. A generation later Misse Ngoh was a member of Los Calvinos when he began to expand the makossa guitar part. Other regular working bands such as Negro Fiesta have survived through long residencies in hotels but there have been few opportunities for groups to develop through touring and recording.

Pop makossa had found its place by the Eighties. And Paris was its epicentre. Moni Bile's definitive 1982 release *Bijou*, recorded in Abidjan, set the tone for the 'new-look makossa'. Bile had taken the master tapes to Paris and begun the collaboration with bassist and arranger Aladji Toure, which opened the way for Cameroonian pop through the Paris studio scene, consolidated a few years later by another team of Sam Fan Thomas and Tamwo, who struck a once-in-a-lifetime monster success with *African Typic Collection*.

Around the same time Antillean zouk music hit Paris and the francophone world, and strong connections were immediately established with makossa. Since the middle of the decade several Antillean musicians had been playing with Dibango, such as keyboardists Jean Claude Naimro and Claude Vamur, bass player Michel Alibo and percussionist J-P Coco, who for a couple of years were alternating between makossa and zouk sessions. The hard-edge 'Martiloupe' music brought a charge of new energy to makossa which offered up another generation of stars at the end of the decade such as Lapiro de Mbanga, Guy Lobe, Ndedi Dibango and Charlotte Mbango.

Culture into Commerce

Cameroon is unique among the West African ex-colonies, in that it is officially a bilingual country, with French and English given equal prominence, although until the First World War it had been a German colony. In effect, Cameroonians look to Paris for cultural and commercial connections, and even the pidgin English hits of Lapiro de Mbanga have been marketed from France. During the 1950s, when African popular music started to become a marketable commodity, Cameroon was exposed on two fronts to the most powerful of these new musics. From the east, especially through the English-speaking territory of Northern Cameroon, came Nigerian highlife. From the south via powerful radio transmitters came Congolese rumba. The full spectrum of discs would have been available in Douala, including the Cuban releases on the famous GV label, but the port town was not one of the coastal hotbeds of musical creativity. In the 'quartiers' there was a frenetic local guitar music called *ambasse bey*, and accordion players enlivened social gatherings or parties. Along with American swing, featured in the big hotels catering to Whites, French variety music met folklore head-on through the accordion.

In common with most African countries individual singer/guitarists, playing outside the highlife milieu, were often the ones who strung together the early threads of a new music. Among the forefathers of Cameroonian pop music were Lobe Rameau (aka Lobe Lobe), Ebanda Manfred, composer of the smash hit *Ami*, Nelle Eyoum and Ekambi Brillant. Before independence there were no opportunities for musicians to record in Cameroon, but some Nigerian labels did take on Cameroonian artistes. Herbert Udemba was one who had songs released on the Nigerphone label. Although singing in the Douala language, his music had enough affinity with eastern Nigerian guitar music to be identified on the label as 'Ibo minstrel style'.

One of the earliest makossa artistes to record was the guitarist and harmonica player Eboa Lotin. Born 1942, Lotin was the son of a martyred cleric who became a Cameroonian national hero. He grew up in a Christian atmosphere where his outlook was influenced by devotional music. His first recordings were released by Philips when he was just twenty years old. Playing guitar and harmonica and singing his own compositions, Lotin developed into a popular star releasing regular hits and becoming a master of makossa. A few years later the guitarist and lyrical composer Misse Ngoh, playing in Los Calvinos, 'modernised' the makossa, using a more adventurous finger-picking style which escaped from the monotonous three-chord system.

But the style which was even more popular at the time was the assiko, played on guitar accompanied by a bottle hit with a stick and other percussion. One of the first exponents of modern assiko to cut a record was Jean Bikoko who arrived in Douala from his home in the Bassa region in 1960, the year of the country's independence. In the newly opened studios of the Douala radio station he recorded *A ye pon djon ni me* which turned into a national hit. With the collaboration of Radio Douala sound engineer Samuel Mpoual, his early records were released on the Samson label, before he switched to a deal with Africambiance. Following several more hits he returned to Bassa to recruit a troupe of 40 assiko dancers, with whom he brought a spectacular show to villagers throughout the country. Also recording for Editions Samson was a musician from the previous generation who had been playing guitar since the 1940s but who was not

Eboa Lotin: known as the Lion, guitarist, composer and early makossa artiste

Moni Bile: pioneer of new-look makossa and Cameroon's favourite singer throughout the 1980s, giving a rare performance in London

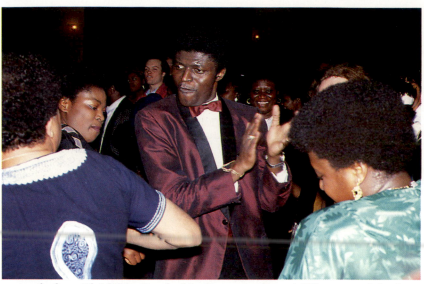

recorded until 1963. Oncle Medjo was almost 50 years old when he found fame as a recording artiste. His records became steady sellers and, like his younger rival, he too put together a 40-piece touring group, comprising members of his family, in which the dance element was as essential as the music.

The third strong style, the bikoutsi, has been most popular around the capital city of Yaounde. Anne-Marie Nzie, the 'Queen Mother of Cameroonian music' has kept the form alive and shaking since 1940. Nzie was performing from the age of eight in her village choir, under the guidance of her brother Cromwell, himself an early music star. She recorded many hits on the Pathe Marconi label, through until the 1980s, when her voice still sounded clear and deceptively young. Hers was a kind of transitional bikoutsi, one step removed from the pure folklore. The populariser of the new bikoutsi, when it came, was Mama Ohandja. Coming from a family of traditional musicians, Ohandja made his break into show business at the age of nineteen, when he found work as a bouncer at a Yaounde nightclub. The owner of the club, Cheramy, was also a bandleader and Mama was able to impress him with his vocal ability enough to join as an apprentice singer in 1961, and a few years later he went with the band on a tour of the country. He quit in 1967 to set up Mandoline Jazz, playing bikoutsi and Ekomot folk styles in a modern way. His first hit came in 1971 for the French Sonodisc label. In 1975 he followed with a new-style bikoutsi number called *Man Enon Wam* and by 1980 he was a national celebrity with his new band Confiance Jazz, with whom he toured Gabon, Equatorial Guinea and Nigeria. His 1981 English-language release *Consequence of Prison* was another big seller, but during the Eighties Ohandja began to slip from view.

Cameroon's other major rhythm, the mangambe, was largely popularised in its modern form by Pierre Didy Tchakounte during the 1960s while he was a teenager. Tchakounte was well grounded in traditional music before taking up the bass guitar. Always interested in experimenting, he created a contemporary version of the Bamileke folk music and started composing songs at the age of fifteen. His recording career took off in the mid-1970s, with his debut release, *Monde Moderne* (Modern World). He made his mark in 1979 with his first national hit, *Mangambe Mythology*, followed up with *Sophisticated Mangambe.*

A contemporary form of 'classical' or formal music has also

been developed by multi-instrumentalist and arranger Eko Roosevelt. Born in 1946 in Ocean Division, Roosevelt learned to play organ at his local church. At college in Douala he took up piano and began playing with student colleagues. He also developed into a skilful guitarist and arranger. Roosevelt interprets African music on a grand scale, arranging for large ensembles which combine orchestral and dance band instruments, particularly for the Cameroonian National Orchestra of which he was conductor. The National Orchestra was founded in 1978 to revive folk music traditions and present them in a contemporary form that would appeal to audiences of all generations and ethnic groups. Comprising 34 musicians, the orchestra toured the regions, playing formal concerts and dances. As well as a public relations arm of the sole political party, the orchestra also provided general entertainment at a time when there were very few opportunities to hear live music.

'Queen Mother': Ann-Marie Nzie pumping out *bikoutsi* for over 50 years

A musician doing the rounds since the early post-independence days was Tokoto Ashanty, a singer, dancer and showman, whose performance incorporated dramatised versions of various folklore rhythms with traditional dances and his bizarre 'zygomatic' vocal style that introduced all kinds of animal sounds into the lyrics, delivered like a sorcerer's incantation while he strutted across the stage like a duck or slithered like a reptile. Claiming that animals provide the models for much traditional dance, he described his stage show as a pan-African celebration of traditional 'animist' symbolism.

The Main Men

Contemporary Cameroonian culture was really brought to life in Paris in the late Fifties by two students who became the country's foremost artists, Manu Dibango and Francis Bebey. Bebey, some four years older than Manu, is Africa's renaissance man, an acclaimed novelist and writer who went on to a multiple career as a film director and head of Unesco's music programme. He is also a composer and guitarist, and leader of the first band Dibango played with after arriving in Europe. Following his best selling novel *Agatha Moudio's Son* in the late 1960s, and an authoritative book on traditional music called *African Music, a People's Art,* Bebey paralleled his literary achievements with his music. In Paris he enjoyed musical adventures with Dibango and other African students. Bebey defined the role of the contemporary African musician when he once said: "The artistic challenge, one I accept, is to use the tools of Western progress and communicate messages of African heritage".

The Sixties was a creative decade for most musicians, and Dibango was well placed to capitalise on the growing musical awareness. In Paris and Brussels he made new friends who opened his ears to the range of jazz, soul and variety music, but his attention was directed back to Africa by the great Zairean bandleader Kabasele. With the realisation of African independence, the Sixties signalled times of change and Dibango joined the independence carnival and launched his pan-African career. He spent two years in Kinshasa with African Jazz and opened his own nightclub, before returning to Yaounde, the capital of Cameroon. He tried to open another club but the administration of the newly independent country was not keen to sanction night life, and the 'ambience' was not conducive to a music career. Undeterred, Manu concentrated on developing his own distinctive sound, recording in Europe and setting up bands in various West African

The Dibango Diaries

Manu Dibango was born in Douala in December, 1933. His family were 'important people'; his father a high-ranking civil servant. As devout Protestants, his parents only approved of church music, but the young Manu surreptitiously broadened his musical perspective from an early age, first with a bamboo flute and later a home-made guitar.

Encouragement and early inspiration came from his first music master, Doumbe Eyango, the son of a priest and director of the church choir, who also played harmonium and violin. At the age of eleven Manu was a member of the school choir when they sang for the visit of the French President General de Gaulle in 1944.

When he was fifteen Manu's parents sent him to France to study for a profession, and where they also paid for him to take music lessons. "I wanted to play violin but I was too old to start, so I did four years of classical piano." Within a few years he had met up with some other musically inclined Cameroonian students including Francis Bebey, and Manu joined his first informal group as a pianist.

Although Bebey was equally inspired by the music of Spanish classical guitarist, Segovia, and by jazz, the repertoire they played for student dances was based on 12-bar blues. Manu's place was at the piano.

"Then on holiday in 1953 a friend lent me his saxophone and he told me, as I had nothing to do, to go and practise this instrument. So I took the saxophone, without knowing that maybe something was going to happen with this thing. After starting to practise by myself, then I had a professor for two years.

"Then I started to play in clubs, every Saturday. That was

in the east of France, and I was the only black playing music so I was very successful at it. Because if you play music, they see you look like Louis Armstrong or someone, but certainly not that you are African.

"So I left my studies in 1957, moving to Brussels where I really started to play music at clubs, more cabaret type of thing - any type of music. I got married there, and was playing with

everybody. First as a saxophone player and later on like bandleader."

In Brussels Manu found a taste of the good life, which his parents had never believed would come to a musician. He had all the trappings of success, including a flash American car and Italian suits.

The Anges Noirs, where Manu was playing, attracted a high-rolling clientele. Congolese delegations had begun arriving in Brussels to arrange their country's transition to self-government, and many passed their evenings at the club. He met the

future Congolese politicians, Lumumba and Tshombe but, more crucially for Manu he made his first contact with the founding father of Congolese music, Kabasele, the Grand Kalle, who accompanied the political delegation.

Firstly on piano and organ, Manu joined Kalle's African Jazz for a marathon recording session in which 40 songs were recorded in two weeks. Threequarters of the songs, he remembers, were composed in the studio. In the meantime he released the first record for the Frech market under his own name, titled African Soul, which staked out the territory he was to make his own.

When Kalle called him to join African Jazz on their home ground he did not hesitate. "I left Brussels in 1960, when Congo (Zaire) became independent and I joined the top band at the time, African Jazz. Playing with Kabasele gave me exposure all over Africa, because he was one of the best-known musicians, and I was not known because I had started to play in Europe. So we did like one hundred singles with African Jazz, through Decca records, the only company with distribution throughout Africa.

"When I went to Zaire I was supposed to stay there two months but because the records we did were so successful we stayed two years, playing almost everywhere. I opened a club named Tam Tam and had my own band. And seeing the African atmosphere, the African landscape, made something in my head and I started to compose. But I had not at that time, a specific style. Sometimes I used to play jazz, sometimes the twist, sometimes Latin music. Before that I was a jazz musician: the singles were African records but when it came to my solo I was playing jazz. I think I started to develop my own style at the end of the 1960s."

countries. For the Congolese market he recorded *Twist a Leo* which scored a big hit in Kinshasa (Leopoldville). His first French success came with *Sweet Pop Corn* in 1968. But although he was spending little time in his home country, he had not neglected his roots; he had already made his first makossa record.

"In Cameroon the makossa started little by little, with two or three influences, with the Nigerian highlife, because we are very close, and also with Central African music, which you can call Congolese music. So the melting, the melange of that made makossa come and develop its own way." His first straight makossa recording was *Nasengina,* released in 1964 for the home market, but his way was about to take a long fruitful diversion into American soul which had already caught his ear, and which became Manu's main motivation in the mid-1960s, when he was based in Paris. Records by Booker T and the MGs and Jimmy Smith influenced his organ playing, while on the saxophone King Curtis became a real inspiration. When Curtis died in 1972 Manu released a superb, soulful homage, *Tribute to King Curtis,* on which he sounds just like the Texas tenorman.

In the other direction there were regular trips to Africa, playing for heads of state and being invited to set up national bands in Cote d'Ivoire, Niger and Benin, where he established the first music 'workshops' ever seen in Africa. He also worked in Nigeria and Togo. Manu usually travelled without a band of his own, picking the best of local musicians, until 1972 when he met up with the Zairean guitarist Jerry 'Bokilo' Malekani, whose band, Ryco Jazz had just broken up. Ryco had been a travelling band, popularising Congolese rumba along the West African coast as far as Sierra Leone and Senegal and across the ocean to Martinique. Jerry has a unique guitar sound which can easily be picked out from the countless brilliant players from his country. His dry, economic plucking can elicit a forest full of natural sounds from the electric guitar. Since their meeting Jerry and Manu have been continual musical associates.

At the time Manu had just persuaded the Cameroonian government to sponsor a record in praise of the national football team who were hosting the African Nations Cup tournament. On one side of the record was the football anthem, *Mouvement Ewondo,* on the other the first version of *Soul Makossa.* "I was very impressed when I went back to Cameroon in 1972 and I listened to the musicians and saw the people dancing. I mean, this connection between the dance and the music gave me the idea to compose, not exactly makossa but *Soul Makossa;* my vision of the makossa which is a traditional dance. So I tried to compose my own makossa with my own culture, because every musician has his own culture, which depends on the environment where you live and the people you know and the contact you have with the people. I had my own chance in 1972 with *Soul Makossa* but before that I played any type of music, from Latin to jazz and even 'real' African music, folklore music. I think if you are going to develop your own thing you must know first what is going on around you." The less enlightened Cameroonian officials who had commissioned the record liked the praise song but hated the revitalised makossa. Anyway, the team lost in the final and fans smashed their copies of the single in disgust. It was not an auspicious launch for the new number, but Manu continued developing the tune, and back in Paris he cut the version which quickly became such an international hit.

Manu moved to New York, where the record had generated its own action. The single and album releases stayed in the *Billboard*

Manu on stage as usual with long-time associate Jerry 'Bokilo' Malekani

Session maestro: Aladji Toure (right) bass player and arranger, at home in the studio environment from where he master-minded countless hits

charts for nine weeks, but sales were lost to cover versions, of which at least seven had been released in the States. A season at the Apollo Theatre in Harlem was seen as a milestone for African music. It also provided hard, professional experience for Manu performing twice daily and three times at weekends on a bill with the Temptations, Johnny Pacheco and Barry White. While in New York he sat in with the Fania All Stars, a salsa supergroup, including Johnny Pacheco and Ray Baretto, at the Yankee Stadium where they played in front of 40,000 people. The sequel to Manu's big hit was the album *Makossa Man,* his first venture into a 24-track studio, a technological facility which many African musicians still dream of using twenty years later.

By the end of 1973 Manu was back in Africa, fresh from the American adventure which had truly sealed his fame. He played in Cameroon and Nigeria before visiting Zaire the next year for the music festival which was part of the circus surrounding the heavyweight title fight between Muhammad Ali and George Foreman. He then made a tour of the Latin American countries and in 1975, was invited to set up and direct the Ivorian national television orchestra, ORTI, in Abidjan. In Cote d'Ivoire, Manu noticed, they did not have their own identifiable music. But the ORTI orchestra went on to later success on a tour of African countries from Congo to Morocco. The band was even called to play at the coronation of 'Emperor' Bokassa in the Central African Republic. In 1976 Manu recorded with the police band of Yaounde. Two years later he cut *Home Made* in Lagos, which became the first gold disc awarded to a foreigner in Nigeria. Back in Paris he launched *Afro-Music* magazine in January 1977. This monthly review and roundup of popular and jazz music coming out of the continent was published only in France but, while interest in African music was growing, the magazine was somewhat premature and after publishing for nearly two years Manu was forced to close it.

In 1978, Manu spread his musical wings a little further when he arrived in the West Indies to record a double album for Island. In the afternoon he would record, in the mornings he was hanging out with Bob Marley at his private studio. The record, *Gone Clear,* was remixed in New York. But he started the Eighties back in Douala where he tried once again to establish a nightclub. He flew in the best and latest instruments with which to develop new talent, and arranged to introduce musicians to the newly-installed television service, but financial circumstances were against him and the scheme failed. Back in Europe, Manu continued his prolific recording schedule, releasing some albums for Africa and others for the European and American market. In 1982 he toured France with the American trumpeter Don Cherry playing every night for several weeks and re-establishing his working connection with jazz.

Breaking out of the Circle

During the Seventies, *Soul Makossa* became an anthem for cosmopolitan, urbanised Africans in the West, and at home it opened up new possibilities for a generation of artistes. Francis Bebey released several hit songs in the mid-1970s starting with *Idiba,* on which Dibango collaborated. In 1975 Bebey won a gold medal at the International Guitar Festival in Martinique, and continued to lecture on and demonstrate Cameroonian traditional instruments. Another guitarist to play a big part in popularising Cameroon's dance music was Toto Guillaume, who made his debut in his home town of Douala with the Black Styls in 1973. He was eighteen. The following year he was inspired by a girlfriend to write his first big hit *Francoise.* Guillaume became a master of the makossa guitar and following his 1975 hit *Mba No Nae,* settled into a career as arranger and session guitarist in Paris. Working frequently with the bass player and producer Aladji Toure, he brought the electric edge to many of the Parisian makossa hits of the Eighties. He was by then also the first choice as guitarist/ arranger for Miriam Makeba's touring band, and while he released occasional hit albums, he appeared to have stepped out of the solo spotlight.

Two impressive women singers came to light in the 1970s. First was a young sensation with a tender, sensitive voice, Marthe Zambo, who first sang publicly at sixteen, and made her nightclub debut in N'jamena, just across Cameroon's northern border. Back home in Douala she worked at the 'Night Spot' and later the 'Jungle' clubs before embarking on a recording career. Under the musical direction of Ekambi Brillant she released several hits making her one of the country's favourite singer/composers through the 1980s.

Bebe Manga was the first Cameroonian woman to attract the attention of international audiences with her 1980 hit *Ami,* written by Ebanda Manfred, one of the fathers of Cameroonian pop. Manga, who has a powerful, high-ranging voice, was born in 1948 to a family of civil servants. A self-taught pianist and singer, she made her debut in a Douala nightclub in 1973. She then moved on to Gabon and Abidjan where, accompanied by Nelle Eyoum, she recorded *Ami,* the song which became a massive hit throughout the West African region. On the back of that success, she toured the Caribbean and Japan and won the French Maracas d'Or award for francophone record sales. She moved to New York where her recording career lapsed, although she sometimes sang with a Haitian band, Tabou Combo.

Manu Dibango meanwhile, had returned from his global success with an idea to "see what is going on in our own culture". Those artistes who had followed his lead in breaking out of closed musical circles had opened up a treasury of home-grown music, and the 'main man' was in a position to help them consolidate and promote a national Cameroonian music to stand against the imported idioms which had dominated since the Fifties. "In the past the influence of Congolese music was so strong because they

Rhythm section: Valery Lobey, Wassi Bryce and Jean-Pierre Coco provided percussive support to a roster of solo stars

117

Renaissance man: Francis Bebey, guitarist, novelist, poet, filmmaker and musicologist

were the ones to have the radio with the biggest transmitter. It was possible to listen to Congolese music all over West Africa, almost twenty hours a day. In our country in the early 1960s, by ten o'clock in the evening there was no more radio. The shows finished. Now if you like the music and it's very hot inside, you go outside and you have the radio and you try to look for where there is some atmosphere, so the Congolese music was there. And for everybody, every night it was a kind of intoxication. In Zaire they have one strong music. There is only one rhythm for the whole country. In Cameroon we can say there are four different types of strong music. Of all these rhythms the makossa is the best known. But the other ones have started and even if I don't understand the lyrics, I like the voicing of the guy who sings and I like the rhythm."

In 1982 the Cameroonian government invited Manu to make a compilation album showing the full spectrum of the country's music from folklore to modern. "They wanted to have a kind of landscape of what is going on," said Manu, bringing a characteristic visual approach to his description of music. The three-album boxed set, titled *Fleurs Musicales du Cameroun* was a classic collection. Starting with a list of some twenty artists, Manu invited each to play one number, and some two, to build up a contemporary picture of the country's music. The project took six months to complete.

The boxed set included two discs of popular styles such as mangambe, bikoutsi and makossa, with the opening disc featuring two sides of folklore music played by Ngumu Pie-Claud and his Medzan Beti group, and Arbogas Mbella playing gospel songs. Others include the National Orchestra's renditions of Aurgo from northern Cameroon, sung by Ali Baba, a dancer, fire-eater and eccentric showman, along with examples of folk music from other regions. Working in collaboration with Manu and the then Minister of Information, Guillaume Bwele, was a total of more than 60 musicians and some 40 technicians, researchers and administrators. The final over-dubbing and eventual mixing were done in Paris. *Fleurs Musicales du Cameroun* was a great example of how a country's music can be 'showcased'. Unfortunately the distribution and promotion of the album were not as effective as the original production and the handsomely-packaged compilation proved hard to find on the record racks, although it did help to resurrect some transitional music styles and gave a creative impetus to several younger Cameroonian musicians.

"It's not ethnic music", chuckled Manu in 1984 as he watched the progress of his single *Abele Dance* in the dance music charts, threatening to be his biggest seller since *Soul Makossa*. Ethnic it certainly was not. The hard-edge electrobeat put it firmly in the hip-hop category, yet its master's lungpower provided the characteristic groove in this hi-tech collaboration with French producer Martin Meissonnier. With a new, heavy-dude image to go with it, Manu made his statement about the boom in world music: 'He ain't ethnic, he's my brother'. It might not have been strictly roots, but the African heritage of *Abele Dance* was never far behind the electro effects, and the riff has become part of Manu's stock in trade.

Manu has always had the most eclectic tastes, and listeners have never been sure just what angle he'd be coming from next. Throughout his varied career he has recorded many different kinds of music, from non-copyright movie background selections and solo piano pieces to the 'Congolese' album, *Negropolitan*, with its instrumentals of Grand Kalle classics. Alternating with the electro-makossa, he recorded mellow albums of 'African melodies' and smoochy jazz ballads. In 1987 he released *Afrijazzy,* which combined various sketches from his notebook into a kind of patchwork symphony. The theme appeared to be an other-worldly voyage in which village memories met futuristic visions. The melodies were often familiar but the arrangements were altogether new. Dibango called all his favourite musicians from the Makossa Gang and some guest stars including Hugh Masekela and a rock violinist. It was by turns eerie, amusing, danceable and provocative. Four years later he continued the journey with *Polysonik,* on which the Douala melodies were threaded through the dance-jazz mix of producer Simon Booth, with a rap contrbution from MC Mello. In the studio during the final mix, Manu was giving Booth visual images and whole scenes which he had illustrated in the music.

The Parisian Posse

During the Eighties Paris became the recording capital of Africa, with a roster of artistes lining up to release albums. Cameroonian singers like Jacky Doumbe, Dina Bel, Nsalle Jojo, Charley Nelle, Hoigen Ekwalla, Pierre De Moussey, Misse Ngoh and Hilaire Penda all had several cracks at success and for some years their music was the most progressive coming out of Africa. There was a core of session musicians behind most recordings, among them Toto Guillaume and bassist Aladji Toure, who became a kind of 'packager', arranging numbers, selecting musicians and organising sessions.

Some of the biggest hits were scored by Moni Bile. One of the few Cameroonians to take a band on tour, Bile's show is polished and professional. The pace and delivery are sharp, with arrangements that emphasise collective effort rather than individual virtuosity. Bile delivers his Douala lyrics in a mellow growl, and he sings almost without pause, the voice blending with the music rather than standing out in front. During the Eighties his records outsold those of the other new-look makossa artistes. Since taking up music professionally in 1981 at the age of 24, Moni Bile has been at the forefront of hi-tech makossa. His first album, *Bijou,* recorded in Abidjan, was the most influential, leading to the first popular boom and opening the way for Sam Fan Thomas, Elvis Kemayo, Lapiro de Mbanga, Guy Lobe and others.

"Dansez, dansez" to *African Typic Collection,* sang Sam Fan Thomas in his catchy 1984 hit song. And dance they did in many countries, making the Cameroonian's *makassi* sound a disco favourite in Abidjan, Freetown, Douala, Paris, London and points west. It was a fusion of African rhythms blended for the widest international audience. Makossa, *cavacha,* assiko, *suguma,* makassi and *tchamassi* were all referred to in the choral response to his minimal lyrics. Based on Thomas' own arrangements, the producer Isadore Tamwo used bright chorus vocals and spicey horn riffs from the Paris session crew to emphasise the catchy hook and the infectious driving rhythm of his version of makossa which he called 'makassi'.

Thomas' hit album was based on a simple formula. His creamy voice delivered internationally accessible lyrics in a blend of pidgin, French and Douala, with few solo verses, except on the occasional ballad. His guitar input was also modest but he showed how to handle clean-cut dance music with restraint and let the rhythm do the talking. Born in Bafoussam in 1952, Thomas has been a professional musician since 1968 when he joined the

Collector's item: Thomas scored one of Africa's biggest dance floor hits. *African Typic Collection* was catchy and of the moment, and a hard one to follow

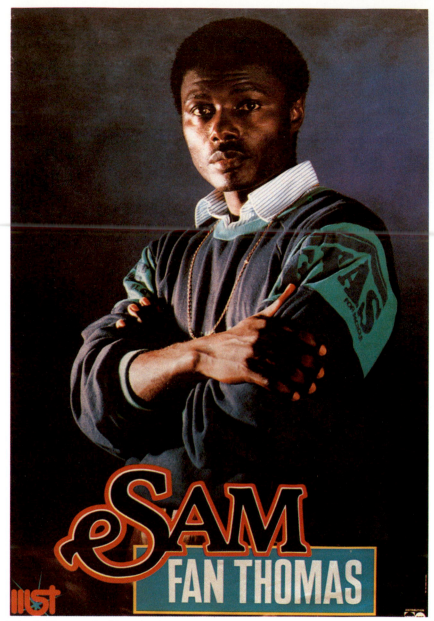

Black Tigers, led by the blind singer Andre Marie Tala, as guitarist and singer. Tala, who became a respected composer and poet-philosopher, had taken up music after he lost his sight at the age of fourteen. His first group, the Rock Boys, evolved into the Black Tigers who released several successful singles in the late Sixties, following which he was encouraged by Manu Dibango to record in Paris. Tala popularised the tchamassi dance rhythm, blending folklore with his own experience of modern music, and also composed for the cinema, including the award-winning music for the film *Pousse Pousse,* on which Thomas also collaborated.

In 1976 Thomas left the Tigers to strike out on a solo career, recording his debut album *Funky New Bel,* at the Satel studio in Cotonou, Benin. His first hit came in 1981 with a song based on a traditional folk theme with support from a chorus of children. Then came 'Typic Collection'. Years later, feet still answer the call to dance the makassi, or as Thomas exhorts in another song from that album, 'Do the foonky, the boogie-woogie. Everybody listen music'. The record had phenomenal sales for well over a year, and was imitated at least twice. The Sierra Leonean studio group of Akie Deen, called Wagadougou, recorded *Freetown Typic Connection*, while another came out of the Caribbean where it was given a soca beat. Thomas followed up with quality albums but it was unlikely that he could re-create such a brilliant success.

Thomas was not the only one to use pidgin English. Lapiro de Mbanga enjoyed the language for its crude wit. He was also seeking a way past the 'boulevard of cliches' which Parisian makossa was travelling. The guitar-playing Lapiro, who had been recording and touring in West and Central Africa since the Seventies, made a big splash in 1986 with the album *No Make Erreur*, featuring a small contribution from reggae man Jimmy Cliff, since when his provocative, polemical lyrics have ensured continued popularity with less affluent Cameroonians.

A pair of musicians whose names became familar from the Paris album credits included horn players Jimmy and Fredo, who eventually released a couple of albums of their own. Like Paris/Douala versions of the Memphis Horns soul section who buttressed so much American music, Jimmy and Fredo were everywhere. Saxophonist Jimmy Mvondo Mvele and trumpeter Frederick Ndounbe-Ngando had teamed up back in Douala during the early Seventies with Ekambi Brillant, and they found themselves together again in the French capital when the recording boom arrived. Their sound, arranged by Fredo, was the stamp of dozens of makossa dance favourites. They have also arranged horns for many other Africans including Youssou N'Dour, Pamelo Mounka from Congo, Pierre Akendengue from Gabon, M'Pongo Love and Les Quatres Etoiles from Zaire, and Mory Kante. In 1985 Fredo went to live in America. His compatriot Vincent Nguini, who had been playing in Dibango's Makossa Gang, joined him later in Washington D.C., where they recorded an innovative 'retro-fusion' album under the name Maloko, juxtaposing American soul classics with soukous guitar backing from the Zairean Syran Mbenza. The album was a mixed bag, but the version of Wilson Pickett's *In the Midnight Hour*, sung straight but ending in a Zairean *sebene*, is a classic curiosity dance number.

Vincent Nguini had arrived in Paris in 1982. Following his debut as a guitarist in a Yaounde nightclub in the early Seventies, he had travelled to Ghana to study music under Professor Teddy Owusu, moving on to Cote d'Ivoire where he formed his own band in 1974. From 1979-81 he attended the Geneva School of Music. In Paris he played guitar and bass for several artistes including Dikoto and Nyanka Bel before joining the Makossa Gang. In 1987 he quit to take his chance in the USA. And his luck paid off in a big way two years later when he was recruited by Paul Simon to contribute the essential Cameroonian ingredient on his *Rhythm of the Saints* album; publicity for which strangely concentrated on the Brazilian input, when much of the music was straightforward makossa, assiko and bikoutsi.

Several other musicians had consolidated their careers as regular members of Dibango's group, in addition to the many whose solo projects were given a boost by a guest appearance or collaboration with the master of makossa. Since making his permanent home in Paris, Dibango's band has been like a school or proving ground for an array of talent. One of the stalwart drummers on many of the Paris sessions during the high point of makossa-mania, and a long-time member of Dibango's band, is Valerie Lobey, considered by many to be one of the finest African kit drummers; his power balanced with finesse and a sense of swing. When rhythm machines became essential to the modern

Chorus queens: Sissy Dipoko and Florence Tity have enlivened many makossa releases

The Makossa Gang, 1984. With Manu, Vincent Nguini, Justin Bowen, Wassi Bryce, Florence Tity, Jerry Malekani and Valery Lobey

studio sound, putting drummers out of business, Lobey had a slim period but was soon back as a programmer of the fashionable machines. One of his colleagues had a similar pedigree and role with Dibango but a harder, more rocky style. Through his many studio contacts Wassi Bryce was chosen to play on Salif Keita's hit album, *Soro,* and soon found a regular job with the Malian singer.

The pianist Justin Tchounou Bowen, who joined the Makossa Gang in 1986, is considered one of the new hopes for Cameroonian music. Following a formal music education in France, Bowen started playing in a piano bar before finding his way into the Paris studios where he recorded on numerous sessions and released two of his own albums. Since 1988 he has been 'chef d'orchestre' of Dibango's band. An arranger and instrumentalist, Bowen has now taken up production, with his first project the solo debut of Sissy Dipoko. Sissy had been a regular chorus singer with Dibango for several years and, along with her colleague Florence Tity Gnimagnon, has appeared on almost as many makossa records as Aladji Toure. The bright vocals of these two ladies became as characteristic of the Paris makossa sound as the snappy horn lines from Jimmy and Fredo. In the late Eighties both women backed away from session work but Florence returned full-time to Dibango's band and Sissy also made occasional appearances. Florence Tity is a trained classical pianist who has started composing in a more contemplative, personal style that, while not exactly makossa, will never be far from it.

At the start of the Nineties, Manu was also joined on tour by one of Cameroon's rising stars, Charlotte Mbango, who sang chorus and showcased some of her own songs. At the time Mbango had released two solo albums which were among the best selling Cameroonian releases, and exposure with Manu helped increase her European following. Mbango, who was born in Douala in 1960, is a granddaughter of Eboa Lotin. She was introduced to music as a young singer with a Baptist church choir and at sixteen she became principal vocalist in her school orchestra, interpreting American country songs by Dolly Parton and Linda Ronstadt. She arrived in Paris in the late Seventies to finish her education and was quickly initiated into the studio scene, where she accompanied many of the top Cameroonian singers. She also worked with female artistes from other parts of Africa including Tshala Mwana, M'Pongo Love and Nyanka Bel. In 1987 Mbango made her first solo recording, produced by Aladji Toure, in which she interpreted a medley of past hits which she called *Makossa Non-stop Nostalgie.* Her music is not exclusively makossa, however, with elements of zouk, Zairean soukous and *kwasa kwasa* varying the excitement, and Mbango has even revived an old Nigerian dance rhythm from the Ibo highlife days of Ikenga Stars. Her second album earned her a gold disc for sales throughout the francophone world and made her a celebrity in Paris and at home.

Burnt Heads, Bikoutsi Beat

They look like a gang of science-fiction urban warriors with their shaved heads, painted bodies, cutaway clothes, designer sunglasses and skateboard body armour. They call themselves 'Les Tetes Brulées' (The Burnt Heads) and their hybrid music is as wild and futuristic as their image. They also play football on stage. Their mix of street-credibility and bush culture revitalised the Cameroonian music scene in 1990. When Cameroon's footballing 'Lions' beat Argentina during the World Cup , Les Tetes Brulées animated the action at the team's all-night party in Milan.

They call their music bikoutsi-rock after the traditional dance rhythm which they have adapted for synthesizer and electric guitars; but what the five-piece band deliver is not so much rock as hyperactive jazz-funk, with a frenetic African dance element.

Bad boys of bikoutsi: Les Tetes Brulées combined street cred and synthesizers with bush music

Bikoutsi is a faster, higher energy rhythm than makossa. The rapid tempo and staccato solos generate a feverish excitement which builds and builds.

The band first took the stage in 1986 in the Chacal Bar in Yaounde, where live local music had been scarce. The founder Jean-Marie Ahanda had just returned from France, where he had worked with several top African musicians and the giants of French-Antillean zouk music, Kassav. On a journey through the forests of southern Cameroon, Ahanda came across the delirious bikoutsi music of the Beti people and he set about fusing it with rock, jazz and zouk into a dynamic pop style. The core of the music, with its fast, multi-layered percussion, remains intact but the delivery, in which the warm acoustic tones of the forest xylophone are hammered out on electronic instruments, took some people by surprise. It was not the first attempt at synthe-sized bikoutsi, however. A few years previously 'Chou Chou Bienvenue' had duplicated the xylophone sound on electronic keyboards creating a kind of zouk-bikoutsi album.

The Tetes Brulées' shock tactics were accentuated by their image. Body paint and 'street' fashions were their stage costume and Ahanda persuaded his collaborators to shave their scalps into Mohican styles or even weirder shapes to create the definitive 'burnt head' look. Cameroonian officials were not smiling when the boys tried to leave the country; haircuts like that would reflect badly on the nation, they announced. Soon Les Tetes Brulées had become known as the bad boys of Bikoutsi.

A meeting with the French filmmaker Claire Denis (director of *Chocolat*) who was working in Yaounde, led to the first European tour for Tetes Brulées in 1988. Manu Dibango presented them at a night given in his own honour at the Francofolies a la Rochelle and Denis made a feature film of the tour, titled *Man No Run*, which gave a big boost to the group's career. The band had recorded their first album in Cameroon and were quickly signed up to make another in Paris, but the sudden death in 1989 of lead guitarist Zanzibar slowed their progress. Back home in Yaounde, Jean-Marie Ahanda had also formed another bikoutsi group, Les Mollets d'Acier, a six-piece outfit including two women, who were playing in the bars of Yaounde in 1990. But Les Tetes Brulées regrouped and toured Europe with a strong five man line-up who could whip up a sweat on the dance floor. And when the football spirit prevailed they brought a ball on stage to demonstrate their close control skills.

Gabon A-go-go

Cameroon's southerly neighbour, Gabon is an oil-rich state with a music business infrastructure out of proportion to its small population, and the envy of more musically productive countries. The capital, Libreville, boasts two 48-track recording studios, Madimba and Nkoussou, and the continent's only short-wave 'clear channel' commercial radio station, Africa No1. It also had a musician/politician in Alexander Sambat, Minister of Education in President Bongo's regime. Apart from some notable exceptions, however, Gabon has provided few artistes of international repute. Since Pierre Akendengue retreated from the scene, Hilarion Nguema has been the only high-profile Gabonese performer.

Akendengue, the blind poet who built his career from political exile in Paris, is an iconoclast whose work defies categorisation. He brought a range of images to bear in his music which made up a synthesis in keeping with the pan-Africanism he espoused. A

AKENDENGUE

PIROGUIER

Hilarion Nguema: satirist and surrealist with a serious streak and a high profile. His music links makossa territory with the rumba region to the south

versatile composer and arranger with eclectic taste and a rich fulsome voice, Akendengue made several fine, crafted albums during the Seventies and Eighties of which *Piroguier* was a career high spot. With arrangements that were never too complex or diverting, Akendengue's albums and his shows covered a wide spectrum of mood and atmosphere. In the words of *Piroguier;* the drum and the song are the canoe which he is paddling to freedom.

Matching him for satire and surrealistic lyrics, but using a more dance-oriented musical formula, is Hilarion Nguema, whose arrangments make a logical connection between makossa and soukous. A guitarist and composer with a social conscience who has been recording since the Seventies, Nguema's songs have included an educational number on Aids, recorded with Jean-Claude Naimro of Kassav, and the 1989 francophone hit, *Crise Economique,* cut in Paris with a makossa session team. The Cameroonian connection has embraced Lapiro de Mbanga, who recorded his biggest hit in Libreville, Elvis Kemayo the one-time artistic director of Gabonese television, and Georges Seba amongst others. Several top Zairean artistes have also recorded there including M'Pongo Love and Zaiko Langa Langa, whose album *Eh N'Goss* was the culmination of their ill-fated relationship with the politician and producer Ngossanga. Subsequently the N'Goss Brothers, led by guitarist Yabiya Rubin, have carried the sponsor's name with a Zaiko-style soukous.

For some time President Bongo's ex-wife was one of the most popular female singers, along with Aziz Inanga, who delivers her electrified traditional music with charm and sensuality. Other Gabonese recording artistes include Pierre Claver Zeng and the big bands Les Diablotins, who released two albums a year through the Eighties, and the police band Massako. The mass female 'animation' groups, Missema and Kakoula Djele de Bongoville, have also made several interesting fusions of party propaganda and Zairean style dance music.

The Rumba Region

Kinshasa, the capital city of Zaire, is the undisputed music centre of Africa. In the entertainment quarter of Matonge the air is filled with exultant rumba from the moment the first record booth opens at 8am until the last nightclubs and bars close their doors around daybreak. Almost all the music heard in the foreground or background, on the neighbour's radio or taxi driver's cassette is local, home-grown produce. And what is first heard here will later be packing dance floors in Europe, America and even Japan as well as the rest of Africa.

No other music in the history of African pop has had such a widespread and lasting impact as the guitar-based music of Zaire and Congo. Known in the West as *soukous*, this quintessential dance pop is still referred to at home as 'rumba'. Since the 1950s, when both the Belgian and French colonies shared the same name, 'Congolese rumba' has moved the dancing heart of Africa with the transcendent quality of guitar playing, the poetic harmonies of the Lingala language and the most sensual rhythms. It creates a unique, dynamic tension which links the often outrageous sentimentality of the songs with the guaranteed euphoria of the improvised dance section known as the *sebene*. One of the most flamboyant countries in Africa, Zaire has provided many of the continent's greatest musical legends and most of its favourite dance crazes.

Congo-Zairean rumba, which is both 'sweet' and dance-inducing, satisfies listeners from widely different cultures. But the way it has monopolised the pop business in so many countries has inspired piracy, plagiarism and outright jealousy. Some cynical observers have stated that all Congo-Zairean music is the same; that the guitarists only play three notes. If so, it only shows there is something remarkable about such a simple formula that has entranced an entire continent, and many outsiders, for more than 30 years.

Whether the local hits are highlife, ndagga, benga, jive, jazz or pop, Congo-Zairean rumba is enjoyed by listeners of all nationalities, ethnic groups and social classes, from Senegal to Madagascar. Variations like the *boucher*, *kiri kiri*, *cavacha*, *kwasa kwasa* and *mayebo* are heard on radio, in bars, and in discotheques, not to mention pirate records and cassettes, and the accompanying dances are eagerly copied. The music's strength lies in the fact that, like the earlier West African highlife, it is a fusion of African and foreign ingredients aimed specifically at a non-tribal, inter-ethnic audience. As 'soukous' it has also made the greatest penetration in Western countries since the mid-1980s, with records outselling almost all other African countries combined. In London, for example, at the beginning of the current decade the major African music retailer's Top 15 chart included fourteen albums by Zairean artistes.

The great rumba dance bands like African Jazz, OK Jazz, African Fiesta, Conga Sucess, and Bantous, which opened up the ears of the continent in the Fifties and Sixties, were followed in the Seventies by a new wave of younger, more raucous groups who effectively streamlined the music for the pop era. The guitar style developed by musicians of the Zaiko Langa Langa family of groups is a sound imitated and sometimes adapted by countless guitar bands in West, Central and East Africa. It also provides the basis for the super-slick Parisian soukous sound of the 1990s, in which more of the original qualities have been whittled away in the

OK Jazz on form: Franco, the Colossus of African music (right) with singer Madilu System in 1987. Franco's biting guitar solos and big-band rumba dominated Africa for more than 30 years

search for crossover success on the dance floors of the West.

Within Zaire, alternatives to the rumba have been muted. In the early Seventies Trio Madjesi developed a Congo soul sound, inspired by James Brown's visit in 1969. During the 1980s Bobongo Stars created a kind of Afrobeat with funked-up traditional rhythms, which they called 'Zairo', for Zairean roots music. Artistes from the eastern region of Shaba such as Kalamu Soul have tried to popularise non-rumba music but, while they might be invited on to national television, the Kinshasa music business is less welcoming. In recent years only Tshala Mwana and, lately, Swede Swede have seriously challenged rumba's dominance.

Land of a Thousand Dances

The contemporary, high-speed, high-fashion soukous which can fill sophisticated Western night clubs might seem a long way from the gentle acoustic rumbas of the 1950s, or even the brassy, big band dance music of the mammoth orchestras, but Congo-Zairean music has evolved in recognisable stages through three generations. The pioneers of popular dance music in Zaire (then Belgian Congo, a much larger territory than the French Congo) were migrant workers who had been moved to the cities or to workers' camps during the 1930s and 1940s, to extract and export the country's vast mineral wealth. Workers were separated from their kinfolk and put to work and live alongside people from different parts of the country and 'imported' foreign labourers. Out of this new, detribalised working class a new social music inevitably appeared. The language used in the east was Swahili. But in Kinshasa, Lingala had become the common tongue among Congo river traders, the military and administration, and this non-tribal, tonal language gave the music an identity which could

Maintaining tradition: folklore music thrives in Kinshasa, and regularly refreshes contemporary pop

be shared by all sections of the population.

Zaire is vast, occupying the heart of Africa and containing peoples who speak more than 250 languages, and without a shared understanding such a homogeneous popular music could never have evolved. In the growing urban centres, traditional rhythms, dances and songs from throughout the region were incorporated into the new fusion. The villagers' traditional instruments, however, were replaced by more practical, and less culturally specific instruments. The huge upright *ngoma* drums, or the wide fan-shaped *lokole* slit-log drums of the Equatorial regions, and the zithers, lutes, lyres and marimbas were abandoned in favour of the more practical *likembe,* or thumb piano, used by most ethnic groups in Central Africa, which musicians could make themselves and play as they walked.

The instrument which was central to the Congo-Zairean sound, however, was the guitar. There is quite a variety of traditional stringed instruments in Central Africa including trough zithers, which use flat, scooped-out, hardwood soundboards, and four-string lutes with strings attached to a neck which protrudes from a sound box. The strings, which are of fixed pitch, are plucked with finger and thumb of each hand. Western guitars had also been heard all along the West African coast since the arrival of Portuguese travellers in the sixteenth century. But during the first half of the twentieth century the instruments were not as common in the western regions of Zaire as in the copper mining area of Shaba (Katanga), close to the then Rhodesian border, where they had been brought as trade goods from South Africa. Many young musicians constructed home-made box guitars, sometimes imitating the curved contours of the real thing, otherwise making do with a simple square box for the body. Locally-made acoustic and electric guitars can still be obtained in Zaire and can prove to be more than adequate in the creative hands of a 'natural' player. Also popular in Congo since the nineteenth century was the *lindanda* or accordion, introduced through the west coast by Portuguese traders who often presented them to local chiefs as trade inducements.

The likembe, accordion or guitar soloists would accompany singing and dancing for parties and informal dances, supported by simple percussion instruments, of which the *patenge* frame drum and a bottle struck with a knife or nail became the most popular. By the late 1930s, such combinations of indigenous and

Antoine Wendo, the first Congolese popular musician to record in 1949, inspired a generation of guitarists but never adapted to the electric age

foreign instruments were being used to animate a dance called the *maringa,* which spread quickly from the work camps to the urban centres, and back into the villages. Involving a slight shift of bodyweight from one hip to the other, this eminently cool expression of an often excitable music was the precursor of the 'rumba' dance which is still central to all Congo-Zairean music. Also popular, but less significant at the time, were dances which reappeared in the electric roots revival of the 1980s, including the 'soukous' and the *zebola.*

Thanks to the wind-up phonograph and 78rpm records which were introduced in the 1920s, the Congolese had become familiar with many Afro-American and Afro-Caribbean rhythms, from the Dominican *merengue* to the South American *tango,* and the *beguine* from Martinique, as well as the more frenetic *salsa* and ubiquitous *polka.* The rumba variant which proved to be the most suitable form for improvisation and adaptation was the *son.* This guitar and drum-based dance music, with its strong African identity, became popular in the early twentieth century in Cuba and recordings soon appeared in Congo. The man who took credit for popularising the rumba in 1940 was the accordionist Feruzi who had arrived in the capital from Lubumbashi (then Elizabethville) in 1927. After working first as an itinerant minstrel with a saxophonist from Guadeloupe, Feruzi later established a band with marimba and guitar to accompany his accordion. Rumba quickly became the generic name for any popular dance music; even West African highlife was sometimes known as 'rumba'.

Another prominent pioneer was Antoine Wendo. Born in 1926 in the Equatorial region, Wendo (whose name was a corruption of the Duke of 'Windsor') arrived in Kinshasa with his guitar on a Congo river steamer in 1941. There he was introduced to the early

Guitar workshop: with Western instruments at a premium Fimbal in Kinshasa do a good trade in cheap custom-made solids and acoustic guitars

Father of Congo-Zairean music: Joseph Kabasele, aka the Grand Kalle, founder of African Jazz and composer of the celebration anthem, *Independence Cha Cha Cha*

pioneers of rumba music, which he recalled was originally played by Sierra Leonean workers. By the start of World War Two, there was a thriving community of 'guest workers' in Lower Congo who had arrived from the west coast. Named after their home regions, there were 'Ghanamen' 'Doualamen' 'Hausas' and 'Coastmen', as well as a community of Senegalese. In fact, the first musical group to be organised and given a name, Excelsior, was formed in 1940 by 'Coastmen', who played an early form of highlife. These people not only brought their own musical influences to the Congo, they also provided a cosmopolitan audience for local musicians which helped to stimulate the synthesis of a non-ethnic popular music.

Several of the foreign ingredients used in the formula for Congolese music were already in place. Christianity was well established in the Congo and the experience of singing Western harmonies in mission church choirs provided the background for many of the later singing stars. Brass bands had been set up in the military and police, to play for public social events as well as ceremonial occasions and fanfares became a feature of funerals and processions. There was also a small, but musically influential, Afro-Caribbean presence in Kinshasa, and several rumba and salsa orchestras visited the city in the Forties to play dance music at the segregated international hotels. In 1942 the first three Congolese orchestras were founded almost simultaneously, with names intended to capitalise on the new taste for international sophistication; 'Americain', 'Martinique' and 'Odeon'.

After Radio Congo Belge was set up during World War Two, these early orchestras, and many solo performers found a commercial outlet for their work, but it was not until the recording studios began operating after the war that the music really established itself. Olympia had opened in 1939, followed by Ngoma in 1948, Opika and Loningisa in 1950 and Esengo in 1957.

Each was run by Greek traders who saw music as a way to promote their retail and distribution businesses as well as a commodity in its own right. Among the first generation of recording artistes were Feruzi, Wendo, and a string of guitarists with a penchant for 'new' sounds, including Jhimmy, who played 'Hawaiian' guitar, Adou Elenga, who was the first to electrify his instrument and, notably, Henri Bowane, who injected a 'Latin' flavour into his finger-picking guitar style.

Many guitar stylists who inspired the early Congolese rumba came from the east, but they were obliged to make fundamental changes to their music, dictated initially by fashion in the capital. Back in the east, the South African musicologist, Hugh Tracey, made the first field recording of Congolese guitar music in 1951, when he 'discovered' the Katangan Jean Bosco Mwenda and recorded his classic composition *Masanga*. But communications in the country were so poor that Bosco Mwenda's popularity in Katanga (and elsewhere following the release of Tracey's recording), was not matched in Kinshasa, the country's centre of influence.

The early 1950s was a period of relative prosperity in Africa, where the Congo had the highest standard of living. Traders were supplied with all sorts of manufactured goods, including gramophones and records. The British company EMI found a natural market in Congo for Cuban records on the GV label. The Congolese reclaimed the rumba and set about making it their own. Many Cuban numbers were covered by local musicians and others were crudely adapted, but Congolese rumba was much more than a copy of the Cuban form. While acknowledging their debt to Cuba, many Congo-Zairean musicians resent the implication that their music is not original. The legendary guitarist and bandleader, Franco, stated many times that his people were being taken to Cuba as slaves long before the music was returned to Africa.

"Many people think they hear a Latin sound in our music," Franco once said. "Maybe they are thinking of the horns. Yet the horns are only playing vocal parts in our singing style. The melody follows the tonality of Lingala, the guitar parts are African and so is the rumba rhythm. Where is the Latin?" By the mid-1950s there would be no confusion; Congolese rumba was about to make its mark, as a host of musicians tried their luck in the studios. The music business infrastucture was now in place.

The Golden Age

The long, productive 'Golden Age' of Congo-Zairean music got under way in 1953 with the formation of one of the continent's most influential bands, African Jazz. Led by the singer/composer Joseph Kabasele, aka the Grand Kalle, African Jazz were to popularise Congolese music across the continent and even overseas, reaching areas where highlife never penetrated. Kabasele, who was born in 1930, has been acknowledged as the music's founding father. He was educated to secondary level before making his musical debut with Georges Doula, a close neighbour in Kinshasa. Kabasele was a comparative intellectual who brought a certain respectability to the occupation of musician, which until then had been largely amateur. He was also an innovator, who introduced new techniques and instrumentation, and composer of some all-time Congolese 'classics'. His band contained several young musicians who went on to become legendary names throughout Africa, including the guitarist Dr Nico Kasanda, the singer Tabu Ley Rochereau and the Cameroonian saxophonist

Future leader: the young Luambo Makiadi grew quickly from 'crazy kid' to 'Franco, My Love'

and keyboard player, Manu Dibango. From its inception African Jazz was hugely popular, especially with the new African bourgeoisie, who were looking outward for international inspiration. Kalle sang in Spanish, French and occasionally English as well as Lingala, and he adapted many of the popular hits on the GV label.

The early recordings show a thin, slightly strained voice which was expressive and emotional, rather than smooth. The band had a light, swinging style built around the solo guitar of Dr Nico and the rhythm instrument of his brother Dechaud. Nico had a unique, languid style of playing which added a completely new dimension to the rumbas, boleros and merengues. Using the tremolo arm on his electric guitar to bend the notes, Nico's solos proved irresistible to those on the dancefloor. Western drum kits were not yet in use and the rhythm section consisted of a double bass, maracas, and timbale. The horn section combined clarinet, saxophone and trumpet, with the woodwind used mainly for rumbas and boleros and the trumpet for merengues and cha cha chas. Eventually an electric organ was added. Throughout the 1950s African Jazz built a reputation as the top dance band in the Congo, although by the end of the decade there was growing competition from several new orchestras. In 1959 Kabasele took the step which launched his international career.

Social unrest in the Belgian Congo had spurred the Belgians into releasing their colonial grip on the country. In January 1959 'Round table' talks were held in Brussels to set the schedule for independence the following year. Kalle was invited to accompany the delegates to Brussels, where he recorded the song which was to establish his popularity far and wide. *Independence Cha Cha Cha* turned a frothy dance number into a celebration anthem, and was taken up in many other countries as they successively achieved their own independence. By the time of Belgian Congo's independence in 1960, it had a thriving music business. Each studio had a roster of bands and there was great commercial rivalry. African Jazz were signed to Opika, while the flagship of the Loningisa label was Kalle's greatest competitor, OK Jazz.

Formed in 1956 by a group of prodigiously talented youngsters, including the juvenile guitar wizard Franco, OK Jazz grew into the biggest, most prolific and longest-lived musical institution in Africa. Whereas Kalle was the 'father' of Congo-Zairean music, Franco was to become the 'Godfather' and one of Africa's favourite sons. His catchphrase, 'You enter OK, you leave KO'd' summed up neatly audiences' expectations whenever he played.

When OK Jazz was founded, Franco was only third in seniority, but the seventeen-year-old had already been working as a session guitarist in the Loningisa studio for three years, under the direction of Henri Bowane. Bowane helped to mould the style of the young prodigy, who had taught himself to play on a variety of home-made guitars. His technique was based on the style of traditional zither players, but as a child he had begun to adapt it to appeal to the 'street kids' with whom he was growing up. Taking a different approach to that of Kalle, Franco developed the folklore elements of the basic Congo-Zairean formula. OK Jazz used the same instrumentation and construction, with early songs that were barely distinguishable from African Jazz, but Franco drew less of his inspiration from overseas.

Although he eventually leapfrogged over Kalle to achieve even greater success, Franco always gave credit to the 'father' of the music. "Kabasele and I were friends, never rivals," said Franco at the time of Kabasele's death in 1983. "He was the founder of Zairean music, and although we were in competition, I came after

Personalised label for Henri Bowane, leader of the Loningisa house band

132

Grand Master: by the mid-1980s Franco's physical presence matched his reputation but to the dismay of countless Africans he was gone by the end of the decade

him. He was the first Congolese musician to record in Europe and after he had visited Brussels for the first time he invited me to record for his label Surboum African Jazz. He made many things possible for me." Kabasele had also invited some of the OK Jazz musicians to play with him in Europe, including the lead singer Vicky Longomba. Vicky had been the virtual leader of OK Jazz, and in his absence Franco consolidated his own position from which he never looked back. Franco developed a hard, dry guitar sound in contrast to the florid runs of Dr Nico and the two distinct styles of Congo-Zairean music began to evolve.

By 1963, African Jazz had begun to disintegrate. Dibango had already quit, after putting his stamp on hundreds of recordings, and now Dr Nico and the young singer, Tabu Ley Rochereau, broke away to set up African Fiesta. Rochereau, born in Ban-dundu in 1940, was another bright young talent, who had brought his first composition to Kalle at the age of fourteen. He became a casual member of African Jazz while still a student, and when the band returned from Europe in 1959 he joined full-time.

Franco: The Legend and the Legacy (1938-89)

Franco Luambo Makiadi, the Grand Master of Zairean music and 'Sorcerer of the Guitar', who died in 1989 aged 51, was a truly larger than life character. For more than 30 years he stood like a Colossus over African culture. He also had a huge following in Europe and the USA.

His long-time competitor, Tabu Ley Rochereau, has called him a monument, a human God. Sam Mangwana said he was unique, like Shakespeare or Mozart, combined with Pele or Muhammad Ali. Many called Franco a genius; some said you might not like him but you had to love him.

Franco was a star before independence, and he survived most of the practising artistes of the 1950s with whom he forged the beginnings of Congo-Zairean music, and outshone them at their own trade as well. But he gave the people of Africa more than music. He gave them a legendary hero of mythical status.

A penniless, half-educated street kid, he achieved considerable power and wealth, but he was above all an artist. As a composer, guitarist and vocalist he was sensitive, observant, and compassionate. Franco was also a great entertainer, who loved to excite a crowd, and was never happier than when making people dance.

OK Jazz developed the most dynamic of big band sounds, full of rhythmic tension, inter-woven guitar parts, powerful vocal harmonies and brassy fanfares. Through it all shone the urgent, metallic sound of Franco's guitar, which he picked with fingers 'like talons'.

Franco was a professional guitar ace from the age of eleven. At seventeen he co-founded OK Jazz. A year later he was dubbed the Sorcerer of the Guitar, and never lost the aura of wizardry.

Franco's business was dance.

But he was also a poet of the people; a cutting satirist, lavish praise singer and witty social commentator in the African oral tradition. To the people of Zaire he provided a running commentary on everyday life, which accompanied them through four decades of immense social change, from colonial times through independence to nationhood in President Mobutu's single-party state.

His collected works must comprise the longest running soap opera never made for TV, and like all good soaps the action often spilled over into real life. There were frequent slanging matches with rival musicians, and run-ins with authority.

In a country where freedom of speech has never been encouraged, Franco balanced on a political tightrope. His satires always hit their target and sometimes he pushed his luck with thinly-disguised criticism of those in power. In 1979 he got a severe warning when he was imprisoned, not for political content but obscenity.

Some of the statistics about the man behind the myth help to put the Grand Master in context. Although he was not tall he looked like a giant, weighing in at 140 kilos at his peak. Since first entering a studio in 1953 Franco claimed to have recorded well over 1,000 compositions on technology ranging from pre-electric 78rpm records to digitally-recorded compact discs. Over 100 of his albums have reached international markets.

His band, TP OK Jazz, included more than 40 musicians and, at at the time of his death over 100 families were reportedly dependent on Franco. He had at least eighteen children.

He had many names, being christened Francois Makiadi in 1938, later indigenised to L'Okanga La Ndju Pene Luambo Makiadi during Mobutu's call for 'authenticity'. His nicknames, sobriquets and titles included Le Fou (the Crazy Kid), Franco de mi Amour (Franco My Love), the Sorcerer of the Guitar, Officer of the Grand Order of the Leopard, Grand Master of Zairean Music, The Balzac of African Music and the Godfather of African Music. His musical associates called him 'Grand Maitre'. He called them 'Le Tout Puissant' (The Almighty) OK Jazz.

With the band Franco appeared in some eighteen African countries and played frequently to African audiences in the francophone capitals of Europe. In the anglophone West his career never developed so smoothly. He only once performed in London, in 1984, and made two short visits to the USA. His records, however, were always at the top of the import charts, a demand fuelled by constant requests from visiting Africans for 'the latest Franco'. If creative output can bestow immortality, the Grand Master will live forever.

Rochereau had a musical background. His mother had been a *griot* and he had started as a youngster in the church choir. His lyrical compositions and expressive singing style earned him almost instant success with African Jazz, and for several years after independence he shared the band's good fortune. Ambition inevitably caused him to break away from Kalle, and when he set up African Fiesta it quickly became a challenger for the position of top band. During the early post-independent years Congolese bands were releasing singles, now on the 7-inch, 45 rpm format, at a prodigious rate, sometimes once a week, and African Fiesta's were selling as well as anybody's.

Rochereau continued Kalle's tradition of 'international' presentation, sometimes singing in European languages, and experimenting with new techniques from Western pop and soul music. The alliance with Nico lasted only two years, however, before African Fiesta split into two bands with the same name, one with the suffix 'Sukisa', the other 'National'.

Whereas OK Jazz had the strength of the region's folklore behind them, Rochereau was looking outward for inspiration. In 1968 he found it. "An idea came to me in 1968, following a big tour of West Africa, which took me from Brazzaville to Abidjan. At the time I could sense a difficulty in penetration. I could see the people knew my music and they liked me well. But when I played, there was not enough passion being generated. So I knew I had to create a spectacular show. I returned to Zaire to create the spectacular which I brought to the Paris Olympia in 1970." The innovations included a fanfare introduction, fancy arrangements with lots of brass and dynamic changes of pace, choreographed steps for the musicians, and a troupe of female dancers. Rochereau's Olympia show broke new ground for African music, introducing it to the

Sorcerer of the Guitar: Franco was unique in many ways, but had been identified as a 'guitar wizard' since his youth

135

Tabu Ley and Mbilia Bel: with Afrisa International the continent's greatest double act, until the 'divorce' in 1988

West and stimulating a revival at home, where there was a swing away from the 'classic' rumba to a more contemporary fusion.

Rochereau's appearance was considered to have been a crucial point in the development of contemporary Congo-Zairean music. But the kudos he accrued was more to do with having appeared in a famous Parisian theatre. With a new band, now called Afrisa International, Rochereau (who took the name Tabu Ley in 1974) consolidated his position as the country's most popular singer, and the only rival to fellow bandleader Franco. Among the many musicians he introduced through the ranks of Afrisa were Sam Mangwana, Dizzy Mandjeku and Ndombe Opteum, but the master stroke in Ley's career building came in the early 1980s with the recruitment of a young dancer called Mbilia Bel from Abeti Masikini's band, who under Ley's coaching was to become the top female singer in Africa.

Throughout the 1960s and well into the Seventies, Congolese music continued to boom, in spite of the horrific civil war which broke out after independence. European record companies were keen to invest in recording the bands to feed their distributors throughout the newly-independent African countries. Apart from the 'pillars' of Congo-Zairean music, there were dozens of other bands cutting records or playing for dancers in the open-air 'Congo bars', which were springing up in both Congolese capitals.

Verckys Kiamuangana: a member of the 'big three' with Franco and Tabu Ley, Verckys went from raunchy saxophone honker to studio boss and music business mogul

In 1965 a local newspaper estimated there were 65 orchestras in Kinshasa alone, while another source put it at over 250. Among those bands which were commercially viable during those two decades were Orchestre Conga, Conga 68, Conga Sucess, Negro Sucess, OK Sucess, Vox Africa, Festival des Maquisards, Grand Maquisards, Bantous de la Capitale, Kin Bantous, Cobantous, Kintul, Cercuil Jazz, Super Boboto, Diamant Bleu, Revolution, Vedette Jazz, and Veve. Almost all the bands were playing virtually identical music, often distinguishable only by familiarity with a singer's voice or a guitarist's inflexion. Any innovations were quickly taken up by competing groups and only something as radical as the sound of Franco's guitar or Orchestre Veve's whirlwind horn arrangements could remain a trademark.

Veve was an orchestra in the 1970s, but by the end of the Eighties it had become the business empire of saxophonist Verckys Kiamuangana. Verckys was a long- standing member of OK Jazz, and one of Franco's 'lieutenants' who brought a powerful energy to the band. Disdainful of the smoochy, vibrato style soloing of the rumba-playing saxophonists, Verckys preferred a rougher, honking style, which combined American soul and R&B techniques with an intense 'folkloric' delivery that created feverish excitement on the dance floor. Developed during the late Sixties, following a visit to Kinshasa by the 'Godfather of Soul' James Brown, the Verckys sound was a characteristic of OK Jazz, until he left to form Orchestre Veve in 1972. Verckys went on to establish a recording studio and pressing plant in Kinshasa, and launched the careers of many of the younger, new wave groups which appeared in the Seventies.

The Congo Diaspora

The Golden Age of Congolese music came to an end, in name at least, around 1974, when President Mobutu renamed Congo-Kinshasa as Zaire. Now there was only one Congo; much the smaller country, with many quality musicians but lacking some of the fanaticism which seemed to drive people on the Zairean side. This is the only place in the world where two capital cities face each other across a river. Since even before its status as the capital of Free France during World War Two, Brazzaville had an image as the prim, respectable sister, like a French provincial town on Sunday afternoon, while Kinshasa was frivolous, disor-

Pigeon Voyager: Sam Mangwana, the singers' singer, worked with the major bandleaders before a solo career took him to recording studios in over a dozen countries

ganised, exciting, and always Saturday night. During the years before and after independence there was relatively free movement between the two capitals and musicians from either side spent much time on the opposite beach.

Several (Brazzaville) Congolese were founder members of OK Jazz, including Jean Serge Essous, a clarinettist and sax player who had originally arrived with his own band Negro Jazz. Essous is the father figure of Congolese, as opposed to Zairean, music. Following OK Jazz he set up the band which was to become a national institution across the water, Orchestre Bantous. A partner in both was a fellow saxophonist, Nino Malapet, who eventually succeeded as band leader. The Bantous evolved into another of the great African dance bands and they maintained an influence on both banks of the river, particularly with the introduction of a new dance craze, the *boucher* in 1965. They also brought the rumba back full circle when they performed in Cuba in 1974.

Other members of the top Zairean bands also came from Congo, including Papa Noel, Brazzos and Master Mwana, while a string of successful vocalists emerged in the 1970s including Youlou Mabiala, Pamelo Mounka, Tchico, and Kosmos Moutouari. After independence there was less exchange between the two countries and the Brazzavillois' output slowed down. In the 1980s, however, the Congolese government opened Africa's first 48-track studio at IAD, and initially all the top Kinshasa bands crossed over to record. Congolese artistes themselves have since tended to slip from prominence while Zairean music has boomed. The differences in the two strands of what had once been a single style became more apparent. Zairean music is vocal-led, and the people are renowned for their word play and verbal wit. With a constantly changing 'argot', composers and vocalists play with the language in a way which inspires innovation from the musicians. The Congolese language, and social atmosphere is more formal, and so is the music. It is arranged in a more classical system with the vocal line seeming to follow the arrangements and singers trying to integrate rather than inspire. The scarcity of equipment and lack of venues in Brazzaville is also a handicap; but then life is hardly easy for the typical Kinshasa musician.

The cultural revolution which Zairean President Mobutu introduced in 1972 under the slogan 'Authenticity' emphasised the need to create a unified nation out of the huge country which had been suffering regional and ethnic wars virtually since independence. From now on the great orchestras would be flying the flag for Zairean music. Indeed, many successful Kinshasa bands did benefit creatively from Authenticity. But the competition was hot and, as the country was suffering an economic recession, many musicians quit Zaire to seek their fortune in other parts of Africa.

Heading out along the west coast went the five-piece band Ryco Jazz, founded by Bowane and including Jerry Malekani, Freddy, Cosmo and Garcia. Ryco Jazz settled in Sierra Leone for several years, touring the region extensively and bringing Congolese music to many countries throughout the Sixties. In 1967 they arrived in the French Antillean island of Martinique where they stayed for four years. An individual who followed their direction a decade later and increased his fame in West Africa was the 'International' Sam Mangwana, aka 'The Pigeon Voyager'.

Mangwana has one of the most tuneful voices in Congo-Zairean music and both Franco and Rochereau have cited him as their favourite vocalist. Born in Kinshasa in 1945 to a Zairean

mother and Angolan father, Mangwana was called to join Rochereau's African Fiesta in the early Sixties. When he left for OK Jazz
in 1972, the rivalry between fans of each band was so passionate
that Fiesta enthusiasts threatened to burn down Mangwana's
house for his 'traitorous' behaviour. But he survived alongside
Franco for three fruitful years before returning briefly to Ley. In
both bands Sam held important positions such as 'chef d'orchestre' and band manager, establishing useful contacts for his later
career. When Fiesta were stranded in Cote d'Ivoire in 1976, Sam
quit the band, taking a core of musicians with him.

Recording in Abidjan, Lagos and Kumasi under the name
African All-Stars, Mangwana launched his own label and released
some of his greatest hits including the perennial *Maria Tebbo*. To
make the music more accessible to non-Zaireans he combined
rumba with Afrobeat, highlife and beguine to create a distinctive
pop-rumba style. After six years in West Africa, Mangwana returned to record with Franco and then embarked on an extended
tour of the continent. He has played in dozens of countries and
recorded in Nairobi, Harare and Maputo as well as in West Africa
and Europe. In 1991 he travelled to the USA, taking as his backing
band some ex-members of the All-Stars now working as the
Quatres Etoiles. He stayed for several months and recorded an
album with some of New York's finest salsa stars, consolidating
his 'international' reputation, and fulfilling his appetite for recording in as many countries as possible.

A friend and colleague of Mangwana's, who left OK Jazz after
four years to try his luck in a different direction, was Mose Fan
Fan. His song *Djemelasi* had been a big hit in Kinshasa but, as a
solo guitarist, he knew he would always be overshadowed by
Franco. In the early 1970s, he began a clandestine recording
career with several colleagues including the OK Jazz vice-president, Simaro Lutumba, the singer Youlou Mabiala, saxophonist
Empompo Loway and others. In 1974, some OK Jazz members,
including Youlou, joined him in Orchestra Somo Somo. The band
survived only briefly in Kinshasa, before Fan Fan moved east.
Arriving in Lusaka he re-established the name Somo Somo, before
eventually moving on to Tanzania, where he settled for some
years. He also visited Kenya, recording several albums for the East
African market. Ten years after leaving Zaire, Mose Fan Fan

Somo Somo: formed by ex-OK Jazz
members in Kinshasa, leader Fan Fan
took the band to East Africa before arriving
in England ten years later

arrived in London where he re-established Somo Somo yet again.

The East African connection was lucrative for many Zairean musicians. Congolese rumba records had been distributed throughout the region since the late 1950s and the music had a firm place in the affections of many East Africans. Other musicians established there included Baba Gaston, who moved from Lubumbashi in the early days and was never part of the Kinshasa nexus. As well as the bandleaders, who often recruited local musicians around a core of Zaireans, there were also individual Congo-Zairean musicians playing in non-rumba bands throughout Africa. The extent of the penetration led some contemporary observers to describe it as 'cultural imperialism'. Eventually several countries tried to limit the influence of 'Lingala rumba' by restricting radio time and not renewing musicians' visas.

One country which shares a common culture with much of Zaire is its southerly neighbour Angola. Although the political situation up to, and after, independence has never been conducive to the establishment of a music business, the country does have something of its own to contribute. In 1979 the ministry of culture founded a national orchestra called Semba Tropical with the purpose of reviving the music industry. As a ministry spokesman explained when the band toured Europe in the mid-1980s: "We had great problems because of the war for independence. When the Portuguese left they dismantled some of the basic structure (by smashing and sabotaging equipment) and we had to start from scratch. After independence there were no bands at all. Those which were formed were not active because they had no instruments."

Semba Tropical's music is a steamy version of the classic Congolese sound, with a Brazilian colouring to the percussion and horn section. It is a showcase band which accompanies some of the country's top solo artistes, the most popular of whom is the singer Bonga. Other bands which have managed to survive under the arduous social conditions include Sensacional Maringa, Os Jovens do Prenda, and Dimba Dya Ngola, all of which have recorded. The South American inflexions recall the flavour of the early coastal rumba before it became repossessed and diffused throughout the African interior.

New wave breakers: Zaiko Langa Langa in the studio. Master guitarist and musical director Matima lays down guitar tracks with Barosa. Dindo and Cele listen in

The New Wave

While the classic rumba bands survived at least until Franco's death at the end of 1989, the 'third generation' of Zairean musicians had been working for twenty years on another bolder fusion of rumba and folklore, known in the West as soukous. This so-called 'new wave' has been dominated since 1970 by Zaiko Langa Langa, the group of 'mods' who brought Sixties Western pop attitudes to indigenous music. "It's like a fetish ", said the band's 'President' Nyoka Longo about their success. "People don't understand the effect of our music on them. But they have to dance. There is something in the tempo which you can't identify but which you can feel."

Zaiko Langa Langa are innovators and their influence can be heard not only in dozens of Kinshasa groups but also in the music of pop bands throughout Africa. The electric guitar and evocative Lingala vocals are at the forefront of all Zairean music, and Zaiko pioneered the contemporary sound which cuts all unnecessary frills to develop those two elements to a fine art. The third vital ingredient is a rhythmic intensity unmatched by any other group, which exploits the Zairean master stroke, the *sebene*, when the melody is suddenly deflected off at a tangent and the rhythm changes into trance-like, repetitive patterns, which can virtually mesmerise people on the dancefloor. The sebene has been central to the success of Congo-Zairean music since its beginnings, and in the age of the 45rpm single it spread over to fill the B-sides of many records. When played live, a sebene can last for over twenty minutes. Zaiko are masters of the sebene, and pioneers of the catch-phrase dance crazes which signify modern soukous.

Founded in late 1969, with a youthful disregard for the preferences of their elders, Zaiko were originally a somewhat

Cultural curiosity: Papa Wemba plugged folklore music into mains electricity, dressed it in designer clothes and invented a fashion religion

Before the big split: good friends in the old Zaiko, Dindo Yogo (right) and Lengi Lenga landed on different sides of the fence

The core of musicians who formed Familia Dei included singers Bimi Ombale, J-P Buse, Lengi Lenga and guitarist Popolipo

samedi 13 DECEMBRE 86 de 21 heures à l'aube

Salle des Fêtes 14ᵉ Arrᵗ de PARIS 26, rue Mouton-Duvernet Métro : Mouton-Duvernet

bal d'adieu

avec le GROUPE CHOC

ZAÏKO LANGA-LANGA

buffet -:- bar -:- spécialités

excitable group of students. They had been exposed to Western pop and were inspired by a percussionist, the late D.V. Moanda, to form a group rather than an orchestra. They made a virtue out of not being able to afford horns and, using just voices and guitars, developed the Zairean equivalent of rock music for the post-independence generation. The available technology was just adequate for the rough-edged sounds of their raw idealism. Zaiko were not quite the first of the groups; they acknowledge the inspiration of the Brussels-based student outfit, Los Nickelos, and Thu Zahina from Kinshasa. But Zaiko tapped the feeling of the time with the name, taken from 'Zaire ya ba koko' – meaning 'The Zaire of our ancestors'. This before the name was applied to the country. Zaiko went on to inspire a whole family of bands in a loose affiliation called 'Clan Langa Langa'.

Each of these bands quickly developed their own characteristics as they took on new musicians. The tone of voice, melodic structure and 'feeling' varied considerably, but their music shared several basic elements. First, none of the groups used horns, which set them apart from the big orchestras. They are guitar bands. While Zairean audiences respond to the sensitivity of the vocals, foreigners have been getting excited by the mesmerising guitar licks and unstoppable rhythms of the sebenes. Back home Zaiko is enjoyed as mainstream culture, continuing in a direct line from the first generation music. Abroad, however, it is often seen as a wild, orgiastic and potentially dangerous sound. This difference in appreciation illustrates some of the misconceptions restricting African music's acceptance in the West.

Other inspirational groups of the early Seventies included the Stukas, who played a ragged electric interpretation of folklore music, with the howling vocals of leader Lita Bembo and intricate guitar picking from the 'Sewing machine' Dodoli, and several bands with alliterative titles, including Bella Bella, Shama Shama and Lipua Lipua. Orchestre Bella Bella, founded by the brothers

Soki Vangu and Soki Dianzenza, established another mini-dynasty. The splinter group Bella Mambo provided singer Kanda Bongo Man with a foothold in music. The brothers last played together in 1974 before going their separate ways in Europe and Zaire. Soki Vangu was never far from the limelight and his last work was a collaboration with Tshala Mwana. With uncanny synchronicity the brothers died, continents and careers apart, early in 1990.

An early graduate of Bella Bella, the giant-sized singer Pepe Kalle, later known as the 'Elephant of Zairean music', went on to establish his own strain of soukous. Born in Kinshasa in the early 1950s, the young Kabasele Yampanya started singing in his Catholic school choir. Later he became a protege of his namesake and neighbour, Joseph Kabasele, aka the Grand Kalle, although he never played alongside the father of the music. By the early 1970s when he joined up with the sweet-voiced singer Nyboma in Bella Bella, Pepe Kalle's voice had acquired the husky, soul-inflected tones for which he became known. In 1973 they had a great hit with *Kamale* and soon launched a new band of that name under the managerial guidance of Verckys. A few years later Kalle formed Empire Bakuba, with whom he forged his career. During the late Eighties Kalle popularised the *kwasa kwasa* dance rhythm and launched a string of albums, supported by foreign tours both with and without Bakuba. He played in Europe, the USA and the French Caribbean as well in West and East Africa, including Kenya where at the beginning of the 1990s he was one of the biggest selling recording artistes.

Few international solo stars have emerged from the Zairean new wave with as much favourable hype as Papa Wemba. Always a provocative showman with a penchant for clowning, Wemba was also unique in that having acquired Western pop techniques, he immediately sought a return to his traditional roots, as if reaching back to pull the rich folklore music into the twentieth century. Wemba's high nasal voice and his agitated folklore rhythms were supported by a line up of serious musicians, first in Isife Lokole and later Viva La Musica.

Big sound of Empire Bakuba: the 'elephant' Pepe Kalle took his name from the music's father but brought his own gruff vocal style

His interpretation of traditional culture included the creation of his own village in the family compound called Village Molokai. He once said it was named after a leper colony run by a famous Belgian priest, which featured in Graham Greene's novel *A Burnt Out Case*. Taking on the role of outrageous outlaw, Wemba was identifying with the 'untouchable' image associated with lepers. His melding of urban and bush culture included a bizarre fashion ingredient; one moment Wemba would be wearing raffia and sorcerer's accessories, the next designer trousers. He eventually took credit for starting the 'sapeur' movement in which clothes took on a quasi-religious significance. A real pop star at home, Wemba made a promising breakthrough into the Western mainstream in 1988 with a rumba/rock album aimed at a crossover, White audience. He also showed his acting talent as the hero of the feature film *La Vie est Belle*, in which he convincingly and humorously played a naive 'bushman' who has to come to terms with the competitive and corrupt lifestyle of Kinshasa. His group, Viva la Musica lived up to their name, and re-appeared in the Nineties with a clutch of new singers, including Stino and Reddy, among whom Wemba reaffirmed his value as a group member.

A partner of Wemba's in the early Seventies was Bozi Boziana, a singer who quit the Zaiko fold more than once. Known to his Kinois fans as 'Grand Pere', Bozi has earned himself a huge devoted following in Zaire, with his plaintive songs and ear-

The Zaiko Langa Langa Dynasty

The full name is Tout Choc Anti Choc Zaiko Langa Langa - known to enthusiasts as 'Zaiko'. One of Africa's most enigmatic outfits, Zaiko have been the top 'youth' band for over twenty years, but outside Zaire they have suffered continuing identity problems which have left the music much better known than the group.

There are, confusingly, two Zaiko Langa Langas, with Grand Zaiko WaWa, Choc Stars, Anti-Choc Stars, and Langa Langa Stars, all closely related.

The name has been hijacked by so many ex-members that Zaiko has become as much an evolving concept as a static group. In addition to those bands, records have been released under the names of 'Zaikomania', 'Zaico' and 'Clan Langa Langa'.

In 1991, however, there remained one core group, containing five members of the original student line up: singer and 'president' Nyoka Longo, guitarists Matima on solo and Zamuangana on rhythm, bass player Bapius and drummer Meri Djo.

Their 22-man team (above), subtitled Nkola Mboka ('Town Boss' or 'Village Headman'), contained vocal stars Dindo Yogo with the quavering 'broken' voice, the tremulous Malage de Lugendo and crooners Adamo, Aziza and Tylon, amongst a front-line of seven. Solo guitarists Shiro and Barosa and keyboard player Alpha created the instrumental euphoria, while the liveliest 'animation' came from Zaire's premier atalaku shouters, Nono and Doudou.

Since the controversial 1988 divorce, a second group known as Zaiko Langa Langa, Familia Dei (Family of God) has also been doing the rounds, including an American tour, with a handful of founder members, notably drummer Ilo Pablo, singers Lengi Lenga and Bimi Ombale, joined by J-P Buse, with guitarists Popolipo, Jimmy Yaba and Petit Poisson and percusionist Manzeku from the old formation.

The pre-20th-anniversary arguments which caused this separation confused the music-loving inhabitants of Kinshasa.

For a while both groups were banned by the musicians union from appearing on TV or radio, but fans tracked down Nkolo Mboka and Famila Dei to the Kimpwanza and Vis-a-Vis clubs respectively. One was sponsored by Skol lager, the other by Primus beer.

It was the most serious fracture in Zaiko's history, but it was only the latest in a series of divorces and defections.

First to leave Zaiko, a few years after its launch, was Papa Wemba, the high-voiced singer who made his name with Isife Lokole, Yoka Lokole and Viva la Musica before settling in Paris where he carved his solo career. He was joined by Bozi Boziana and Mavuelo Somo.

Next to break out in 1981 was the guitarist Manuaku, founder of Grand Zaiko WaWa. A year later Evoloko Jocker formed Langa Langa Stars with Bozi and Roxy Tshipaka. Bozi, the most restless of all, returned from 1977 to 1981, but soon moved on to Choc Stars and later Anti-Choc.

Following the big bust-up of 1988, even the splinter groups fragmented when first Likinga left, then Bimi Ombale, an admired composer and singer with a fragile voice, quit Familia Dei in 1990 to form Zaiko Loningisa, which he later renamed Basilique Loningisa.

In 1991 Zaiko's European fans were shocked to hear that Dindo Yogo, the chef d'orchestre'had not joined them on tour. Yogo's absence left a hole in the front line but Zaiko's strength is in the depth of their squad and the power of their music. Nkolo Mboka survived the turmoil to emerge with an even more fulsome sound, new compositions and a flamboyant stage show. Although ostensibly a group, with no single star figure, they maintain the structure and discipline of the big band days. With seven singers and six guitarists they work on a rotation system, providing an ever changing line-up.

Between tours they spend weeks rehearsing for up to 12 hours a day. New songs and dance routines keep pouring out. In the words of one band member: "Zaiko rises from the flames like the Phoenix." And in its present incarnation it has risen to a high altitude.

boggling arrangements. In 1989 he was the country's Musician of the Year with five albums in the chart. After starting in a Boy Scout band, he became a founder member of the original Zaiko Langa Langa, before launching a series of groups including Minzoto Wela Wela (1972), Isife Lokole with Papa Wemba, (1975) and Yoka Lokole with Manuaku Waku, (1976).

By 1977 Bozi was back in the ranks of Zaiko but he got the itch to break out again and in 1981 joined Langa Langa Stars with two more Zaiko originals, singer Evoloko and the guitarist Roxy Thsipaka. Three years later many of the musicians were offered a deal by Ben Nyamabo to join yet another new outfit, Choc Stars, but after two years Bozi was out. In 1986 he formed Orchestre Anti-Choc, named not just in defiance of his last band, but indicating an antidote to all the old stuff. He was offered a record deal by Verckys to release one album a year, in part exchange for which Anti-Choc were provided with equipment. The deal worked well and Bozi made some great albums for Veve, and some better ones elsewhere, especially with producer Anytha Ngapi.

The Anti-Choc band included singers Fifi Mofoude, Wally Ngonda and Kofi Alibaba, along with guitarists Dodoli, Aimada, Misha, Sadico and Nguma. Bozi has always had a talent for picking musicians, and he caused a reappraisal of the previously male-dominated new-rumba. "I introduced the female component into the music because I thought it would be interesting," he said in 1989, "and I was proved right." His first partner was Joly Detta who had sung with OK Jazz. Next, Bozi recruited a sprite of a singer who quickly made a big name for herself. Déesse (Goddess) Mukangi worked her apprenticeship with Anti-Choc in the Kinshasa clubs like Kimpwanza and Vis-a Vis for a couple of years and made over half a dozen albums with the band.

Detta later returned and Bozi inducted several more women into the Anti-Choc system. Bozi recalls there was some jealousy at first, both between the men and the women, and among the women themselves, but it settled down and they now work happily together, except for (male) singer Fifi Mofoude, who drifted off.

Evoloko Jocker was another founding member of Zaiko who quit once in 1975 to join Wemba and returned later to spend another two years in the group. In 1982 he made his definitive move by setting up Langa Langa Stars with Roxy on solo guitar and Bozi, Dindo Yogo, Esperant and Djanana in the vocal line.

Choc Stars singer Defao: one of a line of vocalists who brought a sweaty intimacy to romantic seduction soukous

Although there have been many personnel changes the band has been kept alive. Known as 'The Joker', Evoloko is an outrageous showman and 'animateur' who took the credit for the *cavacha* dance craze of the early 1970s while still with Zaiko, and encouraged the trend for shouters, the *atalaku*, whose frenzied cries syncopated against churning sebenes, activate the dancers.

The cries of the atalaku are like the bands' trademarks. Often delivered in regional dialects, or nonsense Lingala, their shouts resemble sorcerers' incantations, reflecting the folklore background of many atalaku, who also play percussion, but rarely sing verses. From shouting out the name of the dance, with familiar exhortations to 'get down', 'give it up' or 'put it out', the shouters now include parables, short stories and veiled warnings to rivals, which have no connection with the actual song. The cries are changed regularly to confuse imitators, although a good shout might activate every number throughout a five-hour show. When the Anti-Choc shouters were calling 'salaam elekoum', it did not mean they'd converted to Muslims. It was part of an instructive little tale about how the young Kinshasa bandits, the 'Yankees', creep up and steal the slippers of the Senegalese while they worship at the mosque. Choc Stars' atalaku commentated on a staggering dancer 'Is he sick? No, he's drunk'. Zaiko, who usually play till dawn, had a chant about 'when the cock crows, the bats fly and the sorcerers go home'.

Out of the Verckys stable via Papa Wemba's Viva La Musica came another eccentric fashion victim, the singer Emeneya Kester, eventual front man of Orchestre Victoria Eleison. Emeneya, who cut his teeth in Shama Shama, became a big star on the local scene, with his smooth low voice and savage sebenes. Since the late Eighties he has been searching for a non-rumba sound which he found in the 'Zulu' beat used on his big regional hit *Nzinzi*. But his business strategy was not so clever. He seemed to have frequent problems finding equipment to play with and has often been stuck without a gig.

Choc Stars gradually evolved their own system, which maintained the Zaiko connection through the solo guitar of Roxy, later joined by S.O.S., both able to turn a really curly guitar lick. With their mellow, crooning lyrics, Choc Stars have a softer, more romantic approach than their counterparts. Singers included the tremulous Carlito, the sultry-voiced Debaba and Defao, and the spaced out Djanana. Middle of the Road, many first time European listeners might think, but the intensity is there, held in check by a dynamic tension which opens up the spaces between the notes. The sebene is not so much unleashed as unrolled across the dance floor. Choc Stars were also suffering problems at the start of the 1990s. Their spot at the Madison Square Select had been taken over; Carlito had left to join OK Jazz, Djomali and Djanana had returned to Langa Langa Stars

Up and comers in Kinshasa at the start of the decade, Wenge Musica appealed to the youth market, and while unable to sound a full generation ahead of Zaiko, they did promise a possible line of development. Their new rumba is polished with high-tech instrumentation and fancy arrangements by Alain Makaba, using his experience of producing TV advertising jingles, and their clean-cut 'college boy' looks have begun to charm the youth. Their first album, recorded at the eight-track Bobongo studios, never saw the light in Europe but worked them into public favour at home. Their second release was impressive. Others following the inevitable surge of rumba soukous are Rumba Ray, with lead vocalist Maray Maray, Odeon, Lino Stars and Station Japon.

Dindo Yogo: Zaiko frontliner with the 'cracked voice' and composer who releases regular solo albums

Women from Kasai: photographed in Brazzaville in 1904. Accordions were often given by traders to chiefs who passed them on to their womenfolk

The Female Dimension

The role of women in Zairean music has until recently been predictably limited. In traditional society women often played accordion, and Tshibola earned some renown with that instrument. During the Fifties several women recorded folklore music, following the lead of Pauline Lisanga, but it was as variety singers they later excelled, often as accoutrements of the big orchestras. Early semi-professional artistes included the clear-toned Yenga Moseka, 'melodious' Ebibi and the passionate Bora Uzima. Vonga Ye made a name in the Seventies, but Abeti Masikini set the standard for women stars with her fruity voice, hot arrangements and spectacular dance routines. With her band Les Redoubtables and troupes of male and female dancers, Abeti made her name the hard way by touring as a revue band in Central and West Africa. In the early Eighties she recorded some of her best work in the New Sound studios in Togo. Dormant for several years, she resurfaced in Paris and entered the Nineties with a new show on the road and a successful album.

Making her stage debut as a dancer in Abeti's troupe, the young Mbilia Bel spent four years touring in the show before she was recruited by Tabu Ley, who made a slot for her in the Rocherettes dance troupe. She eventually developed as a singer, duetting with Ley and releasing the first of seven albums together. By 1984 her success was confirmed. Under Ley's tutelage, and singing his songs, she travelled the world. For the six years they were together Ley and Bel were one of the brightest acts in Africa, and one of the few male-female duos on the continent. The marriage broke up around 1988, with much recrimination on both sides and some wild gossip in the Zairean newspapers. The divorce was finalised when she released *Phenomenal*, recorded under the artistic direction of Rigo Star. No longer in Ley's

Style and Fashion in Kinshasa

In the music-mad city of Kinshasa the bars, clubs and discotheques are packed from midnight to dawn with dancers and 'ambiencers' of all ages and income brackets. The night life in the Matonge district is non-stop, as the Kinois dance, drink, eat and generally enjoy themselves. A major part of 'ambiencing' is to be seen to be looking good, and the subtly competitive parading and posing is itself an entertainment.

Through the atmospheric streets majestic mamas, wrapped in swirls of wax-dyed cloth, cruise like schooners under full sail towards the clubs where the classic rumba music of OK Jazz or Afrisa can be heard. Some arrive with heavyweight men of influence wearing the uniquely Zairean 'abacost' jackets which button to the neck; European neckties were outlawed during the 'Authenticity' years of the 1970s and Eighties.

For the Kinois dressing is an important means of self-expression. Younger people who dance to soukous, or new-wave rumba, dress more like the world citizens they aspire to become, sometimes looking as if they've stepped from the pages of a fashion magazine. Crisply coiffed hair and sharp shoes top-and-tail an extraordinary variety of designer suits, trousers and shirts, many of them originals from the top Japanese and European couturiers.

These fashion fans call themselves 'Sapeurs' (Society of Ambiencers and Persons of Elegance). To be 'bien sape' is the most important thing to many young Kinois, who would rather go without food than appear scruffy.

The young people self-consciously flaunting their fashion sense are part of a phenomenon which so grabbed the imagination that it progressed from art-form to a spurious 'religion' known as Kitende (the Lingala word for cloth). The most fanatical followers, like Tity Levalois (below left) and Emeneya (right) consider themselves 'Grand Priests'. The 'deities' are fashion designers like Jean-Paul Gaultier, Armani, Yamamato, Ungaro and Valentino.

The so-called 'Pope' is Papa Wemba, also considered something of a clown or a madman, even by his fans. Over the years he established crazes for three-quarter length trousers, colonial-style pith helmets, and leather suits. In his madcap antics he would balance shoes on his head or pull up his jacket to show off the label while singing the praises of favourite designers. He also enshrined a sapeurs' code, which defined eight stylised ways of walking.

The fashion scene, which took off in the late 1980s, is inextricably linked with music, and was credited by one Kinshasa music magazine with enriching the folklore of Zaire with modern instead of traditional ingredients. The clothes look best when dancing.

Until Authenticity was relaxed in 1990, a woman wearing any kind of Western dress rather than the 'authentic' cloth wrappers, was making a statement, but the limited range of available fashions meant there were fewer obvious trends. It was mainly the young men who took the limelight.

At the other end of the spectrum from the 'Grand' sapeurs, a young Kinshasa group called Bourgeois Uomos recently celebrated the end of the school summer term with a dance. They were wearing clothes of several years vintage but still stylish and, of the nine male singers and dancers, many were in borrowed shoes. Before the show one even had a 'shoe check': instead of testing his microphone he tried a few steps, took off a shoe, examined it, replaced it, spun a few times and left the stage satisfied.

On the dance floor a young girl in elegant pyjama style trousers coolly rode the spiralling rhythms with her partner, gradually hitching one trouser leg inch by inch. A friend danced alone wearing walkman headphones as a symbol of cool. Between songs they posed for photographs.

The sapeur scene is like a re-run of the British mod cult of the mid-1960s. Clothes are seen as the mark of a person, bringing a measure of self-esteem essential to those who dream of living in the far-off fantasy world of Europe.

The 'Grand sapeurs' have access to the European boutiques but how the 'petits' of Kinshasa can afford even copies of designer clothes is far from clear. Many claim they work and save their money, while some confess they neither work nor eat.

shadow, Mbilia Bel started the Nineties with the hard task of establishing a new identity.

The untimely death of M'Pongo Love early in 1990 came as a shock to followers of Zairean music who had become enchanted by her clear voice and romantically soulful compositions. M'Pongo Love had found fame against the odds. She bore a serious physical handicap yet, in a context where women performers were expected to be primarily dancers, she became one of the most popular female artistes on the continent. She had a clarity of voice, a warmth of tone and intimate delivery which set her apart from the handful of top-flight female artistes. But her music was as lively as she was sweet, and M'Pongo could draw a cry of delight or a tear from anyone who saw her perform.

Born in the Bas-Zaire region in 1956, M'Pongo Landu, who was to become known as *'La voix la plus limpide du Zaire'*, had a hard start to life. At the age of four she was stricken with polio, resulting in a paralysed leg which left her permanently handicapped. Undeterred and independent, M'Pongo set her mind on becoming a singer. She studied hard in high school, and later worked as a secretary. Her musical favourites at the time were Miriam Makeba, Aretha Franklin and the Greek singer Nana Mouskouri, whom M'Pongo once cited as a major influence. She began composing songs and performing them for her friends, always with the dream of one day being recorded.

At the age of twenty, her dream came true, courtesy of some 'generous friends'. She began performing with Orchestre Tsheke Tsheke, alongside the guitarist Efumu Mauro, and the same year cut her first record, *Pas possible, Mathy*, under the musical direction of the saxophonist and arranger Empompo Loway Deyese. With the orchestra, M'Pongo toured East Africa in 1977, and with OK Jazz she represented Zaire at the Nigerian Festac festival. By 1980 she had moved to Paris, where she recorded with some of the top Cameroonian session musicians including Eko Roosevelt and Aladji Toure. The 1983 album release *Femme Commerçant*,

Anti Choc: Bozi Boziana moved from Zaiko through almost all the spin-off bands before forming Anti Choc, here with Déesse in 1988

arranged by Sammy Massamba, made her breakthrough to Western audiences.

In 1984 M'Pongo Love released what is probably her most popular album, *Basongeur*, featuring the arrangements of her companion Mauro and some musicians from Les Quatres Etoiles. The same year she was invited to perform in Scandinavia in association with the Year of the Handicapped campaign, and her name spread across Europe as she toured with her group Love Systeme. In Paris, M'Pongo continued working with different musical arrangers, including the Gabonese politician Alexandre Sambat and members of the zouk group, Kassav. Her last release *Partager* was strong and, with a video clip to back it up, it seemed she was set to follow some other Africans into the fringes of international pop. M'Pongo Love, who was mother to three children, was buried in January 1990, at the Gombe cemetery in Kinshasa, where just three months earlier the body of Franco Luambo Makiadi had also been interred. The loss was further compounded by the announcement that her erstwhile arranger and collaborator Empompo Loway had also passed away.

An eighteen-year-old girl who arrived in Kinshasa from her home town of Kisangani during 1977 was particularly inspired by M'Pongo Love whom she had seen on television. Tshala Mwana had already shown her skills as a dancer of the Baluba people's *mutuashi* rhythm, and when she offered her services to M'Pongo Love as a show dancer she became a member of Orchestre Tsheke Tsheke. In those days Tshala had not considered singing, but M'Pongo's visible success gradually inspired her to step up to the microphone. Her musical preferences did not fit the required rumba criteria, however, and she decided she should move out of Zaire to have any chance.

Arriving in Abidjan, Cote d'Ivoire, she teamed up with Bibi Dens, collaborator on her first recordings, and later toured the West Africa region. In 1984 Tshala went to Paris where her first album earned an award for top female artiste. She then turned towards East and Central Africa and by the time she returned home she had consolidated a pan-African reputation. Her albums have been made in collaboration with different artistic directors including Souzy Kasseya and Dino Vangu. In 1989 it was Master Mwana Congo driving the band. Playing at home in Zaire she called in members of Bobongo Stars. In 1990 in her home region of Kasai, Tshala was made a traditional queen, and at the official coronation in Kananga she received the title Shanda Wa Mu Shanda. Always known as the 'Queen of Mutuashi' she now had the formal authority to back it up.

A new voice for the Nineties was the 'Little Goddess', Déesse Mukangi, who had a similar 'voice-print' to the late M'Pongo Love, expressed with energetic enthusiasm. At eighteen the singer had a classic quality and a demure image. Three years later she hit Europe with a glam-punk costume and an extra vitality. She was still relatively inexperienced but had just cut her first solo album in Paris, and had already come a long way from Kisangani. Déesse first exercised her lungs at the time when Zaire was first being stirred by the new-wave bands, but she grew up in a milieu where traditional 'folklore' music had almost as much prominence as the sounds of either big-band or youth music. She claims to know plenty of folklore including, from her father's (Baluba) side, the real Mutuashi.

While Déesse was still a child the family moved to Kinshasa, where the sounds of the Zaiko family hang like an aural forest canopy. Many youths felt the urge to perform, but for girls there

The dancing beat of Kinshasa: to 'play' music means to dance as well as handle an instrument, and paved roads are no obstacle to bare feet

Little goddess: Déesse Mukangi, combining a classic vocal style with exuberant delivery, was groomed for stardom in Anti-Choc

were few role models. Women like M'Pongo (who Déesse remembered for her 'beautiful voice') Abeti, Mbilia Bel and Tshala Mwana were slightly outside the main thrust of the music, which was dominated by flamboyant male vocalists. Her first career break came with Mimi Ley's Afro International. Zairean newspaper reports spoke of a tough little girl who stood up for herself against the crude behaviour of her male colleagues. She denied the tales of shirt ripping, swearing and shin kicking, but obviously has some spirit.

In 1988 she joined Anti-Choc for three productive years, before arriving in Paris where she recorded vocal accompaniment on albums by Dindo Yogo and Koffi Olomide. In 1991 she cut her debut album, but was not tempted to include the hip-hop and reggae styles which she had started to enjoy. "You must not play only modern music", she said at the time. "You must keep in touch with your roots. My first album of four or five songs will be in the style I know. It's the kind of music I've been playing with Anti-Choc. I do have other ideas but they should wait until after maybe

Queen of Mutuashi: Tshala Mwana brought her Baluba music to the fore as the only challenger to rumba

Solo artiste and session player, the Congolese guitarist Master Mwana (no relation) was Tshala's bandleader in 1990

my third or fourth album. If you try to do something too different you risk losing a lot."

Female instrumentalists are rare in Africa and when TAZ Bolingo started playing in the late 1980s, there was only one band on the continent with whom they could be compared, Les Amazones du Guinea. Indeed TAZ did match them in many ways and credited the Guinean policewomen with their early inspiration. TAZ, which stands for 'Troupe Artistique de Zaire' created a version of classic rumba with three-guitar line, a horn section, pumping rhythms and seductive animation. From their base at the Club Self Control, in the Bandal quarter of Kinshasa TAZ built a following, and at the start of the Nineties had released two albums. In 1991 the name TAZ Junior was taken up by a group of young boys; the sons and pupils of the musical mamas.

Soukous by the Seine

Although francophone, Zaire was never French. Its European gateway has always been Brussels and unlike other French speaking Africans the Zaireans have never had the 'incentive' of qualifying for French citizenship. There is a large Zairean community in Paris but apart from a few exceptions they have not blended in with the homogeneous Black French culture enjoined by Senegalese, Cameroonians and Ivorians. The big bands more often record in Brussels. In Paris, solo Zairean musicians have grouped together in ex-patriate alliances, making music together for their own people and, although some of them have adapted it for international 'hot tropic' audiences, their soukous sticks to the trusted formula.

The main exception to the closed system is Ray Lema. At home in Zaire, Lema had a classical training which set him apart from other popular musicians. The church provided the only means of expression for budding keyboard players but Lema, who was enrolled for a career in the Catholic priesthood, took it further, playing the church organ every day and making his concert debut with Beethoven's *Moonlight Sonata.* Music eventually superseded the church as a career and Lema shared his keyboard skills with several top-line artistes, including Abeti, M'Pongo Love, Tabu Ley and Papa Wemba. He also acquired a taste for rock music which did not gell with the rumba-crazy Kinois who thought that musicians playing the feeble rock rhythms were 'walking on each other's feet'.

Lema then had the chance to steep himself in folklore music as musical director of the Zairean national ballet in 1974. A few years later he formed his own group, Ya Tupas, which incorporated ideas from his wide musical experince. The group's first record brought him an award in France and the chance to tour the USA, where he further opened his ears to R&B, soul and jazz music, evolving a personal fusion in which Zairean elements are melded into a cross-cultural cocktail of 'listening music'.

At home, the new music has always been seen as a seamless evolution of original rumba. The first one to break the thread, and discard the rumba element was Kanda Bongo Man. Virtually unknown at home, he took a drastically cut down version of the new-wave music to White audiences in the early Eighties. Singing alone with a four or five-piece band, Kanda went straight for the sebene. He picked the right musicians for the job, including guitarists Rigo Star (ex-Viva la Musica) and Diblo Dibala (ex-Bella Bella), and while his music was going one-way only, it was fast. As he said on his first visit to London in 1983: "Music in Central Africa is dominated by heat and rhythm, and soukous makes everybody dance. Whereas Franco and Tabu Ley adapted the traditional music, so young people are doing something of our own." While older audiences liked slow dancing, Kanda noticed

Kanda Bongo Man: came out of Paris in the early 1980s with a stripped down soukous which has taken him round the world

Tcha Tcho man: Koffi Olomide's crooning style and romantic compositions ensured a loyal female audience

Madilu System: figurehead, if not captain, of the flagship OK Jazz. The only musician Franco ever called by name during a song

Swede Swede: singer and front man Boketshu Premier outside the band's headquarters

described as 'post-punk, neo-traditional', was a battery of drums led by a pair of *lokole* or slit-log drums, accompanied by large upright tambours, western drumkit and assorted percussion. The only 'melody' instrument was a ragged sounding harmonica which, like the drums and voices (and indeed the dancers) locked into hypnotic grooves lasting up to fifteen minutes. The harmonica is a substitute for the accordion frequently used by Mongo village musicians.

The sundama dance is a modern creation, credited to harmonica player Bisasanga, rather than an ancient tradition. The fact that sundama means 'bend over' led to some speculation in Zaire that it might be obscene, but the lead singer Boketshu Premier cited the approval of the mayor of Kinshasa and his wife. Like many other dances, however, the sundama did not lack sexual innuendo. While the pirate cassettes of Swede Swede's performances sold like hot *beignets* (local doughnuts) on the streets of the city, they played through the night at their headquarters in a modest compound, and all over town. Swede Swede's early success rested on word of mouth reputation. The 'banderoles' strategically strung across Kinshasa's roundabouts are the main publicity medium for working bands, and sometimes they implied that Swede Swede were playing in two places at once. In fact this is only half true. In 1990 there were actually four groups working under variations of the name, in different parts of town. In 1989 Boketshu's 'Classique' Swede Swede performed as support act to the Antilles group Zouk Machine and made a big impression. The band visited Europe in 1990 where they made their first recording, although by then the sundama craze had been taken up by Zaire's major artists, including Zaiko Langa Langa, Koffi Olomide,

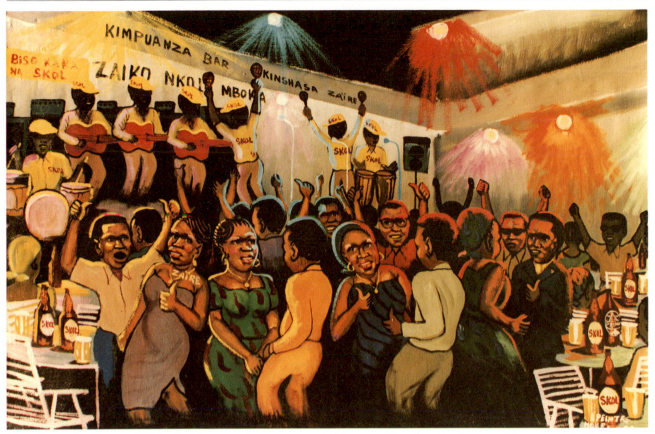

Empire Bakuba and Tshala Mwana. In commercial terms, Swede Swede moved too slowly to prevent the momentum of their own creation overtaking them.

Kinshasa ambience in club Kimpwanza, as seen by the artist Moke, a prominent Zairean painter

At the start of the Nineties, Zaire could still boast the most effective musicians in Africa. The younger established institutions like Zaiko, Viva la Musica and Anti-Choc seemed established enough to survive at least another generation, with continually fresh and invigorating music. Although the days of the big dance bands appeared to be over, the good news for lovers of the 'classic' rumba has been the survival of TP OK Jazz, following Franco's demise. Under the leadership of Simaro Lutumba, the band's vice-president for almost 30 years, the great flagship steamed on. Amongst the singers, Madilu System had become a big star and, together with Josky, Djo Mpoyi, Ndombe, Lokombe and Carlito, maintained their famous 'harmonic force' with lyrics that kept the social debate alive. The first official post-Franco release from OK Jazz proved to be one of the biggest hits in Kinshasa for some time.

The poet: Simaro Lutumba, composer of classic songs and long-time vice-president of OK Jazz, inherited the leader's mantle after Franco's death

But the savage increase in the rate of inflation and the imminent uncertainty of multi-party elections during 1991 sent the music business reeling. Many bands cracked up, as essential musicians emigrated to Europe. For the first time Britain saw a steady flow of Kinshasa bands, as Zaireans began to look outside the francophone world for sustenance. In Kinshasa, the Veve studio had closed down, although Bobongo had re-equipped with digital technology. Musicians from the major bands continued their habit of *zonzing*, playing guests spots on solo records, while new formations were expected from Dindo Yogo and Bimi Ombale. In common with other parts of Africa, Zairean music was facing a major upheaval. And people in those other parts were waiting to see whether Kinshasa could still deliver the goods.

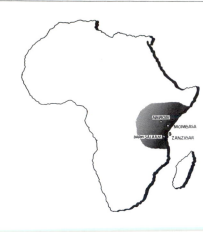

Swahili Sounds

Swahili is not the name of one ethnic group, but it identifies several different peoples, bound together by possibly the best established surviving culture in Africa. It is a society united firstly by the language, Kiswahili, which is used in most countries in East and Central Africa, and is the national language in Kenya, Tanzania and Uganda. It is also one of the four national languages of Zaire and is spoken in Zambia, Malawi, southern Sudan, and along the east coast from Aden to Mozambique and all the Indian Ocean islands, large and small. Swahili is the only sub-Saharan African language to have a tradition of written literature. It also has a vast repertoire of sung poems, and a classical music tradition which owes a lot to Arabic and, importantly, Indian Ocean connections. It is an extremely old culture, dating from the first eastbound migration by Bantu people several thousand years ago. The name Swahili means 'coastal Bantu' (people). While Swahili culture is largely Islamic not all the people who use the language are necessarily Muslim. The historical capital of Swahili literature and the main cultural centre was, until early this century, the island of Lamu, although Mombasa, Dar es Salaam and Zanzibar are also historically important.

The classical Kiswahili, however, is only one aspect of the language. Far more widespread is the informal 'market dialect' known as *kisokoni* which is used throughout East Africa. From the high point of being sub-Saharan Africa's only written literature, Swahili reaches down to isolated peasants and illiterate market traders deep in the interior. As a musical language it helps to bridge the gap between the 'vernaculars' of the 'tribal' cultures

Taarab tunesmith: Abdullah Mussa Ahmed in Uganda in the 1960s with musicians from Tanzania and his first kanoon

and the 'international' language of the urban people. Among the true, coastal dwelling Swahili the crossover point, where the music links ancient custom and modern behaviour, is taarab, a cultural accompaniment right down the East African coast, and as far inland as Burundi. Derived from the word *tarabu,* the name of a type of drum, the music is played by orchestras with as many as 30 or more musicians accompanying a solo singer on a variety of instruments including drums, tambourines, violins, cello, double bass, oud, zither, accordion, organ or harmonium, flutes and recorders. The three line verses in classic Swahili are invariably love songs around which the great interpreters improvise endlessly, and taarab music is played traditionally at weddings and other large family or social gatherings.

The non-classical, everyday Swahili, spoken far inland, is also a vehicle for many musical idioms aimed at a wide audience, just as Lingala and pidgin have been used to spread music's message in Central and West Africa. It has never made such a general crossover, however, and no Swahili bands have broken out of East Africa to the same extent as musicians from other parts of the continent. But there have been at least two all-time classic pan-African songs in Kiswahili, which have become standards, notably *Malaika, Shauru Yako* and *Hulele Hulele,* a version of which made the UK Top 20 in 1968. Swahili guitar bands had their heyday in Kenya in the late Sixties and Seventies, since when the music lost much of its momentum. Several bands, such as Simba Wanyika who began the 1990s with a tour of Europe, have survived, while others have been revived.

Akamba acrobatic dancers perform at Uhuru Park, Nairobi

Since colonial days there has always been more freedom of movement within this region than in any other part of Africa. Nairobi is the hub of East Africa's music industry, and musicians from the neighbouring countries have tended to gravitate there. The traditional music of the inland peoples was predictably rich, with stringed instruments such as lyres and fiddles being used by minstrel style players, accompanied by drums and percussion. The main ethnic groups in Kenya, the Luo and Kikuyu, had also acquired a nineteenth-century taste for accordion playing, and there were clearly defined markets for vernacular music in their regional homelands in Kenya and Uganda.

The first murmurings of a more general, non-ethnic pop music came in the early Fifties from Lubumbashi in eastern Zaire, where guitarists Jean Bosco Mwenda and Edouard Masengo were popularising the Katanga sound, with vocals in Kiswahili. They inspired the first generation of Kenyan guitar pickers such as Fundi Konde, Fadhili Williams, David Amunga and Daudi Kabaka, who played in a style known as the 'twist'.

By the end of the Sixties the region also had a proliferation of local soul bands including the Ashantis, the Hodi Boys and Air Fiesta Matata, led by 'Jodi' and Steel Beautah who used the *nyatiti* lute as a lead instrument on the soul number, *What's that Sound?* The group won a competition to record in Britain, but they split up in London leaving some members behind where they worked under the name Matata. Slim Ali and the Hodi Boys maintained their soul fusion in a different milieu from the bar or dancehall bands who sang in local languages. Slim, who comes from Mombasa, grew up with a taste for soul with an Arabic inflexion which opened the way for tours of North Africa and the Middle East. His crossover sound earned a silver disc in 1977 and in the Eighties he notched up a series of consecutive hits.

A second wave of Zairean music in the Seventies affected the regional idioms once again. This time it was the 'Lingala' music of

Luo roots: Ogwang Lelo Okoth with nyatiti five-string lyre and Paddy J Onono, bass, accompanied by their 'minder'

Kinshasa, which had been 'developed' much further than any other pop form on the continent. In the electric age the Zairean guitar sound was considered essential for any kind of dance band. Lingala music not only had a winning formula of inter-locking guitars, lazy rumba rhythms and peaks of euphoria, but as it had no ethnic affiliation it appealed to the whole population. By the early 1980s the Kenyan government had set up a Presidential Music Commission to find ways of protecting their country's music from this foreign infiltration. For a while the Swahili radio service could only play Swahili music, inspiring many direct imitations which simply transposed the original Lingala with Kiswahili lyrics and melody lines, while trying to retain the 'exotic' element.

Nairobi-based bands like Orchestra Virunga and Les Mange-lepas, which were led by Zaireans, were refused permission to renew their work permits. But the plan backfired. One of the first effects was to boost piracy of music direct from Zaire, while also sending the dance band scene into recession. Discos became more popular than live bands and a cycle of diminishing returns caused a slump in the music business. To this day 'domestic' music, whether sung in Lingala, Kiswahili or 'vernaculars', is struggling. The biggest record sellers among African artistes either come through the Kinshasa-Paris pipeline like Pepe Kalle, or from South Africa like Yvonne Chaka Chaka. Compilations by the late Franco Luambo Makiadi probably sell more in total than any other musician's.

The Colonial Context

The study, manufacture and distribution of East African music has a long history. The first field recordings ever made were done in German East Africa in 1902, only a few years after the British had begun to settle 'their' territories. Most openings for business throughout East Africa had been sewn up by Asian traders by the beginning of this century, and Indian rupees were actually used as currency in Kenya until the end of World War One. By the 1920s these traders were playing music in the form of 78 rpm records, to attract business to their shops, where the new-fangled gramophones were also on sale. The choice included much Asian as well as European and American music, to suit the tastes of the shopkeepers themselves and their prime customers, the British planters. There were no African records available at first but there were enough connections between the early taarab singers and Asian music for someone to identify the potential market among African listeners. There were no recording facilities in East Africa, and the first indigenous musicians to go into a studio were invited to Bombay in 1928, to record for the Indian branch of the British HMV label. The pioneer recording artiste was a young woman, Siti binti Saad, a taarab singer from Zanzibar who became hugely popular throughout the Kiswahili speaking territory, as far as Zaire. Soon after, both HMV and Columbia opened studios of their own in Zanzibar, and Odeon established one in Uganda. By the 1940s dozens of taarab musicians had been recorded, among them two singers of classic taarab whose names are still revered, Maludi, and Musa Maruf.

Popular music also sprang from those people whose traditional culture remained unaffected by the Islamic influence. Any social dance music based on drumming became known as *ngoma* after the word for drum, common to many Bantu languages. There were also popular styles known generically as *dansi* (dance) music, which established the basic group line-up of guitar, mandolin or banjo with percussion accompaniment. Dansi music came in all the local dialects. Early star guitarists were Ally Sykes, Fundi Konde, Peter K. Bernard and Obondo Mugati. One of the first inter-ethnic musical idioms was *beni* associated with marching drum bands. When topical social commentary was added this evolved into a precursor of Swahili guitar band music.

In 1947 the Jambo studio opened in Nairobi. Five years later, under the name of East African Records, its function was changed for use as a pressing plant, but in 1955 it was re-opened as a studio with new equipment. Radio had been introduced to East Africa in 1927 with the opening of the East African Broadcasting Service. This was almost exclusively a service for the White settlers, with little time given to programmes in vernacular languages. During the Fifties, however, the service was expanded with community loudspeakers set up in strategic public places and speaker vans which toured the rural areas. At the same time the African content of the programming was increased. In 1959 the station was taken over as a commercial service and renamed Kenya Broadcasting Service. KBS now offered three services aimed at Europeans, Asians and Africans.

During the late 1950s and early Sixties several top guitarists from Katanga in eastern Zaire moved into Nairobi, endorsing those local musicians who had already begun to emulate their picking styles. Jean Bosco Mwenda, Edouard Masengo and Abelo were the most influential, hosting commercially sponsored radio shows from the city, and along with the Zimbabwean George Sibanda they helped inspire the first generation of Kenyan pop music stars such as John Mwale, George Mukabi and Isaya Mwinamo. The production of 78rpm records was wound down at the start of the Sixties, and in 1963 the South African owned Gallo

Ikwhani Safaa, from Zanzibar: typical line up of a large taarab orchestra

161

company started producing the new 7-inch 45s. Competition came from AGS records and the Equator label with its house band, the Equator Sound Band, and recording artistes Daudi Kabaka, Fadhili Williams, Nasil Pichen Kazembe and Peter Totsi. Many of these musicians were effectively restricted to the studio. Instruments were the property of the recording companies and there was, therefore, no means of pursuing live work. The introduction of jukeboxes made many musicians famous, although few people had ever seen them play. Even today the discrepancy between recording musicians and working dance bands is notable.

The Taarab Tradition

Taarab music has maintained a greater cohesion than other regional styles because it is an essential element of the social life of the coastal Swahili. It is played primarily at weddings, which are massive affairs lasting up to a week, involving hundreds of guests and often spreading out into the street. Although taarab has a function in the general community, it is primarily a women's music, which in the wedding context has an educational role as brides are initiated into the ways of marriage, often these days being advised how to stand up to a husband as much as how to please him. Before the marriage ceremony women dance *vugo* or *chakacha* to drums and percussion, improvising often crude, explicit lyrics. The only men permitted at these evenings are the musicians, although in modern times the sexual taboos are not always strictly enforced. The equivalent men's celebrations are lower-key events, and 'women's taarab' is the most vital form. After the marriage ceremony, the bride sits in state under a decorative tent, while the respective families gather for the real event which means dancing through the night to an improvised repertoire which blends ngoma (drum) dance music with Swahili poetry and Indian movie songs.

Taarab origins have been traced back to Lamu, the ancient

Bandleader Zein L'Abdin Ahmed Alamoody at home in Mombasa

capital of Swahili culture where, in the nineteenth century, the music grew from a combination of *gungu* and *kinanda* dance rhythms enhanced with lyric poetry. One of the earliest documented heroes was Kijuma, a dancer and oud player, who set sail from Lamu in the early 1900s, at the request of the Sultan of Zanzibar, to form an orchestra on the Spice island.

After the decline of Lamu, Mombasa became the main centre of Swahili culture and connections have been noted between the Mombasa style and the Indian lyric form of *ghazal*. Before World War One, Mombasa taarab was championed by Mbaruku, a blind singer and oud player, and its popularity increased during the Twenties and Thirties. In 1931, the band leader Tishi recorded with his taarab group in Marseille for the French Pathe label, and the Odeon company was soon inspired to open a recording studio in Mombasa. The Jauharah Orchestra and Morning Star Orchestra were popular dance bands while, during the Thirties, women singers were the most successful recording artistes. The oud player, Seyyid Ali Baskuta, was one of the seminal figures to arrive in Mombasa from Lamu, as the old Swahili cultural centre was deserted by its musicians.

Siti binti Saad: early taarab superstar, first recorded in Bombay in 1928

As a primarily sea-borne music, Taarab has cultural connections which stretch as far as the Gulf and Asia. The style of vocal expression has been influenced by Indian film music, notably in the delivery of Mohamed Yassin. The music is also closely related to Egyptian forms, particularly the *firquah* orchestras which had an influence on the pioneers of the modernised music of the Thirties and Forties. Singers such as Matano Juma and Zein L'Abdin remained true to original Swahili styles, although there is also a distinction between the 'men's taarab' played by Zein and the more popular 'women's taarab', of Matano and Maulidi, also known as 'Taarab ya Kiswahili'. The form of the dancing which taarab accompanies has links with Arab styles, while a reverse influence has been noted in African-inflected dances of Kuwait. Overland contacts have seen taarab infiltrate as far west as Burundi, where it has been preserved and adapted by people transplanted from Tanga in Tanzania. Some enthusiasts believe the Burundi form to be amongst the 'best taarab in the world'.

In Tanzania women have been more socially liberated than in the more strictly Muslim areas to the north. They were able to sing and perform in public, which would have been prohibited further north. Even in Mombasa, however, women can lose their inhibitions when the chakacha is played, as described by musician Tony Rusteau, on a 1977 BBC television programme about Kenyan music, *Sweet Sound of Honey.* "I like traditional music very much because where I was born you know, there was lots of Swahilis around and the Swahili people they dance the chakacha. Someone is getting married or there is some kind of celebration, then they play this chakacha. It's done mostly by ladies, you know, when they go in circles shaking themselves and singing and at the same time maybe they have a drummer who's drumming and giving a verse. And then the women give the chorus and dancing. There's a lot of body movement in it. You shake your hips very much and usually everybody gets turned on by looking at the best dancer. One girl will curve herself up in such a shape and she'll move so nice, you know. Everybody gets attracted, even the women who are dancing at the time. Really, you know, they put their eyes on that one girl. It's very sexy, it's very nice." Coastal 'tourist' bands have recently updated chakacha music, and one of the pioneers, the keyboardist Chuli, who has since died, had a big regional hit with *Bembe Ya Mtoto.*

Regional Pop Roots

While few East African bands or performers have found fame outside the region, the Kiswahili language was a vehicle for one of the continent's most celebrated ballads. The love song *Malaika*, has been recorded by dozens of artistes, including the doyenne of African music, Miriam Makeba, who brought this romantic song to a global audience. Since Makeba made such a huge hit of it, the song's authorship became a matter of controversy, never satisfactorily resolved. The man who stepped in to claim the credit was the Kenyan, Fadhili Williams, who in the Fifties was a session guitarist and studio assistant with East African Records. "I was only seventeen at the time and the girl looked like an angel to me," Williams later told the BBC. "That's why I named her Malaika, in English it's an 'angel'. I was competing with a certain tycoon, you know the guy was earning a lot of money. And I said, 'Can I get married to you?' She said 'Yes, of course you can, provided you can pay the dowry to my father, there's no problem.' You know the guy who pays the money takes the girl. And so with that I had to lose her. She was married to that tycoon. After that I sat about trying to compose a song. So that she remembers me maybe. So that through the radio, she hears it. Something like this."

The song became the biggest selling record in East Africa during the Sixties. It was recorded at least twice by Williams, and the second recording made in 1963 is the version picked up by

Island of Spice and Taarab

The 'spice island' of Zanzibar, off the coast of Dar es Salaam, was ruled in the early years of this century by the Sultan of Oman. It later became a British protectorate, although as the islanders proudly insist, never a colony. When the British left in 1964 there was a strong movement for 'Africanisation' to prevent Arab domination. There was a thriving 'African quarter' called Stonetown, which is now crumbling but still full of slowly fading memories.

By the 1950s full-sized orchestras were common throughout the city. The top bands were Ikwhani Safaa, (seen, right, in rehearsal), renamed the Malindi Band on government advice following the 1964 revolution, and Culture Musical Club, set up by the government at the same time. Since then these two bands have had a virtual duopoly of the local music business, although there are others struggling in their shadow.

A typical Zanzibar band will include as many as ten singers, with oud, electric guitar, organ, accordion, cello, double bass, flutes and a variety of percussion and drums. Lesser bands

have often done away with the Arab instruments because, ironically, they are too expensive, and have settled for the more familiar line-up of electric guitar, bass, organ and accordion. This is more feasible in Zanzibar than other taarab centres because their music has stronger links with African rhythms and fewer similarities with Asian or Arabic idioms.

Unique to Zanzibar are the many women who have formed their own musical 'clubs', and who employ male musicians to accompany them. The influence of Siti binti Saad, the original taarab recording artiste, has lingered from the late Twenties until today. And now some women of the Sahib el Arry band have taken up instruments themselves. The women's groups have grown out of militaristic marching bands, with names such as the Navy band and Royal Air Force band, which still exist.

During the 1950s the performances of these bands, in which massed ranks of women marched and sang through the streets, became highly competitive. One group hired a boat to leave the island, simply to make a triumphal homecoming on the beach from where they marched through the town. Not to be outdone another competing band took off in an airplane so as to make an even grander re-entry.

As the women tried to outdo each other, the craze reached dangerous levels of enthusiasm with violence breaking out at meetings, until the government founded a unified national orchestra which brought together women from different bands.

Guitar paradise: record featuring Swahili and 'vernacular' dance music, cover painting by Zembi Oteno

Miriam Makeba, and covered by bands all across Africa. Williams, however, received a pittance in royalties. Another claim of authorship came from Lucas Tutu of Mombasa and later a Tanzanian named Adam Salim claimed he had composed the song in 1946 while playing in Nairobi, and that Williams had briefly played mandolin with his trio. Another musician called 'Charo' also claimed credit. The Danish researcher Flemming Harrev has discovered that there was an earlier version of the song with a light calypso beat, recorded around 1950 but, he points out, nobody knew or cared much about copyright at the time and it was the Williams version which 'made' the song if he did not actually compose it.

By the end of the Fifties the infant music business had begun to establish itself with Nairobi as its centre. In addition to recording facilities there were openings for musicians on radio, although the best of the commercially-sponsored spots went to Congolese, notably the Coca-Cola show hosted by Edouard Masengo, and the Aspro show with Jean Bosco Mwenda, who arrived in Nairobi in 1959. There was also a programme sponsored by the East African Railways and Harbours' company, called 'Showboat' which featured the Jambo Boys, led by Fadhili Williams, with Masengo and others, and three-minute musical commercials for luxury consumables like cigarettes and beer.

Kenya's main record label, AIT, started pressing discs at the end of the Sixties. "The industry was much more buoyant then," said the chairman, Ron Andrews, twenty years later. "The emphasis has changed from it being a rural market to an urban one. But there is still an unbelievable number of record labels in the country. You can record a single for £15, a one-take thing that can be wrapped up in an hour and then pressed up in an edition of 350 copies." Although there are adequate studios and dozens of bands making, or seeking to make records, the pop music scene is still dominated by 45rpm singles. Few artistes have had the means to record albums and those which have appeared on the market are usually collections of recent hit singles.

Swahili guitar band music, which reached its peak in the 1960s and 1970s, was a promising combination of elements of indigenous folk styles with Katangan guitar picking and South African kwela ingredients, via the Nyasa sound from Malawi. Bosco and Masengo had inspired dozens of imitators, although many insisted they simply played their 'own' local variation of the regional style. Ben Blastus was one local guitarist who earned a measure of fame from his interpretation of the 'Congolese' idiom. One of the favourite and most famous of the early guitarists who took after Masengo was George Mukabi, who met an early and grisly death at the hands of a girlfriend. He was probably the first to find national fame singing in a local voice. Mukabi initiated the *esukuti* rhythm, named after a Luyia traditional drum and the music associated with it.

Esukuti music was the first idiom to feature guitars, which were unfamiliar to most people in the interior until after World War Two, when returning soldiers gatecrashed the social folk music scene. The *omutibo* music of the elders eventually assimilated the new music, rather than the other way around and, refreshed by a guitar and a ringing Fanta bottle, several small groups began semi-professional careers. Mukabi, who started recording for AGS records in 1956, really popularised that rhythm which was incorporated into electric music, becoming one of the strands of benga. Benga is often considered a Luo music but Kikuyu and Luyia people also play their own benga.

The sound of the electric guitar was originally heard in the 1950s, played by Fundi Konde, reputed to have been the first to play an amplified instrument in the East African bars and dance halls. Instruments were generally owned by the studios and musicians were rarely allowed to take them away, a practice which has restricted the development of live music until today. Equator Records became the main outlet for Swahili guitar music and in the Sixties Diploma recorded the first bands to use two guitars, starting with the Luyia duo of Shem Tube and Justo Osala Omufila, who persevered with acoustic guitars until they electrified in the early 1970s. They recorded under the names Bunyore and Mwilonje Jazz but never played live.

Swahili music was hugely popular throughout the Sixties but during the 1970s its popularity faded as the country's pop music began to suffer in the face of imported records, from both the Western countries and from Zaire. Few bands have survived from that generation although the Maroon Commandos and Morogoro Jazz Band were working into the 1990s. Maroon Commandos was founded as a military band by guitarist Habel Kifoto in 1970. His early recordings for Phonogram included the 1971 hit, *Emily* but the band's progress was cut short tragically in 1972, when their bus was involved in a road accident and several musicians were killed. The Commandos re-formed later and consolidated their position through the Eighties.

There was always fluid movement of musicians throughout the East African region with established artistes and ambitious hopefuls coming to Nairobi from all the neighbouring countries to record and tour. The great Tanzanian bandleader Mbaraka Mwinshehe, who died in a car crash in Kenya, was one of the busiest musical travellers with Super Volcanoes, and other bands including Mlimani Park, Maquis Original, Vijana Jazz, Safari Sound International, Issa Juma, Orchestra Makassy and Super Mazembe, moved regularly between Kenya and Tanzania.

Tanzania, where tribalism was virtually eradicated in the post-independence *Ujamaa* (Togetherness) programme, has a more cohesive musical culture than Kenya, but a comparatively undeveloped music industry. Tanzanian pop-rumba has a bigger, more mature sound than Kenyan music, profiting from the availability of musicians and instruments and the advantages of playing regular live gigs. Dar es Salaam is one of the more active live music scenes for both local and Zairean bands. Throughout the Eighties

Regional favourite: Samba Mapangala, singer and leader of Orchestre Virunga

bands such as Orchestra Safari Sound led by Fred Kasheba, Remi Ongala's Super Matimila, Makassy, Maquis and Dar International were playing almost every night in clubs and dancing bars. The bands, which feature large horn sections, are usually much bigger than the Kenyan counterparts. Many Tanzanian groups are sponsored or employed by large national companies, enabling them to maintain up to twenty musicians.

The man who did most to transpose Zairean rumba from Lingala to Kiswahili and transmit it through the region, was Mbaraka Mwinshehe, leader of the Super Volcanoes. Known as the 'Franco of East Africa' Mwinshehe could play a passable pastiche of the big man's guitar, with a more 'wobbly' overall sound and horn parts similar in feeling to Verckys'. Mbaraka was killed in 1979 in an accident on the Mombasa-Malimbi road, but his music has survived into the 1990s, with pirate cassettes of some of his greatest hits among the hottest sellers in Dar es Salaam. The music has undeniable Congolese origins, but the language gives it a different inflexion. Among the newer bands, Bicco Stars play in a more contemporary style imitating the accents of 'new-wave' Kinshasa groups of the Zaiko family.

The top spot among Swahili outfits has been occupied over the past two decades by Simba Wanyika, led by the singing/guitar playing Kinyonga brothers, Wilson Peter and George Peter. Originally from the western Tanzania region of Tanga, the brothers started with the Jamhuri Jazz Band, before establishing the Arusha Jazz band. They travelled to Kenya in 1972, working in

Benga man: Daniel Owino Misiani,
leader of the celebrated Shirati Jazz

KENYA'S HOTTEST SOUND

Mombasa, where the name of the group was changed to Simba
Wanyika, meaning 'Lions of the Savannah'. Three years later in
Nairobi they found success recording mostly Wilson Peter's
compositions for Phonogram. In 1978 the band split in two, with
Omari Shabani forming Les Wanyikas. Other spin-offs at the end
of the Seventies were Super Wanyika Stars led by Issa Juma and
Orchestre Jobiso, set up by George Peter as a recording outlet for
his own material. In 1982 the Tanzanian government sponsored
the originals on a tour of the country after which they travelled to
Mozambique and Zimbabwe. The band survived through the
difficult years of the late 1980s and finally reached Europe in
1990, where their relaxed handling of steamy dance music showed
up the differences between an authentic working dance band and
the nervous, sometimes star-struck approach of many less experienced performers.

The Benga Beat

Benga missed out on the big chance in 1970 when stories
began to circulate that Amercian soul artiste James Brown had
'lifted' the benga beat for his hit record *Sex Machine.* Benga is the
bass-heavy, up-tempo guitar pop originally associated with the
Luo people, the second largest ethnic group in Kenya, but the
ones who have made the most noise on the music scene. Their
homeland is around the eastern shores of Lake Victoria, in Nyanza
province, where the main city is Kisumu.

Other language groups also use the term benga now, and there
is Kikuyu and Luyia benga, often played by inter-ethnic groups
which sometimes use Luo guitarists, although each has its own
identity set by the tone of the language. Benga was created in the
late 1960s as a response to the dominant Congolese music. The
guitarist George Ramogi is credited with creating the style as a
fusion of his own people's traditional dance rhythms and group
singing, with the earlier Katangan acoustic guitar style and
echoes the *nyatiti* traditional eight-string lyre. When Congolese
music was banned on the Voice of Kenya radio station, the newly-
electrified benga shot to prominence. The musician who success-

fully rode most of the early benga boom was Owino Misiani, founder of Shirati Jazz, the group which helped benga break out of the Luo community to a wider audience. Running close in popularity were the Victoria Sea Kings later known as Victoria Jazz, with two guitarists 'Dr' Ochieng Nelly and 'Dr' Collela Maze fronting the show.

By the late 1970s there was a thriving market for benga. The Luo producer and distributor Oluach Kanindo, who had a chain of record shops throughout the area, would fly in thousands of singles each week from Nairobi, selling more than he would have done in the capital. He was also filling export orders for records by groups such as Shirati and Victoria Jazz in Zambia, Madagascar and even as far afield as the anglophone countries of West Africa. Much benga was also released in West Africa on licence by the French Pathe label, who capitalised on similarities between Ibo guitar highlife and bands like Gabriel Omollo's Apollo Komesha. Kanindo reckoned to record a complete album in a Nairobi studio in one day and have the finished product on sale throughout his network of shops two days later. For a while benga became the dominant beat of the city, pouring out of the 'studio' shacks in the River Road area of Nairobi, like a flood. But to put on profitable live shows in the capital was out of the question and the music's base remained in the west of the country.

More recently, as benga slipped from popularity, the traditional sound of the nyatiti has made a surprising comeback, although the music played has been modified for its new audience in the bars and dancehalls, and by the 1990s nyatiti recordings were outselling benga discs. The top-selling nyatiti recording artiste is Ogwang Lelo Okoth, who began playing professionally in 1954, and whose career has found a late reprieve in the Nineties. He helped develop the music from its role at social gatherings where elders drink home brewed (maize) beer, to a more up-front sound to animate the rowdier drinking and dancing in local bars. For this a smaller instrument with a more penetrative sound is preferred. The nyatiti is often accompanied by the *orutu,* a one-string fiddle of fairly recent origin, popularised by Kapere Jazz, a band formed in 1986 to revive folk traditions.

The Seventies revival of vernacular music spearheaded by benga quickly led to a mix up of musicians and styles, and a form of Swahili benga was popularised by the Luo band, Sega Matata. The Kilimambogo Brothers were also going strong until the leader, Kakai Kilonzo, died in 1990. A Kamba man who sang in Kiswahili, Kilonzo's music crossed over cultural boundaries. Other popular Kamba artistes are Peter Muambi, the Ngolemi Brothers and the Kalamba Boys.

The Kikuyu people have made less of a mark than Luo or Luyia musicians, although they do have star artistes, such as Joseph Kamaru, Francis Rugwati 'The Kenyan Cowboy' and 'Councillor D.K.' Daniel Kamau. Joseph Kamaru, who started recording in the mid-1960s is one of the few vernacular musicians to have established a national reputation outside his own ethnic group, delivering moral and romantic lyrics against a blend of Kikuyu rumba. Kamaru has faith in the quality and originality of his music which he claims has been held back by the shortage of instruments and equipment. Since the mid-1980s he has been reviving and revitalising folklore material from the previous generation, making contemporary hits out of long forgotten songs, including traditional circumcision music which he only slightly 'modernised'.

'Councillor' D.K. Kamau is a guitarist and singer/songwriter who has also maintained contact with his Kikuyu culture, regu-

Roots revival: Kapere Jazz combined one-string fiddle and low-tech percussion in the mid-1980s

larly conferring with the elders of his home village just outside Nairobi and composing songs around their wisdom. Ever since he wangled his way on to a radio show as a teenager to perform his own composition, D.K. has promoted himself and made the music business work for him. He became owner of a bar, two music shops, a couple of farms and other businesses. His level of success is rare, however, and most 'vernacular' musicians are associated with the poorer, working class people who make up the bulk of their audience.

For the Love of Lingala

The main reason for the decline of Swahili and vernacular idioms since the 1970s has been the domination of Zairean (or Lingala) rumba, which flavoured all forms of musical expression including taarab. The influx of Zairean nationals included several competent bands, such as Les Noirs, who could fill the dance floors at the expense of Swahili or benga music, which was often looked down on by the younger, more Westernised customers. Among the first bandleaders to find success in Kenya were Baba Gaston, who settled there in the early 1960s, and Nguashi Timbo whose greatest claim to fame was producing, and not playing on, the all-time classic Kiswahili song *Shauru Yako*. The bulk of their songs were in Lingala, contrasting with the 1950s Katangan guitarists, who had popularised Kiswahili Congolese music before the Lingala variant took such a strong hold.

Baba Gaston, who opened up the country to Lingala music in the 1960s, is often considered one of the 'godfathers' of Kenyan pop. "In Africa you can say that 80 per cent of Africans have got their own music, but when we play the Zairean music it is more exciting than other music", said Gaston on BBC television. Born in 1936 near Lubumbashi, Baba Ilunga Wa Ilunga picked up his early musical training from a Greek pianist, Leonides Rapitis. At the age of twenty he formed the Baba National Orchestra, which he took on an extended tour through Zambia, Zimbabwe and several European countries before settling in Kenya.

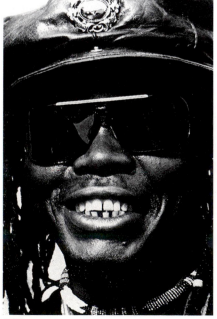

Remmy Ongala: leader of Tanzanian rumba band, Super Matimila

Gaston had a wide-ranging influence on Kenya's music. He once proudly claimed he had played with more than 700 musicians and that his band was a virtual training school. There was another side to the statistic, however, as Hanz Kinzl, manager of Phonogram, the second biggest label in Kenya, spelt out on the same television programme. "Baba is rather an extraordinary person. He has this fatherly image on him, and I think it's quite genuine. In Africa you're wealthy if you have a big stomach. If you can show that you're a big man then you are also regarded as a rich man and an important personality. Which means that he takes the majority of whatever income his music provides him with, to the dissatisfaction of the band members. Consequently there is hardly any band in Nairobi and in Kenya, which has broken up as often as Baba's."

Typical of the East African variant of Zairean rumba is the music of Les Mangalepas, led by Bwamy Walumona, a guitarist and singer from the Kivu region of Zaire, who arrived in Kenya to play with Gaston in 1975. After about a year Bwamy and several band members seceded from the Gaston band and set up Les Mangalepas, which went on to become one of Kenya's favourite dance outfits. In 1978 they earned a gold disc for sales of Bwamy's composition *Nyako Konya*, following which the composer briefly quit the band to play with Viva Makale, although he returned soon after. In the late Eighties, however, Bwamy turned to gospel music and Les Mangalepas appeared to be finished. At the start of the Nineties the band was revived in Harare, Zimbabwe, with new personnel playing songs with English lyrics.

Among the most prolific bands competing for the profits during the early Eighties were Orchestra Super Lovy, Mose Fan Fan's T.P Somo Somo, Orchestre Zaiken, Shika Shika and Vundumuna, the last two featuring guitarist and singer Tabu Frantal who also ran Boma Liwanza during the 1970s. Visiting Zaireans included Sam Mangwana, who charmed his way through the country in the mid-1980s and recorded *In Nairobi* with local musicians. Franco's OK Jazz and Tabu Ley's Afrisa found Kenya to be one of the best markets and both toured several times.

Super Mazembe: one of the top regional rumba groups through the 1980s

Super Mazembe, also regional champions of Lingala music, originally came together in Zaire in 1967 under the name Orchestre Super Vox before emigrating east, settling first in Zambia, then Tanzania and Kenya, where they recorded a string of dance hits during the Seventies, sometimes backing the late Nasil Pitchen Kazembe. They lost their momentum during the Eighties but in 1990 a perceptive businessman relaunched the band, who had been lying dormant in Mombasa, with new equipment, a promotion budget and several international tours.

Orchestra Virunga has proved to be one of Kenya's most enduring Lingala bands, with a hit record, *Malako Disco*, that has earned a reputation abroad as a minor classic. The band's front man, Samba Mapangala grew up in Zaire, where he started singing at the age of thirteen in Super Tukina, followed by a spell in Super Bella. But Samba did not flourish in the new rumba milieu and he joined the eastbound flow of musical talent. It was not a smooth ride. While touring in Uganda in 1979 with Les Kinois the band's bus was machine-gunned by police at a road block. Samba was uninjured but the keyboard player who later joined Les Mangalepas was paralysed below the waist.

Samba persevered and set up in Nairobi with Orchestra Virunga, named after the volcanic mountain in northeastern Zaire. *Malako Disco* proved to be one of those freak hits which typecast the band, setting a high standard for them to maintain. Despite the work permit problems in Kenya which slowed their progress in the late 1980s, they broke out of the dwindling East African market in 1991 with a tour of Europe and a bigger full-blown sound.

The capital city of the region's music industry, Nairobi, is no longer as productive as it was twenty years ago. But throughout East Africa musicians strive to keep their art alive and up to date. In the Eighties a rock crossover hybrid was created by bands like Makonde and OK Jive, with (Bavon) Wayne Barnes and Zembi Oteno and Bonny Wanda. The reggae-benga-funk amalgam of bands like Them Mushrooms maintains the regional rock tradition while struggling to keep pace with technology. There is also a minor resurgence in traditional music. Positive noises have been heard coming out of Uganda since the start of the Nineties, with a boom in recording and cassette distribution of local musicians. Following the path opened up by Sammy Kasule a generation ago and, more recently, the late Filly Bbongole Lutayaa, other artistes such as Daniel Lule, Joseph Nsubuga and Geoffrey Oreyma have successfully tapped overseas connections. Oreyma, who arrived in Britain via France, went straight for the mainstream market with his first crossover album. The fact that such a move is even a possibility should inspire some serious creative effort back home. Whatever the rest of the world is ready for, East African music needs a taste of international glory to re-inspire confidence.

Liberation Music

Zimbabwe was one of the last African countries to achieve self-government which came in 1980, and it was inevitably a late entry to the field of African popular music. The sound of Zimbabwe caught the international ear almost simultaneously with independence, and was greeted in the West as a radical voice of liberation. The result of the struggle had been a victory for Africans over the White man, and for the younger generation it was proof that 'rebels' could be effective. As a socialist/Marxist victory the country's triumph was shared by a whole spectrum of genuine and pseudo radicals. Thomas Mapfumo was the spearhead of the music and his revolutionary credentials were used to promote Zimbabwean culture. International audiences knew he was a rebel when he turned out on his first overseas tour wearing dreadlocks and sporting the rasta's red, gold and green (the pan-African colours chosen for Zimbabwe's national flag).

Zimbabwe was the final stronghold of White settlers north of the Limpopo river. As Southern Rhodesia it was the last remnant of the old Federation of Rhodesia and Nyasaland, formed by the British in 1953 to link the territories which are now Zimbabwe, Zambia and Malawi. The Federation was disbanded in 1963 and Zambia achieved independence the following year, since when the country adopted a high profile in the struggle against colonialism. Malawi became self-governing at the same time. But Ian Smith, the prime minister of Southern Rhodesia, refused to consider majority rule and in 1964 he made his infamous Unilateral Declaration of Independence (UDI), which was intended to keep the country under the rule of the White minority and to block the two political parties, Robert Mugabe's ZANU and Joshua Nkomo's ZAPU.

With the country's cultural development hindered by the long struggle for independence, the connections between a once-repressed traditional form and urban social music are still being actively explored. As elsewhere in Africa, Zimbabwe had a strong cultural heritage, and was not short of traditional or folklore music, but it had a rougher ride to survival than in many other countries. The British who colonised and settled the territory in the late nineteenth century quickly established religious missions and schools and began to impose their own alien values. The fact that much African music had a spiritual and mystical function encouraged the religious bodies to try to suppress it. As an accompaniment to 'pagan' beliefs, music was condemned, along with other 'barbaric' traditional customs. Later, the Church did show more tolerance of African methods of expression and from the early twentieth century *mbira* and other traditional instruments were sometimes to be found in use during Christian worship.

Civilisation in Zimbabwe has a long and respected history, with the ancient fortress city of Great Zimbabwe, reckoned to have been built around 1100 AD, acknowledged as one of the wonders of Africa. The predominant ethnic group are the Shona, who make up some 70 per cent of the population, and who also live in neighbouring Mozambique and Zambia. Historically they have used many instruments in their traditional music including panpipes, harps, drums and percussion instruments. But the sound of their sophisticated mbira thumb piano, which links ancient custom and contemporary pop, has come to the fore as the national music of Zimbabwe.

Thomas Mapfumo: introduced his country's mbira music to the West

CHAPTER NINE

Hotel musicians rehearse on
xylophones in the shade beside
Victoria Falls

The other main ethnic group, the Ndebele, who account for less than one third of the population, live in the southern regions. A sub-group of the Zulu nation, the Ndebele arrived in Zimbabwe as recently as the nineteenth century. As with the Zulus, the Ndebele use fewer traditional instruments, and their popular music has evolved with Western technology. South African music was always popular throughout the region and the early recordings of *kwela* music, played on guitar and penny whistle, caught the imagination. One of the handful of kwela hits which became internationally known in the 1950s was *Skokiaan,* originally recorded by the Bulawayo Cold Storage Band and later covered, along with *Wimoweh,* by countless light entertainment orchestras in the West. The South African connection was kept open by Dorothy Masuka, later Zimbabwe's 'First Lady of Song', who learned her craft performing in variety shows in Johannesburg. These days the relationship is more one-way. With South African pop artistes and reggae musicians direct from Jamaica enticing Zimbabwean ravers, the country's new-found indigenous pop has a hard road ahead.

Birth of a Nation's Music

The foundations of a popular music culture were laid with the opening of the colonially run national radio station. During the days of the Federation, the network was split, with Southern Rhodesian Broadcasting aimed at the Whites, and the African service transmitted from Lusaka. In the early 1950s the Rhodesian Broadcasting Service toured the regions with a mobile one-track recording studio installed in a small truck. The recordists would arrive unannounced in rural locations and tape whatever traditional ensembles they could find. If selected for broadcast on the fledgling African Service radio, musicians were paid one penny per number. The movement of people into the cities which began during the mid-1950s created another outlet for musicians who took to busking on the streets of the larger cities, Harare (then Salisbury) and Bulawayo. The most popular instruments for busking were the guitar and banjo, brought in from the south by traders along with the penny whistles already being played by South African youths with an inspired fervour. Usually accompa-

nied by a *hosho* calabash shaker, these buskers soon spread from the street corners into the bars and restaurants. As in South Africa this local music became known as *marabi*.

Until the arrival of the African Service, the only music available locally on either radio or disc in the pre-pop era of the Fifties was dependent on the very British tastes of the White colonialists. The old BBC Light Programme set the style and the bulk of their output was staid ballroom dance music, with a smattering of early pop, jazz and country standards. As in other anglophone countries the American country crooner Jim Reeves achieved unprecedented popularity which lasted for more than a decade. When the more radical, and relevant sounds of rock and roll, soul and Liverpool pop began to filter through during the Sixties they found their place on the airwaves, and in the hopes of local musicians who tried to follow this exciting new trend.

One of the major successes was achieved by the US soul singer Percy Sledge with his romantic anthem *When a Man Loves a Woman.* Sledge toured the region during the late 1960s appealing equally to Whites and Blacks. Not surprisingly the Beatles were

Mbira, Voice of the Spirits

Although types of mbira can be found throughout Africa, the instrument is probably most developed in Zimbabwe where it has been the vital link between traditional and popular culture. To the Shona people the mbira also has a specific relationship with ancestral spirits and it plays a central role in the bira religious ceremony, when musicians are obliged to play through the night, often sustaining cuts and blisters to their fingers as they maintain the energy level.

Since Zimbabwe's independence the mbira has gained a special significance in the country's culture. During the colonial period public performance of mbira had been suppressed, driving it underground, but following the inspiration of Mapfumo the name is now used as much to identify the electric pop as the traditional music of Zimbabwe. What the groups create with a line-up of electric guitars, bass and drum kit is an amplified version of the music played on a single mbira by such a master as Ephat Mujuru.

Mujuru, a professor at Zimbabwe College of Music in Harare, has been responsible for a surge of international interest in the mbira. In the late 1970s he collaborated with Paul Berliner, whose book The Soul of Mbira *is the definitive work on*

the subject, and he has since visited the US and Canada several times, as well as Australia, Scandinavia and Britain.

Although mbira playing is usually a strictly male preserve some women have recently come

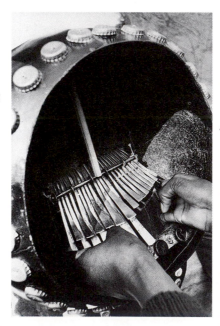

to prominence, notably Stella Chiweshe. Thanks to an understanding uncle who was a full-time player, or maridzambira, she was taught to play as a child. Other players refused to pass on the secrets of the instrument to a woman, as it was traditionally considered a man's

role. It is also believed that once a woman takes on a man's job she will be incapable of doing women's work again.

In fact, Chiweshe has pointed out the physical demands of mbira playing, especially the strength needed in the fingers and the stamina to play for the traditional all-night bira ceremonies.

The uncle, however, was impressed by her insistence and between 1966 and 1974 he shared his knowledge. Thereafter she was accepted as a fully-qualified mbira player. She has made several records and performed with the national dance company where she was called on to dance as well as play. When Thomas Mapfumo made his first visit to Europe in 1984 Stella accompanied him as guest artiste.

"Before independence you were not allowed to play mbira on stage," she said. "Before we were wrapping them up to hide them. Because the missionaries were saying if you do those things it's Satan's work, it's uncivilised, you will all go to Hell. But because it is spiritual, in the people and in the soil, this strong feeling of wanting to play keeps coming back. This feeling was stronger than their words. It is painful, the pain which can only be healed by playing. No doctor could cure that."

Zimbabwe's 'first lady of song', Dorothy Masuka (centre): recording since the early 1950s

emulated and imitated everywhere. While aimed primarily at Whites, Western pop was extremely popular with Africans, who were offered few alternatives. For fresh and exciting African dance music people turned to imports from neighbouring South Africa and Zaire (Congo), and the music which spilled out from those countries inspired two different lines of development.

The popularity of South African kwela was later overtaken by Zulu jive, or sax-jive music which became known generically as *smanje manje*. The rhythm was harder; bass was made more prominent and honking saxophones took over from the lilting penny whistles. When Rhodesian musicians came together in groups it was usually to play covers of these records in a repertoire that would often mix Western and South African favourites. But it was a two-way trade, with several of the early recording successes chalked up by Zimbabwean musicians. Not only *Skokiaan* but other famous numbers, including the all-time classic *Pata Pata*, could be traced back to Rhodesian composers.

The first real star, who claimed credit for *Pata Pata* and several other hits, was Dorothy Masuka who emerged in the early Fifties. Although born in Bulawayo in 1937, to a Zambian father and Zimbabwean mother, Masuka was educated at a mission school in Johannesburg. She started performing at the age of twelve, with the African Jazz and Variety show which launched several top South African artistes, including Miriam Makeba and Hugh Masekela. Dorothy composed and recorded many hits popular throughout the Southern Africa region, including several commonly thought of as Makeba's property. "Miriam Makeba is not just a friend she is more than that," recalled Masuka. "She was already a singer. She is one of those people who admired my singing and probably thought she could take one or two things from me also, which of course she did. She used a few numbers written by me and, because we sound alike, you have to know Miriam Makeba and Dorothy Masuka very well to differentiate."

Stella Chiweshe: transformed
traditional attitudes to female musicians

With a talent she believes is inherited from an ancestor who was a "great singer in the family", Masuka never considered any other career. Her style has changed over the years but she still uses the three-guitar formation which she claims she started as a way to "update the old songs on modern instruments". In the late Fifties 'Aunty Dot's' career took second place to her family and she disappeared from view. In 1964 she performed in Europe before returning to live in Zambia, where she was contracted to Intercontinental hotels. She continued to travel and won an award at the Pan-African Cultural Festival in Algiers in 1969 but, rather than looking for fame, she claims she was fulfilling something that was "lost on the way". During the Zimbabwean independence struggle, she says, she was not so much entertaining as sending messages through political songs and singing at rallies. "Now that everything is where it is, I've come back to finish my duties."

A strong, hard-working woman who admits "there was a period when I used to like my beer," Masuka was looking forward to retiring around 1996. "I don't think I want to go anywhere, because if it's the world people want to see, I have seen a lot of it. I'm much happier under my mango trees at home than anywhere else, because its not the glamour I'm looking for. I've been through the glamours."

The most glamorous prospects for local musicians in the late 1950s were revealed when some city councils began offering contracts to play in municipal beerhalls. The performers were inevitably paid very little but they had some income and a certain amount of security. The British-owned tobacco and soap companies then started looking for bands to sponsor and soon live music was being played in most hotels, beerhalls, bars and restaurants, catering for either Black or White audiences. By 1959, according to the author and musician Fred Zindi, there were some 200 bands working in Harare and Bulawayo. He estimates that by the early 1960s the number had grown to more than 500. Most played Western pop augmented with covers of South African hits, although they were no competition for the real thing, particularly as the South Africans were frequent visitors and had the advantage of records on the market.

The first chance for most musicians came when Teal records was set up in Zimbabwe as a subsidiary of the South African label, Gallo. The other South African major, Gramma records soon followed. Initially all kinds of music were recorded, with traditional mbira ensembles and panpipe players welcome in the studio. For a while Teal persevered with this kind of music, as it was proven to be popular in the rural areas. But country people had less opportunity to buy record players and consume music, and sales were insignificant compared with the European and South African product which the company licensed for local distribution. Eventually, success did come to some of those groups who played African popular music styles like *marabi*, *makwaya* and *jit* (or 'jazz'). Among the first generation were the Green Arrows, who scored the first hit for local music in 1973 with *Chipo Chiroorwa*, the Great Sounds, Harare Mambos and the Jairos Jiri Band.

Competition was also coming from another quarter. Musicians from Congo-Zaire had been visiting the country since the mid-Fifties, and in 1960 Zairean rumba took a serious hold as several dance bands came through via Zambia, including OK Sucess, Orchestre Vedette and Limpopo Jazz, who based themselves in Zimbabwe for a time and began singing numbers in

Shona. A band called OC Jazz settled permanently in the country and changed their name to the Real Sounds of Zimbabwe. They adapted the local mbira idiom to their style, while continuing to play 'copyright' versions of OK Jazz records. A decade later when the 'international' Sam Mangwana passed through he discovered he had blood relatives in the country.

Zairean rumba inspired many Zimbabweans to adapt or transpose the fluid dance rhythm to the Shona language and a new style quickly evolved. The best known exponents of Shona rumba are Devera Ngwena fronted by Jonah Moyo, the Nyami Nyami Band and John Chibadura. Jit music combined some of the Congolese ingredients, notably the solo guitar lines, with a faster rhythm and inflexions which echoed the indigenous marabi and mbira music. Those who used it to spice up smanje manje music included Ndebele musicians Oliver Mtukudzi, and Lovemore Majaivana.

Chimurenga Requests

Business was bland up to and including the liberation war. The vital input which changed the face of Zimbabwean popular music and gave it a revolutionary impetus came from the Voice of Zimbabwe radio, transmitted by Robert Mugabe's ZANU party from their headquarters in Maputo, following Mozambique's independence in 1974. The music programme 'Chimurenga Requests' broadcast revolutionary messages and liberation music to the guerrillas fighting in Zimbabwe. This music was, of course, banned in the White-ruled country and the local musicians who played it were restricted to an underground community. As in many other cases throughout the history of popular music, this gave the musicians even more credibility. Mapfumo, the most outspoken and popular of the chimurenga musicians, managed to sell records aplenty, although they were never played on Rhodesian radio and were not advertised. The song content had to be disguised beneath layers of meaning, a characteristic of African music apparently not fully understood by the White authorities.

As Mapfumo explained to the author Julie Frederikse: "I had to sing my music in that kind of roundabout way, but still a lot of my songs were banned on the air. They couldn't be played on the RBC. So we had to find a way to pirate the music. Instead of going through the radio we would just release a record and straight away sell it to the record bars. We couldn't take it to the disc

Master of mbira: Ephat Mujuru, well-travelled teacher, storyteller and recording artiste

Mapfumo playing his home base at the Queens Gardens, Harare

The Lion of Zimbabwe

Thomas Mapfumo (whose last name is appropriately the Shona word for spear) led the resurgence of traditional music in Zimbabwe by recreating the mbira sound with twin-picked guitars; the hosho calabash with the high-hat cymbal; the stomping of dancers' feet with the thumping of the bass drum. And he added a brass section.

Mapfumo, who was born in 1945 in Marondera, grew up in the home of an uncle with traditional Shona values, who was an enthusiastic organiser of mbira festivals. Later he sang in the church choir and joined an informal vocal group called the Cosmic Four Dots, who performed in the style of the Mills Brothers. For a while he was also a promising saxophone player. By the age of ten he was in a group called the Zulu Brothers singing rock and roll at a time when most people were playing jazz. Before leaving school he also played in the Cyclones.

He left Zimbabwe in 1964 to try to complete his education in Zambia, but returned the following year. Unable to find work, he used his musical skills to earn a living with the Springfields, who originally played a variety of jazz and Western pop including Beatles' songs, before progressing to versions of American soul numbers by bands like Chicago and Blood Sweat and Tears. The Springfelds also experimented by adding Shona lyrics to Congolese style rumba.

Mapfumo eventually became disenchanted with playing covers of foreign music and in 1973, when the group split up, he formed the Hallelujah Chicken Run Band, playing a more African type of rock, influenced by the Ghanaian band Osibisa.

Inspired by their fusion of African rhythms with Western style horns and heavy rock bass lines, Mapfumo began to search deeper into his roots to create a 'pure' African music based on traditional mbira patterns, which would also reach out to the rock audience. First to be given the Afro-rock treatment was his version of Murembo, a traditional song urging people to take up arms to liberate themselves. The record was immediately banned from the radio, and Mapfumo's career as an under-

ground hero was under way.

In 1974 Teal Records set up a local recording division and Mapfumo was one of the first artistes signed by their talent scout. His first 45rpm single for the label was Ngoma Yarira, another traditional song with hidden political connotations. This was just before the height of the Independence war between the Zanu and Zapu guerrilla forces and the illegal UDI regime of Ian Smith.

Following the single, Mapfumo quit the Chicken Run Band to become a session vocalist with two groups, the Acid Band and the Pied Pipers.

The 1977 album with the Acid Band, titled Hokoyo (Watch Out) again attracted government censors who tried to have its release held back. The record company, however, took the commercial initiative and released the album. It was banned from radio, as were all Mapfumo's subsequent songs, but he was popular enough for the records to sell without airplay.

At one stage Mapfumo was picked up by the authorities on the grounds that his music was subversive. Although he insisted that what he played was traditional music sung by his forefathers he was detained for 90 days, without trial. The particular song which raised the ire of the secret service was Send your children to War, a traditional composition which he claimed could have been appealing to either side.

He was released on condition that he play at a rally for the interim Prime Minister, Bishop Abel Muzorewa, to which he was taken at gunpoint. At the rally he played his usual liberation songs, confounding government claims that he had changed sides and was now a supporter of the compromise, pre-independence transitional government.

Mapfumo continued to record and give performances. The record company promoted the discs by playing the music in 'high density meeting places' like beerhalls, shopping centres and discos. Meanwhile, government forces tried to hijack Mapfumo's music for their own cause, flying over guerrilla territory in helicopters with speakers blasting his music interspersed with appeals for the fighters to come out and surrender their arms. It was a singularly ineffective campaign.

jockeys because once it gets on the radio the Board of Censorship gets to know about it and they ban it straight away. So we found that pirating through the record bars was a better way of bringing the music to the people. People wouldn't expect to hear me on the radio because they knew I was banned. They just had to always watch the record bars for the next release."

In 1978 Mapfumo quit the Acid Band to set up his own group, the Blacks Unlimited. Alongside him was Jonah Sithole, the guitarist who had gone furthest in transposing mbira patterns to electric guitar. In their short time together they forged a new more integrated sound, with a solid reggae beat amongst the raw ingredients. By the last days of the Smith regime Mapfumo had become a national hero, young enough to be a revolutionary, yet in the words of his press release, 'singing with wisdom and foresight in a mature voice which demanded the respect due, in African custom, to an older man'.

State of Independence

The big musical contribution to Zimbabwe's independence celebrations in 1980 came from Bob Marley, who unleashed the reggae rhythms which have since pleased many local people more than their own music. The reggae connection has been refreshed regularly throughout the Eighties with visits from top-line artistes such as Misty in Roots, Black Uhuru, Gregory Isaacs and Dennis Brown, as well as British group UB40 and South Africa's Lucky Dube. The Black militancy of reggae suited the celebratory mood, and the ideology, of the new country. The 'struggle' was an important ingredient, and many reggae songs dealt with issues such as unity, peace and the need to look forward. Rastafarianism caught on, with Zimbabwean youths growing dreadlocks and flaunting the rebel image. They also loved the rhythm.

Thomas Mapfumo was no exception. In the mid-Eighties he made his international break with a tour of Europe that greatly expanded the audience for Zimbabwean music and gave incentive to other bands. Albums were being released under licence in Britain, and Mapfumo became a regular visitor. His music had by now matured even further, with keyboards and female vocalists filling out the mbira-reggae fusion, and lyrics maintaining the flow of sharp-tongued criticism. When the Mugabe government was itself embroiled in controversy, he released the album *Corruption* in which he continued his outspoken demands for freedom, liberty and equality in what he then considered his 'neo-colonial' nation.

Jiving Majaivana: Lovemore switched from Western pop to township rhythms

The only artiste who came close to rivalling Mapfumo in the early Eighties was Oliver Mtukudzi, the singer with the husky voice and the 'cough' gimmick. His music is quite different, however, seeming to owe more to the South African *mbaqanga* influence than mbira tradition although, as he says, it is all based on folk music of the region. He acknowledges the influence of Mapfumo, although this is not immediately identified in his own music. Seven years younger than Mapfumo, Mtukudzi recalls writing his first song at the age of sixteen while still at school. When he left school in 1971 he worked for a while, interspersed with several years as a 'layabout'. He bought his first box guitar at the comparatively late age of 23.

Unable to interest his early schoolfriends in forming a group, Mtukudzi took the lonely path of singer/songwriter, and in 1976 he recorded the first of his compositions. It flopped, but he learned from the failure and eventually found a place with The Wagon

Guitarist and bandleader John
Chibadura plays London's Africa
Centre

Wheels Band, whose first recording together, *Dzandimomotera*, was a hit. He left soon after. Before creating his own style Oliver played smanje-manje and Congo-Zairean rumba. In 1979 when the civil war curfew was lifted he took his band, the Black Spirits, on the road touring as far as Zambia, Botswana and Malawi. In 1990 he made his first tour of Europe. Mtukudzi sings mostly in his native Shona with some songs in English and Ndebele. His serious, taciturn manner is reflected in the lyrics which are mostly about sorrow, starvation, poverty and other social ills or natural disasters.

The civil war created a cultural climate which was unhealthy to say the least. But the Ndebele people stayed in touch with their relatives across the border and their music kept pace with the 'Zulu' music from the south. One who had experience of working with South Africans such as Kippie Moeketsi, Caephus Semenya and Sipho Mabuse, was Lovemore Majaivana, who identified strongly with the south. "The political strife in South Africa is also our struggle," he has pointed out. "My brother worked in the mines in Wenela. He spent most of his life underground earning a pittance. He saw many of his colleagues being shot and killed because they spoke for their rights. I think it is wicked."

Like the showman he is, Lovemore couches his social comment in a hard, bass-driven dance beat with a contemporary feel. His youthful image belies the fact that he made his debut in 1967, as a drummer with the Bulawayo group, the Hi-Chords. He soon moved on, working as a singer with a variety of bands in different towns including the capital, Harare, where his rich baritone voice attracted audiences who appreciated cover versions of Tom Jones numbers and other middle of the road Western music.

Unlike some other musicians, Lovemore could never settle into a residency and continued to move from job to job, which

The Bhundu Boys: signed with
Warners, saw the world then parted
with their leader

Gospel truth: Black Umfolosi's choral
harmonies struck a chord in the West

included a spell with the Real Sounds, before teaming up in 1984
with two of his brothers in the Zulu Band, with whom he
developed a more African repertoire. The charms of corny British
pop music had worn thin and even White audiences in the newly-
independent country preferred to hear authentic music from
African bands. Throughout his career, Lovemore has taken a
consistent anti-apartheid stance, with songs like *Free Nelson
Mandela* and *Soweto*. Unusually for a Zimbabwean he sings in
Zulu which can nevertheless be understood by Ndebele-speakers.

Taking on the West

One of the biggest splashes made in the Western music
mainstream in the late Eighties was by the Bhundu Boys, who
after a couple of national hits shot to fame in England, signed a
contract with Warner Brothers for a hefty advance, played a few
prestigious stadium gigs and then appeared to sink without trace.
The name Bhundu Boys, Shona for 'Bush Boys', maintained
solidarity with the guerrillas who had fought the war in the bush.
Brought together soon after independence as a backing band for
a tour by Son Tajura, the five members soon melded into a tight
unit and following the original tour, they continued working the
revitalised post-independence music scene. Their urgent, youthful music occupied a space between Mapfumo's bass-heavy sound
and the high-stepping mbaqanga rhythms of South Africa, with a
Zairean influence on the guitar lines. Their 1985 single *Hatsitose*
stayed at number one in the Zimbabwe charts for three months.

Then they were 'discovered' by a vacationing Scotsman who acquired the licence to release some of their tracks in Europe and invited them to tour Britain.

As a small band, the Bhundus fitted easily into the Europeans' accepted profile of a pop group. For purely practical reasons they could work much harder than a typically large African dance band. Sleeping in boarding houses and travelling in a mini-bus, arrangements were kept simple and they covered Scotland and England during the summer of 1986. Their energetic, economical jit music was taken up by the laconically enthusiastic BBC Radio One disc jockey, John Peel, and for a while the Bhundus became the darlings of the British live music circuit, appearing everywhere from the smallest provincial clubs to major festivals.

That year London was popping with mbira, jit and Zimbabwe rumba. Thomas Mapfumo was making his third annual visit to Britain, and the opening show clashed with Bhundu's. A delegation including Green Jangano of the musicians union and Harare Mambos band, and writer Fred Zindi, were also in town with the Real Sounds. Each band claimed to have been number one back home at the time they left. The Real Sounds are a big band with a rich Congolese flavour, using a front line of four horns and three male singers to blast out ebullient melodies, backed by an enthusiastic rhythm section and authoritative guitar playing. Their show opened in folkloric fashion, with feathered headdresses and leopard-skin cloths. Changing into soccer strip for their hit song *Dynamo v Caps,* in that World Cup season endeared them to the locals and the London-based African community.

Most of the band are not native Zimbabweans. They came from Kinshasa via Lusaka and arrived in Zimbabwe during the Smith regime. In 1981, following Zimbabwe's independence, they were ordered to leave the country but friendly intervention by government ministers enabled them to stay on as 'adopted' Zimbabweans. They continue to play their classic 'Congolese' dance music with elements of mbira infused into the rumba. The songs, delivered in Shona and Lingala, stretch out long and full, giving musicians space to improvise, with the chef d'orchestre and guitar maestro Ghaby Mumba lurking in the darkest corner, almost invisible but always excitingly audible. The Real Sounds made regular European tours thereafter and established themselves as adopted ambassadors of Zimbabwe.

The more frenetic Bhundu Boys suffered a break up shortly after the flash of fame which put them in front of 70,000 Madonna fans at her Wembley Stadium show in 1988. Their Warner Brothers album was not the expected smash hit and soon after the front man, Biggie Tembo, left the four original members to strike out on his own. Musicians waiting at home for a similar break were Robson Banda, the Marxist Brothers, and several artistes who toured the European circuit during the 1980s, including the 'modern traditionalist' Four Brothers, who play fast mbira dance rhythms, John Chibadura, the jit rumba band Devera Ngwena, the Frontline Kids and gospel guitarist Machanic Manyeruke.

Vocal groups which parallel the Zulu harmonisers from south of the Limpopo have also come on apace during the first decade of independence. The Nineties looked promising for Black Umfolosi, an eight-piece acappella group with gospel inclinations, who sing in several languages urging unity and praising those who try to achieve it. Zimbabwe has also begun to offer up its own reggae artistes, following the lead of Doreen Ncube and the Pied Pipers who have been playing a Shona equivalent of the skanking rhythm since the Seventies.

Kalindula Country

Zambia too has a popular music of its own which has lain semi-dormant virtually since the country's independence in 1964. Known as *kalindula* after a one-string barrel bass of that name, Zambian guitar pop has its own identity, although similarities with the neighbouring styles of Zaire, South Africa and Zimbabwe help to place it geographically. In terms of musical development and popularity, however, kalindula does not match up to those powerful sounds from next door, and so far it remains a footnote in the story of African pop. The ingredients of the early music were the usual mix of local traditional idioms and outside influences. The Swahili music of Tanzania had an effect, as did that of Mozambique and the 'Nyasa sound', while South African *tsaba tsaba*, *kwela* and sax jive filtered through from the southern border. In the western region the Angolan *kateke* style became popular in the 1950s, but the biggest impression was made by Zairean rumba which the Zambians took to so readily that, as well as imitating it, they would call in bands from Lubumbashi, just across the border from the Copperbelt city of Ndola and only eight hours drive from the capital.

At the start of the Nineties rumba was still the loudest sound in Lusaka with Zairean nationals playing in most of the hotel bands. Local groups could be found accompanying the beer drinking in the less sophisticated night spots but, like the local bottled beer, their kalindula was not so potent. There is a stronger brew in Zambia, the *mowa* maize beer, but the fomenting of a popular music culture became a low priority during the years of regional strife which placed Lusaka as capital of the Frontline States. During the 1950s the first formal dance bands to earn popularity were the Lusaka Radio Band, the Mapoma Brothers and the Crusaders. Street musicians abounded and, as well as the usual formation of guitar and rhythm section, accordions were

Bush messenger: In the early 1950s, Alick Nkhata (left) provided guitars and recorded local musicians for the Central African Broadcasting Service

Mr Khuswayo (left) proprietor of
Zambian Music Parlour, with staff

quite common. The country's first solo stars were the late Alick
Nkhata in the Fifties, Nazil Pinchen Kazembe who died in 1991
after a 30-year career, and Emmanuel Mulemena, leader of the
Sound Inspectors.

Born to parents from different regions in 1922, Alick Nkhata
had the right credentials to become a 'father' of Zambian music.
He served overseas during World War Two and on his return home
worked with the musicologist Hugh Tracey, making field trips to
record music all over Central and Southern Africa. He later joined
the Central African Broadcasting Service as an announcer and
presenter of music programmes in which he travelled the country
recording all kinds of music and contributing his own guitar
skills. His repertoire was wide, ranging from folklore to Westernised ballads, dance numbers and a form of calypso commentary
which, although never recorded, was remembered as his strongest work. He eventually became Director of Broadcasting but
following his retirement in 1974 he was tragically killed on his

farm during a cross-border raid by Rhodesian forces.

During the war indigenous music suffered under competition from the West and from African neighbours. Ironically, President Kaunda's 1976 'watershed' declaration, restricting radio airplay for foreign music to ten per cent, with 90 per cent reserved for Zambian music, resulted in some devious identity changes among non-Zambians, and the outbreak of Zamrock, in which local bands attempted to recreate the lost noise of Western guitar heroes. Local rock had been commercially viable since the early Seventies with Paul Ngosi, Ricky Illonga, The Witch, Dr Footswitch and Musi Otunya bands among the high earners. But Zairean rumba remained the main attraction. By the 1980s, following the end of hostilities on the southern border, the music scene expanded. With the lifting of the curfew, newly-opened beer gardens offered opportunities for local bands playing an updated form of kalindula; notably Julizya, Amayenge, Shalawambe and the Masasu Band sometimes joined by the blind guitarist P.K. Chisala.

There were three studios operating in Lusaka, including Teal, DB Studios and Khuswayo's Zambian Music Parlour, but in the late Eighties high inflation and a shortage of vinyl scuppered the market for records. Cassettes had become the only viable format but recording and distribution presented a major problem for young bands, who were often confined to playing in hotels and beerhalls in the 'compounds', or townships. In 1991 the new generation included Mashabe, Makishi, Junior Mulemena Boys, Majoza, Oweka Stars and Lima Jazz Band. The formal hotels maintained residencies for Zairean bands while in the township motels local groups like Malaika continued to serve a fixed menu of Kinshasa covers.

Mozambique's clutch on culture

As one of the countries which has suffered most since independence, with civil war since 1975, Mozambique's social life and business have been virtually killed off, but the cultural heritage survives, and types of traditional music which were banned by the Portuguese colonists have been revived.

Back in the Fifties the port city of Maputo (then Lorenco Marques) had a thriving 'ambience' in which local dance rhythms such as the marabenta, majika and shigubu blended South African tsaba tsaba and kwela with the ubiquitous rumba and Portuguese influences and accents. The early stars included Ontonio Williams, Rosa Trembe and Orchestre Djambu.

In terms of traditional music Mozambique is another home of the mbira, first documented there by a European in the sixteenth century, but the most characteristic sound is of the timbila xylophones of the Chopi people which used to be played in mass orchestras with up to 30 instruments.

Timbila music can still be heard throughout the Chopi region but more often played by smaller ensembles. Departments

of government or municipal authorities often have their own timbila bands. The Chopis' instruments are of a design found from eastern Nigeria to Sudan, which uses a flat centre board to hold the keys and the calabash resonators. There are five different sizes of instrument,

some of which are fitted with legs.

Another revived traditional form is tufo music, in which women's choral groups are accompanied by percussionists of either sex. Although there was a sixteen-track studio still functioning in Maputo at the start of the 1990s, the music is propagated primarily by the national radio station, which plays a full menu of traditional and popular music. Typical of local guitar formations are Conjunta Manjacazione (left) with that rare sight in Africa, a woman drummer.

The radio house band Orchestre Marabenta Star and the Ghorwani group keep different strains of popular dance music alive. Successful performers of recent years include Fani Pfumo, Chico da Conceicao, Elsa Mangue Felipe, Alexandre Langa, Danile Langa and Pedro Langa, but in the absence of high-powered national bands, the big musical attractions are often outsiders, particularly from Zaire.

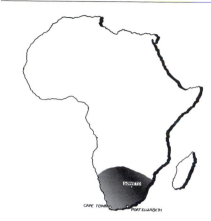

Township Voices

The music of the South African townships, commonly known as *mbaqanga* the 'poor man's soup' is, like other African urban styles, a broth cooked up from available ingredients. Like Rhythm and Blues, the strongest mbaqanga evokes pain and heartache with a yearning melodic intensity and a sometimes audible sense of rage. Significantly, the music also provides some of the hardest bass-driven rhythms on the continent with which to express and dance out frustration and anguish. The flavour of mbaqanga varies from the lurching, raucous Sax Jive of the early 1970s to the impressive 'groaning' vocal style of Mahlathini and the vocal harmonies of the Mahotella Queens to the latest pop hybrid known dismissively as 'bubblegum' which, unlike the poor man's soup, is merely chewed and spat out rather than swallowed.

Mbaqanga was the eventual descendent of jazz, choral and dance idioms dating from the beginning of the century. The first recognisable local style, *marabi* transposed American jazz into a local dialect form, much as happened with highlife in Ghana and rumba in Congo. The tonality of the languages, mainly Zulu, Xhosa and Sotho, generates melody lines which express a range of emotions in a kind of shorthand. The church-inspired vocal tradition of *mbube* was an important input, providing many of the country's greatest singers such as Miriam Makeba, Letta Mbulu and Mahlathini. There was also a fiercely creative instrumental tradition which produced some world-class jazz musicians, notably the trumpeters Mongezi Feza and Hugh Masekela, pianists Abdullah Ibrahim (Dollar Brand) and Chris McGregor, and a legion of pioneering saxophonists such as Spokes Mashiyane, Zakes Nkosi, Kippie Moeketsi and Dudu Pukwana.

An exile for almost 30 years before his return home in 1990, Hugh Masekela had an ambivalent attitude towards both the popular, commercial music of South Africa and those who sought out the more authentic sounds of the townships. "For anyone who has never been in a township," he said in 1987, "what you hear is maybe what the industry is interested in. You don't hear what the South Africans hear. You never know what the real music of South Africa is, you only know what the industry disseminates, what distributors get overseas. In South Africa you can't say there is a real South African music, because we have had Dixieland bands...swing bands, when they were popular in the States. I was in the Jazz Epistles, we had access to all the Western music. And you can't call mbaqanga real South African music because it is played on Western instruments and recorded in Western studios."

South Africa has the oldest established music industry south of Egypt, as well as practical advantages like a high standard of living (for some people), the availability of instruments and equipment, and commercial and cultural connections with America stronger than any other African country's. When diamonds were found in Kimberley in 1867 and gold in 1886, the South African population began to boom, with immigrants arriving from America, Europe and all over Africa to find either their fortunes or a daily crust in the mines. By the beginning of the twentieth century more than threequarters of the mineworkers were from outside South Africa.

From the earliest days all the major international record companies had a stake in the South African industry. The first Black recording artists were Griffiths Motsieloa and his wife, sent in 1930 to record at Decca in London by Eric Gallo, founder of the

'Township Jazz': publicity shot of unnamed musicians for a 1956 show, headlined by The Manhattan Bros and Miriam, with five other bands

'The Empress of African Song': Miriam Makeba with distinctive hairstyle *suki ya maboko*

first domestic record label who was still running the business 60 years later. Among Gallo's subsidiary labels were GRC, RPM, Trek, Unika, Meteor, Trutone and Teal, and he also held the franchise for several major international labels. By 1935 many 'native' music recordings had been made, with more than 300 releases listed by HMV alone. But the audience for that music did not have the economic muscle to make it commercially viable. 'Native' music, considered extremely low-life by the middle classes, relied on cheap, shop bought Western instruments rather than indigenous African instruments which are rarer in the south than other corners of Africa.

Eventually choral music broke through commercially when Solomon Linda, leader of the Evening Birds, and an employee of Gallo, recorded *Mbube*, the name which came to describe the distinctive vocal style. The Manhattan Brothers emerged in the Forties as one of many small vocal groups recruited from the numerous 'evening' or 'night' choirs, and found a ready market for their acappella harmonies. Shortly after World War Two, South Africa launched the continent's first international hit record, *Skokiaan* recorded on a mobile studio by the Bulawayo Cold Storage Band from Zimbabwe. There was also a tradition of theatrical presentation which nurtured many musicians, with the big music and dance variety shows of the Fifties establishing the reputations of all the major stars of the period, often far outside their homeland.

Instruments of Pleasure

Since the late nineteenth century, American minstrel players and ragtime musicians had been visiting South Africa. There were guitars, accordions, fiddles, banjos, harmonicas and penny whistles in the shops, and clients to play for in the boom towns. Records were distributed right across the globe from the 1920s onwards, and in South Africa the most popular products were the latest, hottest jazz from the States. Artistes like Louis Armstrong made a big impact on South Africans, representing, as one musician recalled, the first Black success stories the people had ever witnessed. Jazz was far more popular than Western ballroom dance music, such as waltzes, polkas and sanitised Latin rhythms, and bands like the Merry Blackbirds, the Rhythm Kings and the Dance Maniacs were inspired to create their own interpretations.

The early dance music was a product of the illegal drinking shebeens and, as part of the criminal milieu, it was a dangerous occupation. Incidents of serious violence against musicians are rare throughout the rest of Africa, but in the South African townships there is a sad history of grievous assaults and even the murder of several artistes. Some of the shebeens in the rough 'ghetto' districts like Sophiatown, Jamestown, Dikatole and Orlando (later Soweto) had beaten-up pianos or organs on which musicians began the first marabi synthesis. Dances lasted the whole weekend, with bands starting up when the workers were paid on Friday and playing through until the return to work on Monday morning. During the Forties the sleazy, shebeen-filled Johannesburg district of Sophiatown saw the start of *tsaba tsaba* music, the forerunner of *kwela* and township jive.

Musical instruments were always hard to come by, as musician, writer and filmmaker Molephe Pheto explained. "When it came to instruments like saxophone and trumpet and so on, that was a total mountain to climb...the money was just not there. If you wanted those, it took ages. They were not available in the ghettos. But the guitar was so common, people didn't think much about it, and they didn't think much about the player. Religion, remember, was a very strong influence on us, and the guitar was the instrument of Satan. The religious attitude was that if you played guitar you were going to Hell, whereas if you played the trumpet you were going to Heaven. Well, it's in the Bible somewhere that trumpets shall sound...The Salvation Army had brass instruments all over the place, but no guitar. In fact, to this day I've never seen a guitar there."

The Salvation Army did allow people to borrow instruments, and many took them home to practise on. After World War Two, more instruments were brought home by returning soldiers. Many religious families had old violins left over from the days when they were used in church services, but the general shortage of instruments meant that most people interested in music became singers. Thanks to the church there was a strong choral music tradition, with choirs open to all-comers. Some even had talent scouts who 'discovered' people such as Miriam Makeba and Letta Mbulu in their childhood.

Kippie Moeketsi, a seminal figure in the music's history who died in 1983, was one of those who did get hold of an instrument early on, although he picked up his saxophone technique in an unconventional way with a clarinet and a saxophone instruction tutor. "Once you know the clarinet, the saxophone is a boy," he recalled in a 1981 interview with *Staffrider* magazine. Kippie came from a musical family where his father played organ, his mother

Makeba, 'Mama Africa'

Behind the almost fairytale show business success story which whisked Miriam Makeba from a township singing group to international celebrity, lies an epic tragedy of misfortune, injustice, bereavement, divorce, sickness, exile and, as she revealed in her autobiography, a lethal spiritual madness.

Born into a stable township family in 1932, Miriam's problems began when she was young with the death of her father. Forced to find work, she quickly discovered that music "is a type of magic", which would lift her out of the housemaid's drudgery. There was another type of magic which she revealed would indirectly have just as great an effect on her life, but she made music her career. Even as a young schoolgirl her singing achievements brought disappointment. Chosen by her school to sing for the visit of King George VI, she waited in the rain, only for him to drive by without stopping. The song she would have sung was titled What a Sad Life for a Black Man.

When apartheid was introduced to South Africa, Makeba was just fifteen, but old enough to grasp the consequences of that legislative obscenity. At seventeen, shortly after giving birth to her daughter Bongi, she was diagnosed to have cancer of the breast. Her first of five husbands deserted her soon after.

Her singing career progressed more smoothly, performing jazz standards and kwela melodies in township bars, first with the Cuban Brothers and then the Manhattan Brothers, with whom

she toured Zimbabwe (then Rhodesia) and Zaire (Congo). While touring with them she also experienced some of the most callous aspects of the apartheid system. Trying to find medical help for group members fatally injured in a road accident is just one of the shocking experiences she endured.

By 1957 she was appearing as a soloist in the African Jazz and Variety Review which toured Africa for eighteen months, before landing the leading role in the musical King Kong. The key to her international success was a small singing part in the film Come Back Africa. Invited to the showing at Cannes Film Festival, Makeba became an instant celebrity. She was soon in New York, singing on television and at the Village Vanguard jazz club. Staggeringly for the wide-eyed young newcomer she was also within days performing at the birthday party for President John F. Kennedy. Under the guidance of her new-found friend, the Caribbean singer and businessman Harry Belafonte, Makeba released a string of

memorable recordings including the Click Song, Pata Pata and Malaika, which have remained the basis of her repertoire.

When her mother died in 1960, Makeba discovered her South African passport had been cancelled, preventing her returning home for the funeral. From then until her triumphant return 30 years later she was an exile from her own land, but even the USA, her adopted country, turned its back on her when she married the Black activist Stokely Carmichael.

Black Africa has never rejected Miriam Makeba and, as well as performing for many of the African independence celebrations, she has collected a sheaf of diplomatic passports. She became a friend and confidante of Sekou Toure, the radical leader of Guinea, where she eventually found refuge.

The madness which had been dogging her was, apparently, an inherited state of possession by amadlozi spirits. Miriam's mother had been a conduit for spiritual forces, which she herself could exorcise by performing. She has often talked of being possessed while on stage. But her beloved daughter Bongi could not accommodate the spirits, which eventually led to her destruction.

Makeba's use of music for spiritual exorcise has kept her in tune with her cultural background during that painful exile, while her music has touched countless outsiders. Her catalogue of album releases, international tours and festival appearances have been in collaboration with multi-national bands, including Guineans, Camerooni-ans and Ghanaians, but the spirit of the music is undeniably South African.

Keyboard maestro: Abdullah Ibrahim
(Dollar Brand), virtuoso soloist and
composer of emotive melodies

sang hymns, and his brother played piano. He spent his lifetime
in one of the hardest occupations in the toughest of times, and the
first group he joined might well have been his last: The Band in
Blues was broken up by gang violence.

"In those days the *tsotsis* (gangsters) were rough", Kippie
remembered. "Musicians used to get a hiding from them now and
then. They said we thought that we were clever, and better than
them. Sometimes we would play from 8pm to 4am, non-stop. It
was like that. Sometimes the tsotsis would force us to play right
through up to 9am, by force. We played all the songs they wanted.
I remember one incident in which I managed to escape with my
dear life. It was in '48 when we were still playing at the Bantu
Men's Social Centre. Tsotsis came, man. There were about seventeen, carrying tomahawks, and chopping everybody in the hall for
no reason. After they finished with the audience they came on to
the stage while we just stood glued there, frightened. They began
chopping up our instruments and then we ran for our lives with
the thugs in hot pursuit. One of them chased me down Von

Wielligh Street. It was about 3am. He shouted at me, 'Kom hier, jong, Kippie'. His name was Seven. Fortunately for me, a police van appeared and the thug disappeared. The tsotsis were attacking us for the fun of it. They were from Alexandra township. I think it was not yet the 'Spoilers', it was before their time. Ja, musicians used to have a rough time in those days."

Kippie moved on to join the Harlem Swingsters in 1949. But the band folded after a year. The 1950 Group Areas act which restricted people on grounds of racial classification to live in designated townships, and the general introduction of apartheid, spelt the end for the era of big bands like the Jazz Maniacs, Swingsters, Merry Blackbirds, African Hellenics and the Rhythm Clouds. Kippie was lucky to find a gig with the backing group for the Manhattan Brothers which was expanded from a quartet to a six-piece. The Brothers were the headline band in South Africa throughout the Fifties, and several future stars passed through the band or their theatrical shows.

The Manhattans began as an acappella mbube group called the Jo'burg Boys, with a repertoire of church-influenced songs and an American do-wop style. They gradually included more instrumental parts, with piano and saxophones boosting the choral elements and a rhythm section to make it swing. This was later expanded to take in a complete theatrical show. In 1951 the young pianist Dollar Brand briefly joined the group at the time when the leader Dambuza Nathan Mdledle and bandmaster Mackay Davashe chose to stop playing 'English' styles and devote themselves to indigenous music, in Xhosa, Sotho and Zulu languages. They had recognised that audiences were bored with what they were doing, and their next show, titled *Kings Holiday* brought the public back. Soon afterwards Mdledle recruited Miriam Makeba from the Cuban Brothers, although the musicians were sceptical about this young girl's abilities, Moeketsi believing she would never make their standards. "We thought we were the Guys, if you understand what I'm trying to say. I regarded the Cuban Brothers and Miriam as small fry, let me put it that way." He did acknowledge, though that the Cuban Brothers "were not bad. In fact they started close harmonies in this country based on the American group the Modernaires". Makeba stayed with the band for several years before landing the lead role in the African Jazz and Variety review.

Theatrical 'review' shows became the training ground for the generation of post-World War Two performers. They showcased vocal and dance talents and provided a context for musicians to develop an understanding and mutual respect based on spontaneity and improvisation. Moeketsi, Davashe, Lemmy Mabazo and Masekela came under the musical direction of pianist Sol Klaaste, who arranged and orchestrated *King Kong*, the show based on the life of a celebrated boxer which gave South African music an international identity. Mdledle played the title role and Makeba the female lead. They toured the Southern African region as far as Congo. After two years Makeba left for Europe. She was replaced by Abigail Kubhekathe and shortly after, the *King Kong* cast followed for a production in London.

Moeketsi arrived late in London and was almost immediately committed to a mental hospital after 'going berserk'. He had to leave the show, but he survived electric shock treatment, and returned to the musical base at Johannesburg's Dorkay House, where he helped put together the Jazz Epistles, the "best small band in the country" with Dollar Brand, Masekela, Jonas Gwangwa on trombone and Makhaya Ntshoko on drums.

Dudu Pukwana: a most expressive voice in exile, he maintained the kwela groove with gusto until 1990

IN THE TOWNSHIPS

Big voice choir: Ladysmith Black
Mambazo, the most prolific and
celebrated mbube group

Cries from the Darkness

The best known of the country's many artistic exiles has been called 'Mama Africa', or the 'Empress of African Music', but the name her mother bestowed on Miriam Makeba was Zenzi, from *Uzenzile* (Xhosa for 'you have no-one to blame but yourself'). It seems a harsh sentence, and in retrospect an unfair judgment, to pass on a woman who has endured so much personal suffering in a career lasting more than 30 years. She has brought joy to millions throughout the world and hope and pride to those "exiled within" South Africa. One of only a handful of African musicians to be internationally acclaimed outside the continent, Makeba became a roving ambassador for Black Africa, following the revocation of her passport by the White minority South African government in 1959.

Since then her undeniable talent has been rewarded with a sparkling show business career, but in three decades as a figure-head for the struggle to liberate "the concentration camp which I escaped, but which is my home", she has not been far from controversy, and counter-propaganda. Her marriage to the American political activist Kwame Toure (Stokely Carmichael) left the lingering insinuation that she was a racist, a charge she has denied patiently. "People have accused me of being a racist, but I am just a person for justice and humanity. People say I sing politics, but what I sing is not politics it is the truth," she said in London in 1985. "I'm going to go on singing, telling the truth."

The ability to combine the beauty and the pain of that personal truth, is what makes her one of the truly legendary performers, a part of the history of her times, not just a witness. Her life was peopled with glamorous and powerful figures, and set against a background of international incident.

Business life also had its problems for Makeba. During the Sixties, for example, she played often in Denmark, but on one occasion failed to appear for her show. On returning to the country some years later she was held and actually jailed overnight until a financial penalty had been extracted. In East Africa during the 1970s she ran into further controversy surrounding the classic love song *Malaika*, first thought to be traditional and later claimed by several songwriters.

More recently, confusion surrounded her participation in Paul Simon's 'Graceland' tour. A conflict of opinions on the cultural boycott of South Africa saw the supreme irony of ANC supporters in London picketing a Miriam Makeba performance. In fact they were picketing Simon, who had professed ignorance of any such boycott, but Miriam and Hugh Masekela were lending support. In 1985 she had said she supported the cultural boycott. Two years later she was touring the world with the Graceland review. She had obviously had a change of heart. Since her single-minded concern has been the liberation of her country, Makeba's integrity has never been in doubt. She believed that the propaganda value of music should be utilised – and her voice and presence are one of its most powerful weapons.

When the trumpeter Hugh Masekela set up a hi-tech mobile recording studio in Botswana in 1984, it was the closest he had been to his native country for 23 years. During that period of exile, Masekela, like Miriam Makeba, had forged a prodigious reputation as one of Africa's handful of international stars. Born in Johannesburg, Hugh began singing in his school choir, but once he had seen the film *Young Man with a Horn* he was inspired to try the trumpet. His first instrument was given him by the English liberal churchman, Bishop Trevor Huddleston, and with it he entered the burgeoning jazz scene, centred around Nkosi, Moeketsi and others based at Dorkay House.

In 1961, soon after arriving in London he met Harry Belafonte, who later arranged for him to study in the USA. There he released his first major hit, *Grazing in the Grass*, but his follow-up album had a political content which proved too provocative for the American distributors and the record was held back. He then formed his own label, Chisa records, with producer Stewart Levine. By the early 1970s he was playing with two township friends, Jonas Gwangwa and Caiphus Semenya under the ironic name Union of South Africa. He also recorded in London with Dudu Pukwana, but before long he returned to Africa.

His first stop was Guinea-Conakry where he taught music for a year, before moving to Zaire and finally Nigeria, where he met up with his friend Fela Kuti, with whom he travelled to Ghana. There he was impressed by Hedzolleh Soundz who opened the show for Fela. They recorded together in Lagos and Hugh took them with him to the States. In 1974 he went back to Zaire with Manu Dibango for the famous 'Rumble in the Jungle' championship fight between Muhammad Ali and George Foreman. He recorded with several Zairean musicians and along with Dibango made a film, which was never released. About these collaborations he once said, "I am very close to Franco, Rochereau, Fela and all the big artistes from Africa, because I think we are a new entity on the entertainment scene, because Africa has only been free for 30 years and people have just made contact with Africa."

In America he collaborated on a crossover attempt with Herb Alpert, set up by his old colleague Caiphus Semenya. But the two

Man with a horn: Hugh Masekela in New York retracing the jazz journey

Three Jazomoloo: Jacob 'Mzala'
Lepers, bass, Ben 'Gwigwi' Mrwebi,
sax, and Sol Klaaste, piano

trumpeters' styles did not meld satisfactorily. Then, at Christmas 1980, he returned to Lesotho with Makeba to play at a huge festival in front of 100,000 people. Back in London he set up Jive Zomba records with Levine and in 1984 he bought a mobile 24-track studio, which he shipped out to Botswana. The first recording was *Technobush*, one of his most accomplished albums, combining funky Western elements with the emotional drive and melodic intensity of mbaqanga. The instrumental accompaniment was provided by the Soul Brothers.

Then came 'Graceland', the controversial issue which upset some European anti-apartheid groups. Masekela's opinions were made clear in 1987. " It was so positive, as it reached so many of the European middle and upper-middle classes who never otherwise would have stopped barbecuing in the backyard, or sailing or surfing or skiing. And they found they liked the music and then found it was part of a big international controversy. To that extent it was great that the cultural boycott came out in public. It put a lot of pressure on those even who opposed it, because it did great things for a lot of people, and it also got solidarity groups and liberation movements to review their thinking."

Many of those liberation groups had been inspired by other South African exiles, including a clutch of jazz players who, although identified with a wider, world community, constantly referred to the struggle back home. Since World War Two, jazz had provided a focus for many fine instrumentalists, particularly piano and horn players. The Jazz Epistles recorded the country's first jazz album, as opposed to 78rpm single, at the start of the Sixties, and their pianist Dollar Brand made his break for freedom in Europe and America, where he was encouraged by Duke Ellington. Unlike other exiles, however, Dollar returned home to share his worldly knowledge with his old colleagues in the Cape Town suburb of District Six. On one of his visits, after he had taken the Muslim name Abdullah Ibrahim, he began a collaboration with the young sax player Basil Coetzee, which led to the landmark recording of *Mannenberg*, a signature tune for both musicians.

Dudu Pukwana, from Port Elizabeth, was also an aspiring piano player in the early Fifties when he went to Cape Town to play backing for a vocal group, performing alongside Chris McGregor's Blue Notes. Dudu sat in with them during their set and made an impression. But as McGregor himself played piano, Dudu was encouraged to take up sax, an instrument which he made so much his own that just one note would be enough to recognise his powerful, emotion packed style. With him in the Blue Notes were trumpeter Mongezi Feza, bassist Johnny Dyani and drummer Louis Moholo. Invited to the Antibes jazz festival in France in 1964 the Notes departed South Africa, never to return.

They eventually settled in London, where the band kept their marabi-kwela vision alive under the name Brotherhood of Breath. In 1969 Dudu formed Spear with drummer Julian Bahula. In 1977 he travelled to Nigeria with Jonas Gwangwa, Moholo and Bahula to play at the Festac festival. Bahula had taken his ticket to exile in the band of Philip Tabane, named Malombo after the traditional drums which Bahula battered unrelentingly. Along with pianist Mervin Afrika, singer Pinise Saul, guitarists Lucky Ranku and Russell Herman, and tenor sax player Frank Williams, these consititued a core of township musicians who could be heard regularly in London through the Seventies and Eighties, playing in variations of Spear, Zila, Jabula and District Six. In 1990 Dudu died, leaving Louis Moholo the only survivor of the original Blue Notes.

Sounds of Soweto

When radio was launched after World War Two most Black people could not afford a set. Only White music was played and although they did get a chance to listen in while working as servants in the White's houses, they were not much interested . A radio rediffusion service was first introduced in Orlando (Soweto) and, as Molefe Pheto remembers, "Boxes were put in every house in Soweto. It came on whether you wanted it or not, but basically it was propaganda...At the same time they had to have Blacks controlling that, so there was Black music...but our relationship with radio was very peripheral. The people who were really interested in radio were the mine workers. We used to laugh at these guys when they carried their ghetto blasters. There would be about fifteen of these guys listening and dancing to this thing. They used to play it in the streets...The miners would sacrifice a lot to buy a radio". The influence of radio on the artistic community was not so great but in the Fifties the broadcaster K.E. Masinga had started producing the first short programmes of African jazz music, supporting the emergent generation of players in small bands like Dollar Brand, Zakes Nkosi, Kippie Moeketsi and Dudu Pukwana.

Another sound of Soweto came from makeshift street-corner groups, usually small boys who developed their own kind of skiffle music, a poor boys' interpretation of American big-band swing. Known as *kwela* it apparently arose spontaneously in South Africa and neighbouring countries. Innovative youths adapted jazz, swing, and jive or R&B music to fit their limited resources. The most common combinations were based around guitar, banjo and penny whistle players, usually with a one-string box bass. Their street music soon adopted the name kwela, from the Zulu word meaning 'to get up', 'get on top', 'move'. Throughout the Fifties and early Sixties kwela combos could be seen and heard on almost every street corner of Johannesburg, attracting crowds of Black and White spectators. The music's popularity spread the names of artistes like Spokes Mashiyane and 'Little' Lemmy Special throughout Southern Africa.

Kwela also penetrated much further. By chance the penny

Little Lemmy Special helped spread the pennywhistle sound round the world during the Fifties

Chief 'groaner': Mahlathini pioneered
a vocal style and revived his career
with international tours in the late
1980s

whistle caught on as a novelty sound in Britain and in 1958 *Tom
Hark* by Elias and the Zig Zag Flutes stayed in the British charts
for fourteen weeks. Others like *Mbube* (aka 'Wimoweh' or the 'Lion
Sleeps Tonight'), *Skokiaan* and the original version of *Swinging
Safari* were taken up and 'Little' Lemmy Mabazo even visited
London at the age of twelve to promote the music.

During the Sixties kwela was boosted into the electric rock era
with amplified guitars and bass, saxophones to replace penny
whistles, organs and drum kits. Street musicians graduated to
the instrumentation that had been available to jazz and variety
musicians for two decades. The new sound was known as 'Jive';
there was Sax Jive, Accordion Jive, Organ Jive and Vocal Jive.
This hot new music coincided with the introduction of 45rpm
singles and the heyday of the South African record market. One of
the labels on which jive music was released was Smanje Manje,
meaning 'now, now' or 'things of today', which became a generic

name for the jive style popular throughout Southern Africa.

There were scores of jive artistes being recorded on a range of labels throughout the late Sixties. Some recording bands existed only on disc, while others collaborated with different singers. The most popular jive artistes included West Nkosi, the Soul Brothers, Boyoyo Boys, Big Voice Jack and Marks Makwane. Nkosi was one of a string of leather-lunged saxophone players who led the honking on the raunchiest Sax Jive variant. Others were Lulu Masilela, Lemmy Mabazo, Alex and his Alto Sax and Thomas Phale. One of the best-selling jive bands during the Seventies, the Boyoyo Boys earned themselves twenty gold records, seventeen in a space of four years. Formed in 1969, the Boys enjoyed a successful recording and touring career for fifteen years, until the drummer Archie Mohlala was stabbed to death in a shebeen fight in 1984. The band hung up their instruments for a while, until the American explorer Paul Simon heard their tapes and inspired a revival.

The vocal tradition, with roots in church choirs and American acappella do-wop formations, continued to develop alongside the instrumental music with dozens of both male and female Vocal Jive groups such as the male-voice 'Abafana' ('Boys') bands and the various 'Queens' and 'Girls' outfits. One of the foundations of modern choral music had been Alexandra Black Mambazo, founded in the early Fifties by Aaron Lerole, with a style that was followed by Ladysmith Black Mambazo, who found international acclaim some 30 years later.

In the Sixties Lerole went on to direct the Dark City Sisters led by Joyce Mogatusi; pioneers of the first mbaqanga sound which incorporated three-part American style harmonies with indigenous rhythms and electric guitar. Along with the Flying Jazz Queens, the Sisters started a trend throughout the region for three-women groups and were forerunners of the Mahotella Queens. The female partners were not self-contained bands, however, but worked in front of R&B-inspired instrumental sections who retained their own working names, such as the Makgona Tsohle Band.

Another element which soon became essential was a deep-voiced male 'groaner' to share the limelight and exchange call-and-response lyrics. Eventually there were many gruff-throated bass singers, but the original was Mahlathini, who made his debut in 1962 as a teenager with the local band Alexandra Black Mambazo, for whom his brother Zeph played penny whistle. Two years later when his voice broke into the distinctive growl, the youth was disconcerted. "Everyone was so worried about my voice; no-one knew what to do about this loud and deep voice coming from my mouth. Then my mother took me to a witchdoctor and it was discovered this was my natural voice. So we all stopped worrying and I started singing like a new man."

Mahlathini made his first commercial breakthrough with the Dark City Sisters, putting his personal stamp on several of their hits. Under the guidance of producer Rupert Bopape, the man behind many of the jive singles, he switched allegiance to the newly-formed Mahotella Queens with whom he shared a string of hits throughout the 1970s. Mahlathini's career was revived during the late Eighties when his music finally broke into the international market, through releases by sympathetic British independent labels and his associations with Simon and the televised Mandela birthday celebrations. He toured Europe and Japan and in the Spring of 1991 he made his second tour of the USA, playing some 60 dates.

Mahotella Queens: popularised the three-part vocal mbaqanga style of the Dark City Sisters, and sang backing for Mahlathini

Early days: Kippie Moeketsi on clarinet with musicians from the Manhattan Brothers in the early 1950s

Expressions of Freedom

The freedom for Black people to express themselves had long been denied by political, cultural and commercial constraints, and South African musicians have had to develop a resistance mentality. Instrumental heavyweights communicated intense, non-verbal messages of pride and survival, while playwrights, poets and choral groups have carried a literal message at funerals, political rallies or secretive 'underground' functions.

The beginnings of a resistance music appeared in the Forties among urban community groups who started to express their social concerns in singing. "The tunes mostly came from the churches," recalled Molephe Pheto. "Because of the urban situation these were modernised and adjusted, made much more rhythmic because the church tunes were formal. The people were freer outside church so they jazzed them up a bit, adding some rhythms, and they also changed the lyrics. So a church song would be picked up in one popular language and then through that language you hear about the problems of the community. During those days the songs were not confrontational. They were very subtle. That was when the oppression was really at its highest in the Forties."

Professional musicians had further problems. "Exploitation is something most musicians complained about," said Molephe. "There were no political organisations, these were just musicians feeling that something was terribly wrong and I feel that was political. Another political issue was the night pass. The musicians worked at night, and on their way home they'd be stopped by the police, so songs of protest started around that police harassment. It was not so much a political movement but they were protecting themselves and complaining about how hard the police were making it for them to work. Problems with the studios began as well because they didn't want to be involved in those things. The studios, as a result, suggested different approaches in the songs. So the musicians found they wanted to say something but couldn't because they were being silenced by the studio. Then there was the general political awakening. In the 1950s the ANC was the only political party, and they had a little cultural thing. They were singing to meetings and huge rallies. When the ANC choir was formed that brought retaliation. Politically things were beginning to take shape. But the popular songs were about complaining and not resolving issues.

"In the mine areas the songs are total protest. These people were recruited or became uprooted from wherever they came from, plunged into Johannesburg without their families, without anything. Here there is a resemblance of slave revolt in their songs. On Sundays when the miners were off work they would start singing. The songs, however, were disguised through what we now know to be the miners' dance. In the city people were afraid to dance because there is a stigma, but it broke through because they realised that through the dance they could relay the messages of protest and the *indunus* ('Boss boys', in contact with the foremen) could not translate it to the master, because it would be difficult for the indunu to explain that when they dance a certain movement they mean, 'you, the White man'. Some of the dances portrayed the White people, how cruel they were. So in the dance they could confront the system totally.

"Political awareness was growing and the Black Americans were up for their rights in the Sixties, and all those things were happening, so eventually you got groups subtly beginning to talk about events and issues and eliciting a response from the people." One of the current stars who rose through the political milieu is Mzwakhe Mbuli, the 'Poet of the Struggle', whose passionate verse

Liberation lyricists: the ANC Choir brought the message home at party rallies

Stimela: leader Ray Phiri went from dancing with vocal groups to township fusion

animated political rallies for years. He gradually added instrumentation leading, in 1990, to the formation of a full-time band, the Equals whose forceful township music carried the poetry and the politics to the people.

The cultural boycott organised by the ANC helped concentrate international support against apartheid. In Britain members of actors' Equity and the Musicians Union withheld their works from performance in South Africa. The reciprocal agreement, however, preventing South African artistes performing abroad, sometimes appeared plain ludicrous. Among the first to suffer at the hands of British unions were the Malopoets whose planned appearances in London during 1985 were banned by the MU. They later based themselves in continental Europe. Until the late 1980s, the boycott rule was also applied voluntarily to record imports mainly on the grounds that any money paid for discs would simply disappear into the coffers of the South African majors. The dislike of people working in the independent music sector for major labels was compounded by their hatred of the racist regime. Some saw they were depriving not only their customers of worthy music, but also a whole generation of South African musicians of any chance to break out of their predicament. Among the first releases of South African pop to be waved through the selective boycott were *Zulu Jive* and *Indestructible Beat of Soweto* compiled for the Earthworks label, and *Soweto Street Music* and *Soweto Compilation,* released after consultation with the ANC by the English independent label Rough Trade.

However, the fate of South African music was not solely in the hands of the ANC. While the debate about 'selective' or blanket sanctions was warming up, there were already murmurs of a 'post-apartheid' crossover filtering out of the country. Coming from a White man, the message surprised and amused Europeans who took to Johnny Clegg in different ways. Clegg, known in France as the 'White Zulu' is unique among African performers. Born in England, he spent most of his childhood hanging out in township shebeens, developing a deep affinity with Zulu culture, before studying social anthropology. He is fluent at Zulu guitar styles and adept at the complex *indlamu* dance steps. With his childhood friend, Sipho Mchunu, Clegg launched Juluka, but Mchunu left in 1985 and Clegg re-grouped with Savuka. Playing for racially mixed audiences, he broke down barriers at home, while the curiosity value of a White man wearing animal hides and being able to dance well earned him his biggest fame in France. In the 1990s, the non-racial group Mango Groove attracted similar interest in the West.

But it was another White man who really opened the can of worms. Paul Simon's 'Graceland' project was controversial not just because he broke the boycott by working in South Africa, but because he naively thought it was not applicable to what he was doing. A little more awareness of the culture he was exploring might have earned him wider international respect, although among South African musicians the episode is considered to have been a good thing, opening doors for a range of artistes from Mahlathini and Ladysmith Black Mambazo to Stimela, Sipho Mabuse and the Soul Brothers.

Stimela is a township fusion band formed by the guitarist Ray Chipika Phiri, originally to back Sipho Mabuse and other recording artistes. Phiri started as a dancer with the Dark City Sisters vocal group before setting up the Cannibals, who survived through the 1970s. In the early Eighties he formed Stimela, releasing several acclaimed albums which caught the ear of Simon, who recruited him for the Graceland project and subsequent tours. Sipho Mabuse tapped the pulse of the modern township with his *Jive Soweto* title. Sipho is a multi-instrumentalist who seemed to have an ear for what was fresh and exciting in contemporary South African music. Originally known as 'Hotstix' for his drumming ability with the group Harari, Mabuse straddled the line between bubblegum pop and electric roots music, seeing himself as an infiltrator helping create social awareness behind the commercial lines. Mabuse broke into music with a band called the Beaters, playing music inspired by the Beatles. With the name changed to Harari, and a style which fused mbaqanga with American soul and disco, the band pioneered the Seventies Soweto soul sound. In 1984 Mabuse went solo. His album *Burn Out* with the song *Jive Soweto*, on which he played bass and keyboards as well as drums, brought a new disco feel to contemporary township jive.

His follow-up album brought him to the notice of Western record companies and in 1987 he was shuttling regularly between South Africa and Britain, where he eventually signed a deal with Virgin, who released two albums. The second, *Chant of the Marching* had a mixed reaction in South Africa. The show business press noted that Mabuse had now taken to 'political preaching', no doubt influenced by his new outside perspective on South Africa. In London he was continually being asked about the political content of his songs and his part in the struggle. Taking the lead offered by the exiled Makeba and Masekela, Mabuse had introduced a message element, although he held on to his old pop fans with the 'Hotstix' style they 'know and love'.

Township champions the Soul Brothers, who have already swept much of the world, claim to be the country's most popular recording group, with sales of over four million albums accumu-

'Hotstix': multi-instrumentalist Sipho Mabuse brought pop presentation and technology to the township groove

lated before they embarked on their 1991 world tour. They came together in Johannesburg in 1974, when bassist Zakes Mchunu and guitar player Tuza Mthetwa of the Groovy Boys joined up with drummer David Masondo to play backing for the Mthembu Queens vocal group. When the Queens split up, the musicians remained together and the drummer Masondo doubled on lead vocal. In 1976 they changed their name to the Soul Brothers and took on keyboard player Moses Ngwenya (Black Moses) who became one of the most influential mbaqanga musicians. Another newcomer was vocalist American Zulu. With Tuza's Zulu guitar picking style embellished with ideas he picked up from Western pop, and Moses' inspirational keyboard playing, the Soul Brothers found almost instant success. Their second single *Mshoza* became one of the biggest selling mbaqanga hits of all time. In 1979 they were shattered by the death in a car crash of Tuza and the band's saxophone player, but they managed to re-build the band and stayed at the top of their trade.

In 1982, following the departure of American Zulu the remaining core of David, Zakes and Moses released the album *Isiphiwo* which sold almost three quarters of a million copies in the first year. But they suffered another set-back with the death of Zakes, also in a road accident, and lay dormant before rising once again in 1985. With a new line up totalling thirteen musicians, the 'honey-voiced' Masondo and keyboard wizard Moses toured frequently in Southern Africa and finally made their first overseas tour in 1990. A second tour in 1991 took them to USA, Europe and Australia, where they played the prestigious Sydney Opera House. Considered to be the best-selling recording group in South Africa, the Soul Brothers have all the trappings of success. The senior members are reportedly super-rich and the South African popular press delights in showing them posing alongside their swimming pools and Mercedes cars.

Bubblegum and Beyond

Two women who came to the fore in the late Eighties did more than any other South African artistes to reap the rewards of international success. Yet the music which made Yvonne Chaka Chaka and Brenda Fassie rich and famous was just too commercial for many listeners, who noted the mbaqanga had been smoothed almost out of recognition. This was straight pop music they judged, albeit with a thumping township bass and back beat, no better than 'bubblegum' music. Well, pop music has always been aimed at young audiences and the kids liked it enough to buy the records.

Brenda Fassie made her debut in 1970 at the tender age of six, singing the Temptations' song *Papa was a Rolling Stone* in a group called the Tiny Tots. She had been named after the American Sixties country/ rock and roll singer Brenda Lee, but the family were in no position to start her on a musical career, and when she was fourteen she ran away to find fame in Johannesburg. One year later, with her mother's blessing, she joined a vocal trio called Joy. She then moved on to a group called Family and recorded *Weekend Special,* which became an instant pop hit. Renamed Brenda and the Big Dudes, the group went on a successful tour of Southern Africa. Brenda then spent two years on her own before rejoining the band in 1989. The line-up now included composer/ arranger Sella Chicco Twala, with Brenda's brother Themba on keyboards and her sister Lindi providing vocal accompaniment.

Singing a mix of sanitised mbaqanga and soul or country ballads, and often sounding uncannily like her namesake, Brenda

Brenda Fassie: a powerful performer of 'pop' mbaqanga

was neither roots nor radical enough for her critics, but she presented her somewhat anodyne material with energy and intensity. A powerful performer and a genuine pop star, whose marriage was attended by 40,000 fans, Brenda felt insulted by the 'bubblegum' tag, claiming that although her music is for fun, she was always thinking about the struggle. When Nelson Mandela was released the world's press carried pictures of him hugging Brenda Fassie. And her simple peace-and-love lyrics do contain messages of solidarity, as the title of her album, *Black President*, suggests. On her first European tour she showed her capability at traditional folk dance and directing a children's choir.

Internationally, Brenda's path had been opened up by Yvonnne Chaka Chaka whose 1988 album *Umbqombothi* was a massive pan-African hit which she followed up with tours in Zaire, Kenya and Nigeria with her backing band Taxi. In Kinshasa in 1989 she

Proud to be African: Yvonne Chaka
Chaka, taking on Africa and the West

played to a full house of 70,000 at the national football stadium.
Then in Nigeria the following year she made a three-week concert
tour to capitalise on the commercial success of selling more than
600,000 authorised copies of the disc which must have been
pirated in equal numbers. With her face featured on billboards
and television commercials, Nigerian labels bid to release her
follow up album, *Be proud to be African,* which contained a remix
of *Umbqombothi,* by a hit-shot 'dance music' producer from
London. Yvonne had realised her ambition to become a big star in
Africa before taking on the West.

A third member of the bubblegum brigade, Rebecca Malope,
who rose to fame in 1989, was surprisingly forthright in her
assessment of the modern pop. "The problem is that what we sing
today has no future," she told the South African popular press.
"It's not the kind of music one would want to listen to for years to
come. We appear to be all singing with the same direction and
style. You listen to one of us and you've heard us all."

However short her musical future, Rebecca's story is a classic
version of the rags-to-riches fable. Brought up without knowing
her mother she ran away from home with her sister at the age of
fifteen to join a band. Living in a coal dealer's backyard in a 'shack
full of holes', the girls went without food when they were not
working and at times became desperate. Their luck changed when
they met a member of Stimela who brought them to Johannesburg. In 1987, after two years trying, Rebecca won a national
talent competition with prize money and a record contract. In a
move to trace her long-lost mother, she recorded *Mama Come
Back,* and set out for the rural areas to try to find her. It was a
happy reunion for the girls and their mother who returned to
Soweto together, amid promises of a new house from Rebecca.

Jazz, gospel, R&B and disco-pop have all inspired South

African music trends through the generations, and the country's biggest solo attraction at the start of the Nineties has tapped another international idiom which has appeal throughout Africa. The music is reggae and the singer is Lucky Dube. Lucky made his debut singing rock music with some school friends, playing a guitar paid for from profits of a 'stage play' he produced. He later linked up with Richard Siluma in the Love Brothers playing mbaqanga, and made his recording debut in 1979, before turning elsewhere for inspiration in the mid-Eighties.

He found it in reggae, a rhythm which has been tugging at the youth across Africa. With his band, The Slaves, Lucky's first reggae album was *Rastas Never Die*. His third release, *Slave*, became the first album of any kind to sell more than 300,000 copies in South Africa, surpassing the Soul Brothers' previous efforts. The subsequent *Prisoner* proved to be a big seller in Nigeria and Zimbabwe. He also starred in a movie, *Getting Lucky*, for which the soundtrack album brought him a gold disc. With a high ranging voice, a delivery compared with the Wailers' Peter Tosh, and a solid reggae band with a strong choral element, Lucky Dube has found success far from his home territory. He has toured in Southern Africa and the States and his vision of African reggae has appealed to listeners across the globe.

Bound for success: top record seller at the bottom of the continent, Luck Dube's reggae reached as far as the States

Afropop: an American radio show broadcast nationally and relayed in Europe by BBC

Music in the Marketplace

All the signs are that African music is on the verge of a big change, perhaps a complete metamorphosis, even without the political, social and economic upheavals facing the continent in the 1990s. Africa is a youthful continent, with over half the people in many countries under twenty years of age. By the start of the 21st century the population is predicted to grow from 650 million to 900 million. There are already millions of educated, talented young people ready to participate in the overdeveloped modern world. With the ability to function in both systems, African 'world citizens' can reach the fruits of technology, while rooted in age old realities. The hard part is reconciling culture with commerce, and making a living at it. As Manu Dibango said, "The show can be good, but the business is bad".

Although the music business is chaotic, the popular music of Africa is tightly structured, with formal conventions and a reliance on 'systems' that define the musicians' role. For a long time musicians have been dissatisfied with the 'feudal' structure of African music, which extends down from 'producers' or patrons donating random amounts of cash, through the ranks to the lowliest musician. In 1979 the Ghanaian musicians union went on strike with the slogan, 'We are musicians not band boys', yet the attitude still lingers. The system of apprenticeship provides a practical education but the hierarchical structure of the big bands can suppress young talent. Or, as Nyoka Longo, president of Zaiko Langa Langa, puts it: "One of the things musicians have to combat is egotism. Some of the older band leaders were too proud to keep in contact with young musicians." Zaiko, on the other hand is regularly refreshed with up and coming talent.

Even the most progressive artistes who wish to break out of their closed circuits maintain contact with the source of their work which, as countless musicians acknowledge, lies in the folklore, or culture of the people. In maintaining this vital continuity artistes as diverse as Franco, Sunny Ade, Youssou N'Dour, Nico Mbarga and Alain Makaba of Wenge Musica have insisted they are bound to play their 'own' music, drawing on what has always been there, and spicing it occasionally with Western ingredients that Nyoka Longo calls 'gimmicks'.

For a long time African music has been dependent on outside patronage from the West. Unless they are introduced by an acceptable, White, celebrity figure, African performers have a hard time attracting mainstream media interest even though their shows may be as popular and profitable as domestic pop 'stars' who continue to sustain interest. Controversial or not, Paul Simon's 'Graceland' project in 1987 exposed certain African pop idioms to a truly global audience. He was not the first Western popster to explore the continent, but his timely introduction to

township mbaqanga came just as other people in the West were turning an ear to the rest of Africa.

Many African musicians might well have felt nauseous that it took a middle-of-the road White minstrel to make the biggest commercial breakthrough for their music. While many graciously admitted that it was beneficial for African culture to be dipped into the Euro-American mainstream, others were apprehensive that whatever idiom fed the mass market would be assimilated into a kind of exotic wallpaper, with a short lifespan lasting only until the next fashion swing, and its social, psychological and spiritual function would be devalued. To the average Western pop fan, Paul Simon and Peter Gabriel might appear to have done more towards an Afro-fusion than Manu Dibango, Fela Kuti, Sunny Ade, Youssou N'Dour and Salif Keita combined. But it might be just another illustration of the continuing one-way trade with Africa.

It is no coincidence that those five major African stars were encouraged by Western record labels to collaborate to some extent with 'commercial' guest stars and producers: Dibango with Bill Laswell and Herbie Hancock for Celluloid; Kuti, whose *Army Arrangement* was remixed by Laswell with Jamaican rhythm men Sly and Robbie; Ade, with Stevie Wonder an aimless guest on his final Island album; Youssou N'Dour who played with Simon and collaborated and toured the world with Peter Gabriel, and Keita recording with Joe Zawinul. The initiative has usually come from the West rather than Africa, but up until Keita's 1991 project none had achieved the desired commercial effect. Youssou no doubt profited from his deal with Virgin, but the label baulked at trying to recoup their recording costs and abruptly dropped him, as Island had done with Ade. Apart from Dibango, who alone seems able to step from one circle to another on his own creative terms, Africans get scorned for compromising their music, while people

Africa's music media: as in the West, magazines have been a part of pop music culture since the 1960s, transcribing hit lyrics and gossiping outrageously about the stars. Few survive more than a couple of seasons

Africa No1: the only pan-African commercial radio station

Ballet dancers: Les Ballets Africaines from Guinea transpose traditional culture to Western theatre stages

like Simon and Gabriel are praised for enriching theirs. And they get credit for 'discovering' African music once again. Ironically, the late, great guitarist and bandleader, Franco, felt quite bitter that no Western pop 'star' had approached him for a collaboration. Franco claimed many times that he would always remain true to his own culture but, as he also said, music has no frontiers. People like Eric Clapton or Mark Knopfler could have picked up a whole book of tricks from the 'Sorcerer of the Guitar'.

Africa is a producer of raw materials to the world and, as with coffee, groundnuts or copper, its music does not get a fair deal on the world market. As Dibango explained in his introduction, the void which has opened up between producer and consumer, between Africa and the developed world, is the continent's most pressing problem. Along with its mineral wealth, Africa's music has been plundered, manipulated and exploited, and some brokers want to further 'refine' it to suit Western tastes. The connection between culture and commerce, although alien to African custom, has been understood well enough by Africans in the music business, but there are cultural as well as political and economic factors conspiring against professional artistes in all media; not least the 'festival syndrome'. The Ghanaian writer Ayi Kwei Armah writing in *West Africa* magazine in 1985, put the festival mentality into a clear perspective. Culture, the author insisted, is a process not an event, and its existence depends on calm continuity rather than spectacular extravagence; like a continuous, nourishing drizzle, rather than a torrential thunderstorm. Armah was talking specifically about the excessive cost and illusory benefit of a pan-African cultural festival planned for 1986 in Dakar which was finally cancelled in 1988, but the comments are appropriate to music presentation anywhere. Armah argued a convincing case that such festivals are counter-cultural,

Sound seller: a neighbourhood record shop pumps the latest hits on to the streets of Kinshasa

diverting needed resources and energy from everyday expression. The author points out that people in the West don't wait for festivals to absorb the best of their own culture; they live it daily.

The presentation of 'alien' cultures is another matter, and in the West festivals provide a structure of first-rate facilities for the largest number of visiting artistes and present them to a huge catchment audience. But there is often an unsatisfactory balance from the audience's perspective, in that the festival, rather than the participants, becomes the entertainment. Despite, or because of, the expansive stages and mammoth sound systems, these are usually not ideal situations to see performers or hear the best of their work, and the event is often remembered long after the performance has been forgotten.

Of course, the carnival atmosphere affects performers also and they often carry fonder memories. The major pan-African festivals remembered with pride by participating artistes following the World Festival of Negro Arts in Dakar in 1966 were Algiers 69, and the 1977 Lagos Festac. These expressions of African unity and cultural diversity were expensive public relations follies. Festac hosted artistes from 75 countries over a period of weeks on a scale more like a cultural Olympics than a weekend picnic. There were smaller, more selective events in Algiers in 1984 and Goree island in 1987 and huge music spectaculars accompanied such occasions as the Ali-Foreman fight in Zaire, Zimbabwe's Independence celebrations and the Africa Games. But the Live Aid and Mandela benefits, televised from London, did little to promote the music of the continent they were focusing on, while the African community's own 'self-help' fund raisers, such as 'Tam Tam Pour L'Ethiopie' and 'Africa for Africa', received scant media coverage.

Trading in tunes: the Congolese recording company IAD display their wares at a pan-African trade fair

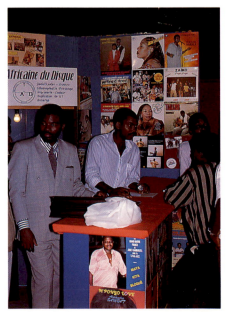

Rather than running up huge debts on the more flamboyant events, which are now beyond even imaginary budgets, Ayi Kwei Armah made a case for coordinating national cultural policies to give African film makers, writers, artists or musicians access to facilities in Africa, rather than forcing them abroad. For that, however, the whole system of artificial borders, political patronage, trade barriers, incompatible technology, currency restrictions, poor communications and other colonial legacies would have to be changed, presupposing a united Africa, which seems a long way off. As Manu Dibango said, the music is in the image of Africa, isolated and scattered but not yet shattered.

Presidential patronage or state sponsorship have underwrit-

Crossing cultural frontiers:
Ghanaian drummer 'Speedy' Nii
Moi Acquaye blows a didgeridoo,
behind him South African Julian Bahula
beats his malombo drums

Taxi Pata Pata: London based ex-
patriates from Zaire, Zimbabwe, Kenya
and points west

ten the music industries in many African countries since independence, but as the era of single-party rule comes to an end,
some established orchestras are sure to opt for retirement.
Commercial sponsorship offers one possible lifeline. But national
companies, even selling international brand names, often have no
relation with their counterparts in neighbouring countries, and
there is no reciprocal benefit in sponsoring foreign tours.

Occasional flashes of commercial inspiration have come from
the CFA franc zone, where companies in countries with low music
profiles, such as Benin, Togo, Gabon and Congo (Brazzaville),
have built modern, hi-tech studios attracting artistes from neighbouring countries. Nigeria is well equipped for studios, and has
now been joined by Ghana as a 48-track power. The vinyl pressing
plants had almost all closed down by 1991, but cassette technology opened a more direct route from studio to distributor. The CD
format, although expensive, is attractive to African musicians, not
just for its quality and durability but also because of the
continuous play format, which has appealed to fuji star Ayinde
Barrister, who recorded in London in 1990 for Globestyle. "I prefer

this compact disc to anything," he said. "Here I can sing for the first 30 minutes, stop and play the next 30 minutes. One hour of settled music is like playing ten hours non-stop."

In several African countries, smaller, eight- and sixteen-track studios are also mushrooming, particularly as national radio and television stations demand more locally made advertising commercials. Historically, radio has been the best self-promotion medium for music, reaching the most isolated villagers but, throughout the vast continent of Africa, there are only two commercial stations, Radio Syd a local FM station serving The Gambia's tourists, and the 'clear channel' short wave station Africa No1, from Libreville, Gabon. All other stations in Black Africa are government owned and fairly strictly tied to national policy. For many years literate urbanites in the major capitals have been informed and entertained by music publications carrying lyric sheets and show-biz scandals. In the mid-Sixties Franco launched his own title *Ye!* to counteract some of the gossip carried in the existing papers. A decade later, Dibango aimed for a more international readership with *Afro-Music* magazine. During the Eighties the growth of overseas interest inspired *Africa Music,* a Nigeria/UK publication which survived five years, folding just as the business started taking off in the West. The French title *Afrique Elite,* provided a more complete and tasteful picture of African culture, but it succumbed to the recession in 1991.

Franco-fusion: Parisian band Adioa bring Senegalese touch to urban reggae

Bringing it out of Africa

Within Africa, the role and status of popular musicians varies greatly. Some administrations seem largely indifferent, or unwilling to support their artistes, while others push certain favourites, and /or restrain 'bad messengers'. Most states have national 'ballets' or 'cultural troupes' as symbols of unity, which occasionally make foreign forays. But the domestic propaganda value of popular dance bands is rarely equated with international PR, even though the slightest help given to those musicians invited abroad could be used to national advantage.

Audiences in the West have so often been disappointed by the non-appearance of African bands, that certain musicans have gained for themselves and their countrymen an indelible reputation for unreliability. Problems of communication range from simple misunderstandings of language and social habits to unreliable telephone connections and erratic airline scheduling. The perennial visa problem, which affects most promoters, can often be traced to poor organisation at either end, and within Europe there is a further culture gap between French and English speakers. Ironically, the British immigration authorities, on refusing entry to a francophone star in 1989, stated that from their point of view African musicians posed few problems as they always had somewhere else to go next.

In the West the record labels, shops, distributors and media which provide the infrastructure for the 'niche market' of African music, struggle gamely to supply a steady, nourishing drizzle of culture, but the 'world music' tag chosen in 1988 by a clutch of British distributors has outlived its usefulness. It was vaguely demeaning to bracket the world's strongest music with culturally incompatible curiosities, and it also quarantined the music well away from the more vital popular 'dance' culture. Consumers of African music are by now well enough educated to know which styles suit their own tastes. Manu Dibango said at the start that music should not be judged by where it comes from, although in

Hilife International: helped raise interest in Europe during the mid-1980s before scattering

effect that is what happens as soon as the language is identified. There is something about the environment that attracts listeners to Zaire, Zimbabwe, Cameroon or Senegal and most enthusiasts know exactly which direction to turn their ears. The days of a continent wide, catch-all sweep are over. The introductions have been made and now it is up to the customers to make the choice.

African musicians have been touching base in Europe for several generations, if only to record work which was then sold back to consumers in Africa. Since World War Two, West and South African jazz and dance band musicians have integrated themselves into the British scene. In the Sixties, Ginger Johnson, Gasper Lawal and Speedy Acquaye brought a percussive boost to rock. There was no contemporary dance music, apart from odd pockets of kwela, although in the 1960s the young music student, Fela Kuti formed his first band in London. On the European mainland Dibango went a different route, integrating with the local scene, before stepping back to Africa and farther afield.

European-based Afro-fusion had its best chance in 1970 with the success of Osibisa, but until the Eighties the African community was not cohesive enough to provide ex-pat participants on both sides of the stage. The current British interest in popular dance sounds started with Europeans bringing it back from their travels and linking with African musicians in bands such as Jazira and the Ivory Coasters. London-based bands surged forward with African Connexion, Hilife International, Somo Somo, Taxi Pata Pata, and Abdul Tee Jay's Rokoto. In the 1990s a new formation, Big Musica, was replenished from the growing Zairean community. Cameroonians, Nigerians, East Africans and Zimbabweans have also tried to replicate their homeland ambience. One who went the other way via piano bars and jazz clubs is the Nigerian keyboard player and composer Juwon.

The current 'movement' took off in London in 1983 on the back of the Greater London Council's cultural policy, with a series of shows that launched Youssou N'Dour, Sam Mangwana, Les Quatres Etoiles (Four Stars), African Brothers, Akendengue, Toure Kunda and Kanda Bongo Man. Unconnected, but crucial to the myth-building was the one and only visit by Franco and OK Jazz, on the rebound from their American debut.

In France, African culture is often taken more seriously than in Britain, and as there was no competition from French rock until the middle of Eighties, Parisians accepted the tropical mix as part of mainstream culture, with organisations such as Africa Fete massaging the market for visiting bands. In Belgium the Zairean community is more close-knit and more insistent on maintaining a musical connection with the homeland. Even the great OK Jazz, who had been visiting Europe since the 1960s, only started to consider the available Western audience in the early 1980s.

In London there have been so many music movements and cliques that 'foreign' idioms have had a hard time, but as a hub for the international distribution of specialist music it serves well, linking anglophone Africa, Europe, America and the Far East. Few of the independent record labels are exclusively African, and even the premier label/distributor, Stern's African Music, who anticipated the interest back in 1983, has diversified. Some of the small labels have done justice to the music but the majors have frequently floundered. In Britain, radio has given poor service, with no Black disc jockeys on the case and intermittent enthusiasm from a handful of 'cosy' presenters over the last decade. African sounds have even been ignored by 'innovative' new jazz and dance music stations. The printed media gave it a better run for a while, often generating interest in new, unheard sounds, until editors became confused at the proliferation.

In the USA, distance is an obstacle for touring large bands, but there is at least a nationwide African music show on National Public Radio called 'Afropop', with a knowledgable African presenter, Georges Collinet. Musicians on the domestic scene have tended to slip into jazz or mainstream music, although the drummer and bandleader Babatunde Olatunje has been a stalwart supplier of Nigerian atmosphere while an authentic juju band has been formed in Washington DC by ex-members of Ebenezer Obey's band, and in Oregon the Ghanaian, Obo Addy, keeps highlife alive. The Gambian 'electro-griot', kora player Foday Musa Suso anticipated the 'Worldbeat' fusion with the Mandingo Griot Society, and worked with Herbie Hancock on the Los Angeles Olympic theme music. In Canada there is a thriving Ghanaian community to support highlifers from the Pat Thomas/ Native Spirit camp. Musicians inside Africa also have their eyes on Japan which has a huge appetite for variety, and juju, soukous and mbira stars make successful visits. There are specialist publications and a good market for CDs.

Records, radio and discos only provide half the story, however, and African music's real dynamic energy comes from live performance. Show promoters are nervous about the inconsistency of the market, with interest in some artistes slumping after peaks while others maintain a mythical status. There is an aura of uncertainty surrounding most appearances, but for the music to prosper outside Africa it must be accepted as much as possible on its own terms. Bands frequently play all night at home, and confining them to two-hour shows is restrictive. Occasional all-nighters have shown that if a big name band can play till dawn, the dance floor stays full. Music may have no frontiers but it does face a time barrier. 'African time' has derogatory connotations, but the African time-scale is unhurried, open-ended and full of possibilites, and in music the journey is more important than the arrival. As Barrister put it, "You know I play for nine hours non-stop. That means I have become addicted to playing for a long time. The

Music for the masses: the Gambian National Troupe at a Womad festival in southern England

Niche marketing: African music is slowly growing out of its specialist 'ghetto', but vinyl albums and the cosy record shop will soon be a thing of the past

Local sponsorship provides a useful ground breaker for visiting performers but commercial benefits are hard to evaluate

musical spirit in me does not allow me to have a proper rest if I don't digest all my message."

It takes a large, disciplined outfit to play for nine hours, and the days of such behemoth bands are numbered. The dance orchestras have faded away, except the OK Jazz juggernaut which should be able to circle the world like a Zairean music version of the Harlem Globetrotters. The squad system in which extra musicians were taken on to play specific parts, rather than existing musicians changing their style, is almost obsolete. Hi-tech studio gadgets, synthesizers, and audiences' low expectations have made many musicians redundant. Yet the differences between a 21-piece band and an eleven-piece outfit become evident when they are called to keep a dance floor filled all night.

New Horizons

While remaining faithful to their roots and the primary audience at home, musicians are continually looking forward for the vital element that will boost them into world fame: dipping into the cultural baggage to revive traditional rhythms while keeping pace with technology. Recent folklore fashions have come from the Wassoulou region of Mali and Swede Swede's Mongo music from Zaire. Hi-tech fusions like Madilu System's rumba-rap and Maloko's soul-soukous have more than novelty value, and might well be re-invented in the future. Afrobeat is sure to sound out again from Nigeria, possibly connecting with hip-hop and go-go rhythms. Reggae is obviously stirring a new pan-African fusion in a range of languages, or environmental flavours.

Many university educated, technologically aware and computer literate young Africans want to play progressive, modern music and any ambitious artiste will try for the widest market and the biggest audience within reach. As young musicians struggle to escape the closed cultural system they have been brought up in, many attempt to by-pass the 'world music' bottleneck and go straight for the global jackpot. By the end of the century this new surge should be evident in the wider world. African music will continue to infiltrate Western idioms and, maybe, one of the crossover studio experiments will hit gold.

Louis Moholos' Drum Orchestra (right): the pan-African orchestra is a common ideal for many musicians, but hard to realise

A face for world music: Salif Keita's voice reached far, even selling canned beer to the Scots

Musicians like to cross over, it is often their listeners who hold them back. Western audiences, often satiated with choice, have pegged their allegiance to one or another pop style – in what has been described as a 'tribal' division. This reconstructed tribalism enshrines the indifference, chauvinism, or covert racism which holds the music back. Given the European's fear of the unknown it is amazing that African music has got so far. A well known truism in magazine publishing is that a Black face on the cover is a liability. In America, an African face is even more so. Even supportive, specialist publications like the American *Reggae and African Beat* and the English *World Beat* have to contend with this marketing prejudice. Similar attitudes seem to apply to mainstream radio and television, where there are no young Black presenters dealing with the music.

Many Africans are hurt and perplexed by the West's indifference to their culture. Their own artistes give real value for money; in terms of workmanship, creativity, art or stamina, they do the business. With the demographic shift in the world's population, young Africans will be reaching deeper into the West, and as Westerners become acclimatised the music is sure to grow. The assimilation necessary for people to pick up on an alien culture takes time. Time is something African musicians know much about, and they are the ones able to create most with it.

The Record Rack

A selective discography of some of some recent bestsellers and classic albums available outside Africa since the 1970s.

Islamic Inflexions

Oum Kalsoum, *Azkouriny*, SONO 142 [CD]
Cheikha Remitti, *Ghir El Baroud*, MLP 306
Cheb Khaled, *Hada Raykoum*, TERRA 102
Bellemou Messaoud & Cheb Ourrad Houari, *Le Pere du Rai*, WCB 011
Chaba Zahouania, *Medahates*, CAD [cassette release]
Chekikene, *Ya el Hadhra*, RIM [cassette]
Jil Jilala, *Ghir el Baroud*, KAN [cassette]
Nass El Ghiwane, *Chansons de Nass El Ghiwane* BUDA 8267-2
Dissidenten and Lem Chaheb, *Sahara Elektric*, ORB 004
Lhaj Lhoucine Touali, *Songs*, TCK [cassette]
Ait Menguelet, *Ettes, Ettes*, Triomphe Music [cassette]
Various, *Rai Rabels Vols 1 & 2*, Earthworks
Yalla, *Hitlist Egypt*, MLPS 1040
Abdel Aziz El Mubarak, WCB010
Aster Aweke, *Aster Aweke* TERRA 107

Sounds of the Sahel

Les Ambassadeurs, *Best of...*, CEL 6640
Orch, Poly-Rythmo, *Zero + Zero*, TAN 7007
Bembeya Jazz, *La Continuite*, SLP 61
Les Amazones *Au Coeur de Paris*, SLP 76
Super Biton, *Afro Jazz du Mali*, BP 13
Youssou N'Dour, *Immigres*, EMV 10
Jali Musa Jawara, *Fote Mogoban*, OVLP 511
Salif Keita, *Soro*, ST 1020
Ali Farka Toure, *Ali Farka Toure*, WCB 007
Mory Kante, *Akwaba Beach*, Barclay
Orch. Baobab, *Pirates Choice* WCD 014
Ismael Lo, *Mbalax New Look*, Celluloid
Oumou Sangare, *Moussoulou*, WCB 021
Baaba Maal, *Baayo*, CIDM 1061
Alpha Blondy, *Apartheid is Nazism*, ST 1017

The Highlife Zone

Guy Warren *Africa Speaks - America Answers* DL8446
E.T. Mensah, *All For You*, RETRO1
Koo Nimo, *Obasarima*, ADRY 1
S.E. Rogie, *The Palm Wine Sounds of S.E. Rogie*, Rogiphone R2
Sweet Talks, *Hollywood Highlife Party*, 635 4034
African Brothers Band, *Agatha* BNELP 01
Prince Nico Mbarga, *Sweet Mother*, RAS 6
The Ramblers, *Hit Sounds of the Ramblers*, DWAPS 25
Fela Kuti, *Everything Scatter*, PMLP 1000
Victor Uwaifo, *The Best Of...Vol 1*, POLP 046
Sunny Ade, *Juju Music*, ILPS 9712
Barrister, *Fuji Garbage* CDORB (CD only)
Jewel Ackah, *Electric Highlife*, AS 4010
Shina Peters, *Ace* CBS N 1002
Majek Fashek, *Prisoner of Conscience*, MLPS 1030

Makossa Movers

Manu Dibango, *Soul Makossa*, CRLP 503
Electric Africa, CEL 6114
Eboa Lotin, *Gratitude*, TSI TSHI 002
Bebe Manga, *Ami*, SIIS 10
Various, *Fleurs Musicales du Cameroun*, FMC 001/2/3
Les Veterans, *Au Village*, TC0007
Sam Fan Thomas, *Makassi*, TAM4
Lapiro de M'Banga, *No Make Erreur*, TSHI-TSHI003
Moni Bile, *Makossa Ambience* MBK 114
Guy Lobe, *Mon Ami a Moi*, AT 068
Jackie Douleur, *Beneground*, Kanibal
Charlotte Mbango, *Makossa Non-Stop*, AT 072
Les Diablotins, *A Paris, Vol 4*, DB1763

Pierre Akendengue, *Nandipo* SH10045
Hilarion Nguema, *Crise Economique MH 107*

The Rumba Region

Joseph Kabasele & African Jazz, Vols 1 & 2, 360 142/ 143
Franco & OK Jazz, *Mabele*, 360 056
24eme Anniversaire, FRAN 004/5
Mario & Reponse de Mario CD8562 (CD only)
Tabu Ley Rochereau, *En Amour Y a Pas de Calcul*, GEN 101
Mbilia Bel, *Keyna* GEN 114
Sam Mangwana, *Maria Tebbo*, SAM 02
Nino Malapet, *Mokilimbembe*, MP33004
Zaiko Langa Langa, *Nippon Banzai* PZL86-87
Ici Ca Va - Fungola Motema, MOTO1/ PZL82-84
Papa Wemba & Viva La Musica, *Franco Presents...A Paris* FRAN007
Les Choc Stars du Zaire, Espera 6989/24
Anti-Choc, with Bozi, Detta & Deese, *La Sirene*, AMG 101
Emeneya *Nzinzi KL 04*
Pepe Kalle, *Gigantafric*, ORB 062

Swahili Sounds

Various, *Songs the Swahili Sing*, OMA103
Zein & Party, *Mtindo wa Mombasa*, ORB 066
Various, *The Music of Zanzibar, Vols 1 & 2*, ORBD 040
Nguashi N'Timbo, *Shauri Yako*, ASLP 936
Various, *Tribal Songs of Kenya*, POLP 316
The Nairobi Beat - Kenyan Pop Music Today, Rounder 5030
Super Mazembe, *Kaivaska*, V2263
Samba Mapangala & Orch. Virunga, *Malako Disco*, AR 0986
Remmy Ongala & Super Matimila, *Songs for the Poor Man*, Real World/Virgin
Simba Wanyika Original, *Kenya Vol. 1*, AMG 0003
Super Wanyika, *Singalame* ANAC 15
Shirati Jazz, *Benga Blast* EWV13

Various, *Guitar Paradise of East Africa*, EWV
Shem Tube with J. Osala & E. Okola, *Abana ba Nasery*, ORB 052
Various, *Luo Roots* ORB

Liberation Music

Thomas Mapfumo, *Chimurenga Singles* ELP 2004
Chamunorwa, Mango
Ephat Mujuru, *Rhythms of Life*, Lyrichord
Junior Mulemena Boys, *Tribute* ZMLP 70
Bhundu Boys, *Shabini* AFRI 02
Jonah Moyo & Devera Ngwena, *Taxi Driver* KKO-1
Four Brothers, *Makorokoto*, COOK 014
Black Umfulosi, *Unity*, WCB 020
Stella Chiweshe, *Ambuya?* ORB 029
Oliver Mtukudzi, *Zvauya Sei?* ZIL 209
Real Sounds, *Harare* ZML 1015
Various, *Zambience* ORB 037
Various, *Zimbabwe Frontline*, EWV 9
Alick Nkhata, *Salapo*, RETRO4
Eduardo Durao, *Timbila: New Chope*, ORB

Township Voices

African Jazz Pioneers KAZLP14
Miriam Makeba, *Sangoma*, 925637-1
Abdullah Ibrahim, *Mannenburg*, KAZLP 101
Dudu Pukwana, *In the Townships* EWV5
Hugh Masekela, *Technobush* HIP11
Mahlathini & Mahotella Queens, *Thokozile* EWV6
Soul Brothers, *Jive Explosion*, EWV8
Ladysmith Black Mambazo, *Classic Tracks*, Shanachie
Stimela, *Look, Listen and Decide*, HUL 40109
Various, *Indestructible Beat of Soweto, Vols 1,2 & 3* EMWV14, EWV1, EWV17
Mzwakhe Mbuli, *Change is Pain* SHIFT18
Sipho Mabuse. *Burn Out* HUL 509
Brenda Fassie, *Black President*, SBK
Yvonne Chaka Chaka, *Umbqombothi* RBL123
Lucky Dube, *Slave*, CEL 66834/1

Bibliography: *Sources referred to and further reading*

African Encyclopedia, Oxford University Press, London, 1984

Akpabot, Samuel Ekpe. *Foundation of Nigerian Traditional Music*, Spectrum, Ibadan, 1986

Anderson A.M. *Music in the Mix: The Story of South African Popular Music*, Raven Press, 1981

Bebey, Francis. *Musique de L'Afrique*, Horizons de France, 1969. [English language edition, African Music; A People's Art, Lawrence Hill, New York, 1975]

Bemba, Sylvain. *50 Ans de Musique du Zaire-Congo*, Presence Africaine, Paris, 1984

Bender, Wolfgang. *Sweet Mother: Afrikanische Musik*, Trickster Verlag, Munich, 1986. [English language edition, University of Chicago Press, 1991]

— (Ed.) *Perspectives on African Music*, Bayreuth University, 1989

Berliner, Paul E. *The Soul of Mbira*, University of California Press, 1978

Brincard, M.-T. (Ed.) *Sounding Forms: African Musical Instruments*, American Federation of Arts, New York, 1989

Cathcart, Jenny. *Hey You! A portrait of Youssou N'Dour*, Fine Line Books, Whitney, Oxford, 1989

Charters, Samuel. *The Roots of the Blues, an African Search*, Quartet, London, 1981

Chernoff, John Miller, *African Rhythm and African Sensibility; Aesthetics and Social Action in African Musical Idioms*, University of Chicago Press, 1979

Collins, E. John. *African Pop Roots, The Inside Rhythms of Africa*, Foulsham, London, New York, 1985

— *Musicmakers of West Africa*, Three Continents Press, Washington, 1985

— *E.T. Mensah, King of Highlife*, Off the Record Press, London, 1986

— (Ed.) *My Life, by Sir Victor Uwaifo, The Black Knight of Music Fame*

Coplan, David. *In Township Tonight*, Longman, London, 1986

Davidson, Basil. *Africa in History: themes and outlines*, Weidenfeld and Nicolson, London, 1968

Dibango, Manu, with Rouard, Danielle, *Trois Kilos de Cafe*, Lieu Commun, Paris, 1989

Duodu, E. A. *Symbolic Movements in Ghanaian Dances*, University of Ghana, Legon

Euba, Akin. *Essays on Music in Africa*, Bayreuth University, 1988

Ewens, Graeme. *Luambo Franco and 30 years of OK Jazz*, Off the Record Press, London, 1986

Frederikse, Julie. *None But Ourselves: Masses vs media in the making of Zimbabwe*, Raven Press and Zimbabwe Publishing House, 1982. Heinemann, London, Ibadan, Nairobi, 1983

Gambaccini, P. with Rice, T. and Rice, J. *British Hit Singles*, Guinness, London, 1991

Graham, Ronnie. *Stern's Guide to Contemporary African Music*, Zwan & Off The Record Press, London, 1988

Harrev, Flemming. 'Jambo records and the Promotion of Popular Music in East Africa', *Perspectives on African Music*, Bayreuth University, 1989

Hommage a Grand Kalle, Editions Lokole, Kinshasa, 1985

Hudgens, Jim and Trillo, Richard. *West Africa: The Rough Guide*, Harrap Columbus, London, 1990

Jenkins, J. and Olsen P.R. *Music and Musical Instruments in the World of Islam*, Horniman Museum, London, 1976

Kazadi, Wa Mukuna. 'The origins of Zairean Modern Music: A socio-economic Aspect', *African Urban Studies*, Vol 6, 1979-80

— *Trends of nineteenth and twentieth century music in the Congo-Zaire*, Regensburg: Musikkulturen Asiens, Afrikas und Ozeaniens in 19. Jahrhundert, 1973

Knappert, Jan. *Four Centuries of Swahili Verse*, Heinemann, 1979

Kubik, Gerhard. *The Kachamba Brothers' Band: A study of neo-tradi-tional music in Malawi*, Zambian papers No9, 1974

La Musique Africaine: Reunion de Yaounde, Unesco, 1970

Lee, Helene. *Rockers d'Afrique*, Albin Michel, Paris, 1988

Lonoh, Malangi Bokengele. *Essai de commentaire de la musique Congo-laise Moderne*, SEI/ANC, Kinshasa, 1963, 1969 and 1970

—*Negritude, Africanite et Musique Africaine.* Centre de Recherches Peda-gogiques, Kinshasa, 1990

Makeba, Miriam, with Hall, J. *Makeba, My Story*, Bloomsbury, London, 1988

Manuel, Peter. *Popular Musics of the non-Western world*, Oxford Univer-sity Press, Oxford, New York, 1988

Matondo, Kanza. *La Musique Zairoise moderne: Situation actuelle et perspectives d'avenir.* Conservertoire National de Musique et d'art dramatique, Kinshasa, 1972

Moore, Carlos. *Fela, Fela, This Bitch of a Life*, Allison & Busby, London, 1982

Mutwe, Credo. *My People: writings of a Zulu witchdoctor*, Anthony Blond, London, 1969

Nketia, Kwabenah J.H. *The Music of Africa*, Norton, 1974, Gollancz, 1979

New Grove Dictionary of music and musicians, Macmillan, London, 1980

Olema, D. 'Societie Zairoise dans le miroir de la chanson populaire' *Canadian Journal of African Studies, Vol 18, No1*, 1984

Oliver, Paul. *Savannah Syncopators: African retentions in the Blues*, Studio Vista, London, 1970

Oliver, Roland, and Fage, J.D. *A Short History of Africa*, Penguin, London, 1978

Ranger, T.O. *Dance and Society in Eastern Africa*, Heinemann, London, 1975

Roberts, John Storm. *Black Music of Two Worlds*, Praeger, New York, 1972. [Morrow Paperback, New York, 1974]

Stapleton, Chris and May, Chris. *African All-Stars: The Pop Music of a Continent*, Quartet, London, 1987

Trillo, Richard. *Kenya: The Rough Guide*, Harrap Columbus, London, 1988

Wallis, R. and Malm, K. *Big Sounds from Small Peoples*, Constable, London, 1984

Waterman, Chris. *Juju: A Social History and Ethnography of an African Popular Music*, University of Chicago, 1990

Zindi, Fred. *Roots Rocking in Zimbabwe*, Mambo Press, Harare, 1985

Issues of the following magazines have also provided useful reference:

Africa Music, London and Lagos
African Beat, London
African Sunrise, London and Lusaka
Africa Journal, London
Afrika, Amsterdam
Afrique Elite, Paris
Afrique-Asie, Paris
Afro-Music, Paris
L'As des As, Kinshasa
Blues & Soul, London
Black Beat International, London and Harare

Disco Hits, Kinshasa
Folk Roots, Sussex, England
Keskidee, Essex, England
Musical Traditions, Essex, England
Reggae and African Beat, Los Angeles
Stars, Kinshasa
Straight No Chaser, London
Take Cover, London
Tradewinds, London
West Africa, London and Lagos
World Beat, London

Photographic credits

Pierre-Rene Worms; Cover, back cover, pages 5, 25, 37, 57, 65, 77, 109, 116, 125
Adrian Boot/Island; 21(b), 48, 49(t), 51, 105, 154, 172. Adrian Boot; 38, 39, 101
Jak Kilby; 10, 11(b), 12(b), 18(b), 19, 22, 53(t), 80, 81, 83, 88, 96, 99, 108, 174, 191, 196
Michael McIntyre; 13(t), 29, 128(b), 137, 145, 148, 152
Steve Williams; 141, 151, 153(t), 173, 176, 177(b), 180, 208(t)
Wolfgang Bender; 20(b), 28, 36, 53(b), 61(b), 97, 98, 182
Eddie Bru Mindah/John Collins; 11(t)
John Collins; 35, 78(b), 82, 84(t & b), 85, 87, 91, 98, 102
Ben Mandleson/Globestyle; 24, 126, 158, 160, 161, 162, 164, 169, 185,
Werner Graebner/Globestyle; 163
Hugo Glendenning/World Circuit; 49(b), 181, /Mr Bongo's 213
Diana Stone /World Circuit; 41

World Circuit; 30,,43,69,72,76
Charles Easmon; 90, 92, 93
David Lodge/Island; 47
Island/Mango; 48, 68
Jean Bernard Sohiez/Mango; 48, 211
Robyn Martin/Triple Earth; 55
Trevor Herman/ Earthworks; 167, 168
Hai Roseboom; 133
Patrice Dubois; 123
Publishing Africa; 192, 197, 200, 201, 203, 204, 205
World Beat; 64, 76, 193
Lucy Duran; 97
Malamini Jobarteh; 58
E.T. Mensah; 86
Manu Dibango; 110
Zambian Information Service/ David Nkhata; 183
Bailey's African Photo Archives; 186, /Jurgen Schaderberg 194, 198
Megan Green; 33
Hulton Picture Library; 46
Graeme Ewens; 8, 9, 13, 14, 15, 16(t & b) 17, 31, 56, 58, 60, 61, 62, 63, 71, 73, 74, 89, 104, 108, 112, 114, 115, 117, 121, 127, 128, 129, 134, 135, 136, 138, 140, 141b, 142, 144, 146, 149, 152, 153(b), 156(t & b), 157(t & b), 177, 184, 190, 210, 213, 215

Publicity material was provided by Island/ Mango records, Virgin/Earthworks, WEA/ Warners, Barclay, Stern's African Music Centre, Triple Earth, Globestyle, World Circuit, Celluloid, Oval, Sonodisc, Eddy'son, RetroAfric, Boogie Down Productions
Copy photography and retouching; Gary Woods

Artwork and illustrations
Megan Green; 19, 42, 94,, 118, 129, 173 and maps
Kofi Ankobra; 100, 214(t)
'Moke Art'; 157
Zembi Oteno; 165

Acknowledgements

Molephe Pheto and Dorothy Masuka were interviewed by Mamello Pheko. Nana Ampadu and Amakye Dede spoke to Charles Easmon. Victor Uwaifo was talking to John Collins. Hugh Masekela quotes were extracted from an interview by Rene Williams with Brian Creese of NMR Productions. Quotes from Kenyan musicians in Chapter 8 were taken from the BBC television documentary *Sweet Sound of Honey*, broadcast in the 'World About Us' series in 1978. Ray Lema was interviewed by BBC television for *Under African Skies; Zaire*, broadcast in 1989.

The discography was compiled with the assistance of Ronnie Graham, editor of *Stern's Guide to Contemporary African Music*, Andy Morgan and Nick Carnac.

The author and editors would like to thank the countless musicians and enthusiasts who have knowingly or unknowingly provided information for AFRICA *O-Ye!*, in particular Manu Dibango, whose musical career inspired the idea for this book several years ago, and who provided such a pertinent introduction. Further motivation came from the late Franco, Luambo Makiadi.

The greatest help in gathering information came from Mamello Pheko, Charles Easmon, Phil Stanton, Florence Tity Gnimagnon, Rick Glanvill and Gary Stewart. Ronnie Graham, Musah Joh, John Collins, Wolfgang Bender, Lucy Duran, Wayne Barnes and Trevor Herman have also provided invaluable assistance, as have Ben Mandleson and Roger Armstrong of Globestyle; Don, Robert, Lois, Dominic, Ruth and the staff of Stern's African Music Centre, Nick Gold and John Crosby at World Circuit, Jumbo van Reenen and Rob Partridge at Mango, Gaylene Martin, Andy Morgan, Nick Carnac, Vincent Kenis, Nish Matenjwa; Keith, Wala, Kwesi and all at the Africa Centre, London, Pamela Abeyie, Obinna Anyadike, Justin Morell, Nsimba Foggis, Biolo Binganzenza, Moussa Awuounda, Mwana Musa, Joss Bokken, Laye Bamba, Nzita Mabiala, Atafuka Mbuze, Malambo Ma Kizola, Maxwell Nwagboso, Yewande Keleko, Charlie Gillet, Chris Howe, Kofi Adu, Fred Zindi, Kwabenah Fosu Mensah, Abdul Tee-Jay, Iain Scott, Martin Sinnock, Richard Finlayson and David Nkhata. Those to be thanked for supplying live African music in London include, Stuart Lyon, Wilf Walker, Kelefa, Nii Osam and Kitenge-Linkoyi.

Among musicians, I would like to acknowledge all those who have spared time to talk; they are too numerous to name all, but most have appeared in the text. Among those who have given particular help, encouragement or hospitality are Sam Mangwana, Mose Fan Fan, Gilbert Benamay, Nyoka Longo and members of Zaiko Langa Langa, Lutumba Simaro and members of OK Jazz, the late Alhadji Bai Konte and Allah Seck, Malamini Jobarteh, E.T. Mensah, Jerry Malekani, Don Cherry.

More general thanks go to Roger and Angela Burnett, Dr S.J. Green, Olwen Green, Clarice Ward, Bob Luzolo Mbemba, Margaret Busby, Mopanzi Sango, Kofi Ankobra, Susie and Tshala Mundy-Castle, Andre Gnimagnon, Marijka Skipp and the commissioning editor at Guinness Publishing, Honor Head. Special thanks for underpinning and overseeing to M.G.

The author also wishes to thank the publishers of the following titles for publishing contributions over the years, of which some elements have been used in the preceding chapters: *Africa Music, Africa Now, African Sunrise, New African, West Africa, World Beat,* and Compass News Features, London.